Help Thou Mine Unbelief

Scientific, Historical, and Spiritual Evidence of God

By Nancy Phippen Browne

Copyright © 2014 Nancy Phippen Browne
All rights reserved.

ISBN: 1494255626
ISBN 13: 9781494255626

No part of this book may be reproduced in any format or in any medium without the written permission of the publisher. This work is not an official publication of The Church of Jesus Christ of Latter-day Saints. The views expressed herein are the responsibility of the author and do not necessarily represent the position of the Church.

Contents

Preface	ix
Introduction – God-Science Conundrum	xiii
1. Evidence of Divine Creation	1
In the Beginning	3
A Divine Designer	6
Uniform Law of Nature	8
Matter, Energy and Spirit	10
The Creative Period	12
Worlds without End	15
The Expanding and Inflating Universe	18
The Multiverse and Eternal Progression	20
Conclusion	23
2. The Origin of Life	25
How LDS Educators Approach Evolution	31
Divinely Guided Evolution	34
The Predictability of Chance	35
Medical and Biology Experts Weigh In	36
Fixity of Species	38
Death and Decay	39
Unique Abilities of Humans	40
Making Sense of the Origin of Man	41

Garden Story Meanings	45
Conclusion	47

3. Spiritual Communication — 49

Spiritual Phenomena are Part of Being Human	52
The Brain as a Conduit	54
Communication through Dreams	57
Dreams Connect Us with God	59
Visions are Spiritual Gifts	64
After-death Communications	68
Conclusion	72

4. Near-death Experiences and the Afterlife — 77

Out-of-Body Experiences	82
Children have NDEs	84
The Blind Can See	87
Atheists have NDEs	88
NDE Elements and LDS Beliefs	89
What Research Studies Reveal	96
Interpreting the Experiences	100
Conclusion	104

5. Avenues to Miracles — 107

Power of Faith	107
Optimism Builds Faith	111
Righteous Actions Required	113
Prayer, the Ultimate Conduit	117
Personal and Prophetic Revelation	123
Distinguishing Revelation from Reason	126
Miraculous Intervention	129
Stories of Miracles	132
Understanding the Miracles of Jesus	134
Conclusion	136

6. Origins of Religion	139
Differences and Similarities of World Religions	141
Reasons for so Many Theologies	145
Deviation from True Doctrine	145
Bible Stories Appear in Other Cultures	149
Scripture Stories: Fact or Fiction	153
Adam and Eve and the Garden of Eden	155
Noah and the Flood	157
Tower of Babel	158
The Message in the Story	159
Book of Mormon Authenticity and Symbolism	161
Gospel Globalization	167
Conclusion	170
7. Salvation of the Dead	173
Spirit World Evangelization	174
Degrees of Glory	179
Justice and Mercy	182
How Many Will Be Exalted	186
Wayward Children to Be Saved	190
Advantages to Conversion Here Instead of There	194
Conclusion	197
8. Symbolism and Ritual	199
Societal Symbolism	200
Religious Symbols and Rituals	203
Symbolism in the Scriptures	207
The Temple	211
The Endowment in Antiquity	212
The Handclasp	214
Names	215
Drama	215
Creation Drama	216

Ancient Origin of Sacred Clothing	217
Garments as Coverings	220
Aprons	221
Robes	222
Caps	222
Embracing the Symbolism	223
Conclusion	226
9. A World of Evil, Tragedy, and Challenge	229
Satan is Alive and Well	230
Global Evil	233
Tools of the Devil	235
Moral Agency and the Fight against Evil	239
People are Inherently Good	241
The Biology of Goodness	244
God Provides a Balance	246
Why Bad Things Happen	249
Conclusion	253
10. Inherited Attributes of Deity	257
The Transforming Power of Forgiveness	263
The Reality and Mission of Jesus	266
Building Testimonies	268
Attributes of God	272
Errors of Man-made Creeds	274
Who is God	275
We are not Alone	278
Conclusion	280
11. Help for the Doubting Thomas	283
Questioning is Not a Sign of Weakness	284
The Spiritual Value of Evidence	287
Science and Revelation Work Together	289

Avoid Stumbling Blocks	290
Revelation through Pondering and Meditation	294
Physical Benefits of Meditation	295
Stories of Inspiration	297
The Love of God is our Rudder	300
Conclusion	302

Notes 307

Preface

Do you find yourself sitting in Church listening to the faith promoting stories of others, wondering why you have so few of your own? Is there a touch of envy in your heart at the descriptions of stirring temple insight people receive, that you seldom, if ever, experience? Do you wonder what's wrong with you for your inability to sense and recognize the whisperings of the Spirit or even fathom the very idea of God? You want to believe. You'd like to feel what others feel instead of being the consummate Doubting Thomas who lives his or her religion with a raised eyebrow. If you are dogged by such questions and more, it is you I seek to reach.

Doubt is not necessarily unhealthy if it motivates us to search for answers and seek a deeper communion with the Spirit. But if left unchecked long enough, doubt can menace the soul and infect the spirit with dubious messages that weaken the divine nature within us. Many people seem blessed with an abiding faith. They never seem to struggle with testimony because somewhere deep within, they just know the gospel of Jesus Christ is true. But many more, I suspect have doubted at one time or another, with one principle or another. Often, they can manage the various faces they must wear within the Church community to keep their doubt concealed, but when something traumatic happens and they need faith the most, the emptiness of feeling spiritually alone can become overwhelming.

It's somewhat like the story in the book of Mark when a man brings his son possessed by a "dumb spirit" and asks the Savior to heal the boy. "Jesus said unto him, if thou canst believe, all things are possible to him that believeth. And straightway the father of the child cried out, and said with tears,

Lord, I believe; [and then he hesitated when he realized his faith was weak and pleaded] help thou mine unbelief" (Mark 9:23&24).

I must confess that I too have felt the unease of doubt about God and his Church, and understand all too well how unbelief can fester like a sore that won't heal. For me, it was largely a matter of seeing science and religion as incompatible. I simply couldn't grasp in my limited earthbound mentality, the idea of a Supreme Being with supernatural powers, creating worlds without end. Equally unsettling were tenets suggesting we are literally his offspring, will live forever, and will have the opportunity of becoming like him someday. The whole thing was really out there, and I simply could not imagine it.

Most people I have known and served with over the years never knew about these misgivings, because my whole background and persona reflected religious strength and testimony. I was born into an active LDS family, was faithful to my baptismal and temple covenants, served a full-time mission, married in the temple, and raised three wonderful children in the ways of the Lord. I served in many capacities within the wards and stakes where I resided and tried very hard to reach out to others to help them wherever I was needed. In other words, I was a typical Latter-day Saint woman.

But underneath it all, I was a Doubting Thomas. Despite my activity in the Church, there was always within me a steaming cauldron of doubt and insecurity about the very belief system to which I had dedicated my life. Most of the time, I could keep the pot on simmer because after all, I would tell myself, any religious belief a person professes is simply a matter of choice anyway. I chose to believe, just like everybody else. But still that persistent little voice of doubt would bubble up until, from time to time, the cauldron would boil over requiring yet another Herculean effort to get the lid back on.

It wasn't until the passing of my 88-year-old father and the reaction to it I saw in my mother that I decided to make this literary journey to find for myself the reality of God. Up until my father's passing, I had never heard a sliver of doubt escape my mother's lips or see it in her actions. She was a stalwart Latter-day Saint through and through and raised her children to be as well.

She mourned my dad's loss as would any devoted spouse. She expressed how much she missed him especially in those lonely hours after dark when a loving companion can bring comfort and security. She recounted memories about him to all who would listen and spoke of the posterity they created together with reverence and pride. She responded as one might expect given the loss of her eternal mate, but in the mix of it all she also began to express doubt.

She would pose questions to me and others about whether she would really ever see her beloved husband again. "I've believed in God and the gospel my whole life," she said, "and now when my faith is truly being tested, I can't help but wonder if any of it is really true. I miss my husband, and I'm starting to doubt."

I had long conversations with her to try to buoy her up and give her answers that would fill this new void in her otherwise unshakable testimony. It was forcing me to dig deep into my own soul for answers that just weren't completely there. I wanted to know too. Would I see my dad again? Is he at rest now with God in the spirit world? Is God real? So it was on the heels of this deeply profound experience that I decided once and for all: I needed answers. My mom needed answers too, so I became determined to get them.

In the research and writing of this book, I had three hopes. The first was that I could put to rest my own incessant doubts about the existence of God, and the second was to assuage my mother's uncertainty and give her reassurance that life with my dad would indeed go on. The third was to help others who doubted find a semblance of inner peace and be newly motivated to ask God to "help thou mine unbelief."

The journey of this writing has taken me into areas that were new to me both temporally and spiritually, which ultimately, I'm thrilled to say, transformed and solidified my own testimony to the point of true conversion. I not only am stronger in the gospel, but also feel a tangible connection to my Heavenly Father like never before. I am at peace with the notion that we simply don't have all the answers and that true evidence of God is manifested in my spiritual relationship with him. I am learning how to deepen that relationship each day and am rewarded in ways that have taken me to pinnacles of understanding and clarity beyond anything I ever imagined. My testimony is now resolute with a firm belief that God lives and that Jesus is the Christ, and that a prophet of God leads this Church to help us toward our goal of eternal life.

I know these things after using a two-step process to find truth. The first was digging into science, history, and theology to provide a foundation for tangible evidence, and the second was embracing a spiritual relationship with Deity through prayer and pondering. I found I needed both components to come away, once and for all, truly converted to the restored gospel. It should be understood that while I extensively quote scientists, scholars, prophets, apostles, and learned Church educators, the conclusions I draw within these chapters are my own. I feel those conclusions are in keeping with LDS theology, or at least, do not deviate from it. I make this distinction because there isn't always stated Church doctrine for every theological topic of interest. Because of that, we must use the light of Christ, the Holy Ghost, and our own research from the "best books" to embrace answers that build our individual faith.

I am not a scientist or a theologian; far from it. I am, however, a bit of a digger. With a degree in journalism and years of work as a reporter and editor for various publications, including some time at the *Church News*, I have a penchant for researching and pursuing answers to tough questions. I tried to harness this "news hound" energy of mine into researching what the scientific as well as theological experts had to say. I relied heavily on the words of Church leaders and educators to validate the messages within these pages and provide possible answers that ease doubts and motivate readers to seek an even greater spiritual witness.

In the end, scholarly evidence can help increase faith as it unravels some of life's greatest mysteries, but it can never replace a spiritual connection with God. I hope your journey through these pages will bring you that connection.

INTRODUCTION

God-Science Conundrum

*I*t would be so easy if science could prove religion in our quest for truth and vice versa. Many people hold tenaciously to one or the other and won't allow for even the slightest deviation in what they believe. Sadly, by doing so, they miss out on incredible possibilities that could broaden their understanding and illuminate truths that are right at their fingertips. The more I studied this conundrum, the more I discovered how absolutely cohesive God and science really are. They provide more harmony than dissonance and in those areas where it may appear that neither side has a conclusive answer, there is enough agreement to maintain a working symbiosis.

The Savior said, "Ask, and it shall be given you; seek, and ye shall find; knock, and it shall be opened unto you" (Matthew 7:7). Science and religion can actually harmonize because both involve a spirit of inquiry that seeks out truth. Since the gospel welcomes and incorporates all truth, both science and religion have important roles in separating fact from fantasy.

God's counsel to Joseph Smith opened a world of resources for learning truth: "Teach ye diligently and my grace shall attend you, that you may be instructed more perfectly in theory, in principle, in doctrine, in the law of the gospel, in all things that pertain unto the kingdom of God, that are expedient for you to understand; of things both in heaven and in the earth and under the earth; things which have been, things which are, things which must shortly come to pass; things which are at home, things which are abroad; the wars and the perplexities of the nations, and the judgments which are upon the land; and a knowledge also of countries and of kingdoms" (D&C 88:78-79).

Other prophets also have taught this principle. Brigham Young said, "All wisdom, and all the arts and sciences in the world are from God, and are designed for the good of his people."[1] He also reminded us that we are obligated and indebted to God for the benefits that flow to us from the truths He has revealed, whether "scientific or religious."[2] President Harold B. Lee stated, "All truths, whether called science or religion, or philosophy, come from a divine source."[3] Spencer W. Kimball said modern scientific findings "harmonize with revelation through the ages."[4] He also said, "No conflict exists between the gospel and any truth .... All true principles are a part of the gospel of Jesus Christ. There is no principle that we need to fear."[5] Ezra Taft Benson once stated that Mormons "have no fear that any discovery of new truths will ever be in conflict with ... any fundamental basic principle which we advocate in the Gospel." He affirmed his comfort with "any new truths, whether discovered in the laboratory, through the research of the scientist, or whether revealed from heaven through prophets of God."[6]

It is clear that God sees no conflict in putting science and scholarship right alongside revelation and spirituality in establishing truth. It is also clear that mankind has assimilated elements of science over time in a kind of evolution of belief.

History shows us that flanking even the most rudimentary discoveries in science since early man, is evidence of various cultures in worship of a deity. Ancient Egyptians held such strong belief in their gods that they built massive pyramids to honor them. Ancient Greeks worshipped Zeus, early Romans worshipped Jupiter, and the Aztecs in Mexico offered human sacrifice to keep their god happy. Today, Hindus believe in the triad of Brahma, Vishnu, and Shiva; Islamic theology espouses Allah as being above all comprehension; and of course, Christians worship the God of Abraham, Isaac, and Jacob, and view him as the only true God.

Though I've only mentioned these few, the list of deities today and throughout history is enormous, to say the least. Why is that? What is it that pushes humans to seek out and ultimately devote their lives to a supreme being? Some argue that the ancients believed in a God because their limited world view and sometimes barbaric lifestyles easily led them to Pagan-type ideologies. In today's modern world with its ever accelerating technological advances and scientific breakthroughs, some find it ludicrous that people still believe in a Supreme Being.

Those who adopt science as their main purveyor of truth simply can't understand why any intelligent, rationally thinking person would continually look to the supernatural for answers to their existence. They can't grasp why people so tenaciously hope that things they can't see are nevertheless true. Could it be that we humans have always gravitated toward God because we are connected to him as his children? Could it be that as God's literal offspring, we have a spark of the divine that makes us long for the filial connection we once had and a desire to find our way back home? Could it be that the longing, yearning, all-consuming need to know God is not because we are delusional people who need some outside support to get through life, but because we are connected like an umbilical cord to a Heavenly Father who loves us?

Atheists often suggest that belief in God exists to bridge the gap between what we can understand about life and what we can't. They purport our use of religion is a crutch to help us limp through life, buoy ourselves up, and give our lives meaning. Science, they say, can now explain what has historically been inexplicable. Those gaps in information and evidence that supported the need for a belief in God in times past have now been filled making a belief in God superfluous. And while this argument may seem logical on its face, scientists are usually the first to say they don't know everything.

Historically, many scientists actually held a strong belief in God because they grew to acknowledge a spiritual element to the universe. Even Albert Einstein, one of the greatest minds of all time, couldn't completely disavow the notion of God. While developing his general theory of relativity, his calculations led him to draw only one conclusion—there had to be a beginning. (Later, Hubble discovered the universe was expanding, which further verified this requirement for a beginning). This troubled Einstein because it meant the universe and all that it holds must have been created by a deity, something he had always rejected. Ultimately, he became a deist—a believer in an impersonal creator God, who "did not concern himself with fates and actions of human beings."[7]

The atheist, or just the simple Doubting Thomas who would like to believe in his heart of hearts, is sometimes duped into thinking the scientific method is the *only* way to investigate, research, and find truth. They limit their quest to only what they can see and touch. We can't see and touch gravity. We can't see and touch thoughts. We can't see and touch atoms, yet we know through evidence that each of these things is real.

Think about it. For God to create the vast expanse of the universe, he, himself, would have had to exist far beyond the limitations of his creation and the science associated with it. Therefore, in our efforts to find him, we would likewise need to look beyond the laws of physics for more cosmic measuring devices that could lead to his doorstep.

Consider the account of Korihor in Alma 30, who antagonistically argued against the existence of God in the Book of Mormon. Gerald Lund, LDS author (*Work and the Glory* series), Church Education System director, and former General Authority, put it this way:

"Korihor will consider only evidence that can be gathered through the senses. In such a system, it is much easier to prove there is a God than to prove there is not a God. To prove there is a God, all it takes is for one person to see, hear, or otherwise have an experience with God, and thereafter the existence of God cannot be disproved. But here is what it would take to prove there is no God:

"Since God is not confined to this earth, we would have to search throughout the universe for him. We assume God is able to move about, so it would not be enough to start at point A in the universe and search through to point Z. What if after we leave point A, God moves there and stays there for the rest of the search? In other words, for Korihor to say that there is no God, based on the very criteria he himself has established, he would have to perceive every cubic meter of the universe simultaneously. This creates a paradox: In order for Korihor to prove there is no God, he would have to be a god himself! Therefore, in declaring there is no God, he is acting on *faith,* the very thing for which he so sharply derides the religious leaders!"[8]

It's an astoundingly complex topic and one in which volumes of literature have barely scratched the surface. After pouring through these volumes, it's easy to conclude there is no way to prove or disprove the existence of God using empirical scientific methods. This methodology excludes anything that cannot be tested with our five senses. But while there is no *scientific proof* of God's existence, there certainly is an abundance of evidence—evidence that can create fertile ground for a seed of faith to be planted and nourished (see Alma 32).

From a biblical perspective, God has not left us alone and without verification of his divine signature all around us. In fact, we learn that the world is replete with evidence of God, so much so that we are "without excuse" if we reject him (Romans 1:19-20). Paul said to "prove all things," (1 Thessalonians. 5:21), and to use reasoning instead of blind faith in matters of God and his plan of salvation (Acts 18:4, 19). In essence, though we can't see God, he is evident in every facet of life. In any court of law when there is no smoking gun, a preponderance of evidence will provide a conviction every time. It is that kind of evidence that helps establish the groundwork for the existence of God and the restored gospel.

As we explore what science has to say about our universe in the coming chapters of this book, it's important to acknowledge scholars are continually learning about our world. What was once considered truth in science in the past is often disproved as new information is discovered. As Christians, and Mormons in particular, we are instructed to seek out and embrace truth wherever we find it. But if scientists go beyond or fall short of what they can actually prove, we are not obligated to buy into their theories.

I have presented scientific theories and scholarly writings on various topics because they made sense to me personally. Some people may have no interest in what these secular experts have to say because their faith is sufficient the way it is. But others will be keenly attentive to scientific and historical findings and conclusions because their faith may require the added value of physical evidence. There's nothing wrong with this, and in fact, great blessings will surely come to anyone who sincerely seeks out God and Christ wherever they may be found.

CHAPTER ONE

Evidence of Divine Creation

One can imagine the ancients looking upward from their primitive encampments in awe of the vastness of space without the slightest clue of what was actually out there. But over the centuries, science carved out a tenable foundation for understanding the universe. As primordial scientists started to fashion rudimentary instruments for piercing the skies, humans began to get a glimpse of the enormity of the universe. Today, thanks to more than two decades of incredible images from Hubble, the world's first space-based optical telescope, we are given a window into space through unprecedented photos of the farthest reaches of our galaxy.

I remember being spellbound while watching the IMAX movie, "Hubble 3D," where viewers were taken on an exhilarating visual ride through the Orion Nebula, a vast star-making factory 1,500 light-years away. We soared through Orion's immense canyon of gas and dust and past enormous stars that illuminated and energized entire regions of space. We explored infant solar systems and journeyed through the Milky Way into a field of 170,000 stars in a giant cluster. The movie just scratched the surface of some 15,000 galaxies, many of them 13 billion years old, stretching billions of light-years across the universe.

The iconic Hubble has connected us to our universe like nothing else in modern science. It's only a matter of time before we forge new frontiers in space exploration when its successor, the James Webb Space Telescope, is launched in late 2018 to replace Hubble. One can only speculate and wonder at what further reaches into the cosmos we may yet go, providing additional answers to our origins.

When we begin to fathom, even slightly, the vastness of the universe, we see how inadequate words are to describe it. We characterize the universe as immeasurable, limitless, and infinite and still we are sorely lacking in just the right words. Notice that those same descriptions used to delineate the universe are consistent with or even identical to the words we often use to describe God and his power. When doubters express their inability to grasp the concept of an omnipotent, omniscient, omnipresent God, they, like most of us, also have trouble grasping the infinitesimal immensity of the cosmos. Both are mind-boggling, both are other-worldly, suggesting an interconnectedness that seems to hold the keys to unlocking all truth.

As we explore the evidence of creation, we should understand that it is not only acceptable, but also beneficial, to look at science as a way of adding beauty and clarity to gospel doctrine. Evidence is always a great defender of truth by pointing out error, and provides broader meaning and perspective for the honest seeker of truth. Elder Neal A. Maxwell counseled, that learning through discoveries would help "make plain and plausible what the modern prophets have been saying all along."[1] President Gordon B. Hinckley said that evidence derived from scientific and historical research can "be helpful to some" and "confirmatory."[2]

It's the melding of research with revelation that provides the confirmatory weight so many of us need for faith to flourish. Until we accept how interlocked science and theology are, even the explosion of information we enjoy today as compared with the ancients, will not be enough to provide sufficient answers to many of our questions. It's amazing what we know, but equally amazing what we don't know. As predicted by Paul, we are truly "ever learning and never able to come to the knowledge of the truth" (2 Timothy 3:7).

In the Beginning

Let's take a look at some of what we know, or think we know, about the beginnings of our universe. Science is positive that our universe sprang into existence as a "singularity" around 15 billion years ago. Singularities are zones that are thought to exist at the center of "black holes." Black holes are areas of concentrated gravitational pressure which are so intense matter is actually mashed into infinite density.

Somewhere along the way these singularities suddenly inflated [the big bang], and changed from an exceedingly dense, incredibly hot, infinitesimal ball of *something* into the size and temperature of today's universe. It continues to expand and cool to this day with humans living on a perfectly prepared planet circling a star that is surrounded by several hundred billion other stars. This all exists in a galaxy within a cosmos that began as an infinitesimal singularity which just suddenly appeared for reasons unknown.[3]

What an incredible scenario. Taken at face value, it is difficult for our finite minds to grasp. But the takeaway here for Mormons is that when big bang theorists use it to support creation *ex nihilo,* which is creation from nothing, it is at total odds with Mormonism. We do not believe in creation from nothing. However, the big bang theory itself, without the component of creation *ex nihilo,* is not at odds with Mormonism. In fact, there is no Church doctrine about it one way or the other.

When studied scientifically, and not theologically, there is a big glaring hole in the singularity narrative. If existence itself was created by the bursting of this singularity, then elements of it would have had to exist in some fashion already. In quantum mechanics we learn that a certain amount of energy is *always* present. There is no such thing as the idea of a great void, nothingness, or empty space because empty space, science has learned, is filled with a menagerie of particles, waves, fields, energies, and interactions, many of which we don't currently understand.[4] Our universe is dominated by the mass-energy of empty space and it always has been. What science really means by the idea of empty space is the emptiest possible state that possesses the lowest possible energy: The state from which no further energy can be removed. This is the *ground state* or the *vacuum state*—a possible point at which a big bang could have occurred but not from a literal and absolute nothing.[5]

Why is this important? Because it would suggest that in order for our universe to come into being, there had to be a true "beginning,"—not just something out of nothing—where creation is produced by that which creates: God. The big bang theory is largely ignored in Mormon creation discussion because of the lack of real evidence. How can you test and measure something that happened billions of years ago? However, the theory can certainly be discussed in light of where it intersects with truths revealed through God's prophets. For instance, we know there were actually two creations, the first spiritual and the second temporal (see Moses 3:5), which neatly fills in the glaring holes in science's explanation. The fine, sub-atomic matter or energy that was used to form all things spiritually in the first creation was also used in the creation of atoms, chemical elements, and larger entities that came later in the second.

With this in mind, there is no reason to reject the basic premise of the big bang as long as we include the hand of God in the process. Mormon scientist William Lee Stokes put it this way:

> "The original, invisible hydrogen and helium created at the big bang were dispersed into space until the tendency to fly apart was overcome by gravity, and they began to condense into large, dark clouds called proto galaxies. Eventually, still under the influence of gravity, matter at the centers of individual clouds became so heated by compression that thermonuclear reactions began [as in the Sun]. The most notable result was the appearance of light. The invisible became visible, and the process of creating visible, solid elements was under way. The meaning of Genesis is the same. Matter created as 'the beginning' is depicted as 'without form and void' (Gen. 1:2), a good description of the dark, unorganized phase of creation. Then the majestic command, 'Let there be light'

(Gen. 1:3), makes the invisible visible, and the more complex steps of creation can proceed."[6]

The creation *ex nihilo*, out of nothing, argument in the big bang continues to be science's hallmark in cosmology [the study of the origins of the universe] and is presented to the general public as "fact." Seen in that light, it is literally based on a guess. Many astronomers, mathematicians, and physicists have discredited creation *ex nihilo*, while many others cling to it tenaciously as "the" scientific explanation for our existence.

Creation *ex nihilo* is probably the one doctrine of science and mainstream Christianity that is most emphatically denounced in Mormonism starting with Joseph Smith.

> "Now I ask all the learned men who hear me, why the learned men who are preaching salvation say, that God created the heavens and the earth out of nothing, and the reason is they are unlearned; they account it blasphemy to contradict the idea, they will call you a fool ... The word create came from the word *baurau*; it does not mean so; it means to organize; the same as a man would organize a ship. Hence we infer that God had materials to organize the world out of chaos; chaotic matter, which is element, and in which dwells all the glory. Element had an existence from the time he had. The pure principles of element are principles that can never be destroyed. They may be organized and re-organized; but not destroyed."[7]

In the book of Abraham's account of the creation, we learn that the Gods formed the heavens and the earth out of preexisting materials (see Abraham 4:1. 12, 14-16). This goes against centuries of Christian dogma, which insists that God created the universe from nothing. But Daniel C. Peterson, BYU professor of Islamic Studies and Arabic, pointed out that once again, the book of Abraham is supported by current research. He said the doctrine of *ex nihilo* creation is simply not in the Bible—anywhere. Furthermore, ancient Jewish texts explain that God created the universe by giving form to formless matter. This is what was taught among the Jews and early Christians until the Greek philosophy of creation *ex nihilo* began to influence Christian thinkers during the second century after Christ. The doctrine gradually replaced the truth and became widely accepted in mainstream Christianity.[8]

Scientific parlays into factors that argue for both are readily available for those who want a more in depth look at it, but for purposes here, physicist Fred Adams wrapped it up well. He said, "The big bang does not represent creation *ex nihilo*. Cosmic history began at a particular point in time—the moment we denote as $t = 0$. But before that point we do not assume that there was nothing at all in existence. Energy is the currency of the cosmos, so this incorrect assumption would imply that an extraordinarily large violation of energy conservation took place at the beginning of time."[9]

Any discussion of the big bang theory should include an understanding that the term "big bang" is used in two ways: First, for the whole expansion period of the universe and second, for the assumed moment of origin at time zero. There is very little that science knows about the origin. It knows much more about what happened afterward.

A Divine Designer

The amazing design and intricacies of the universe suggest they didn't happen by chance, but were the workmanship of a divine designer. A masterful painting, for example, couldn't just spring into existence on its own. The undeniable truth is that a painter had to have painted it.

In the Book of Mormon, the prophet Alma taught, "All things denote there is a God; yea, even the earth, and all things that are upon the face of it, yea, and its motion, yea, and also all the planets which move in their regular form do witness that there is a Supreme Creator" (Alma 30:44). A look at a few of nature's truly miraculous workings can serve as stark evidence of God as the artist and architect of the universe.

The Earth. If the earth were not at the distance it is from the sun, it would not be capable of supporting much of life as we know it. The earth remains this perfect distance from the sun while it revolves around it at a speed of nearly 67,000 mph. It also rotates on its axis, ensuring the appropriate amount of warming and cooling each day. Even the tiniest variance in the earth's position to the sun would make the earth incapable of sustaining life. Also, our moon is the perfect size and distance from the earth to create the gravitational pull so important for ocean tides and movement that keeps water from stagnating. And it does all this while keeping our massive oceans contained within the boundaries of the shorelines.

The earth is also perfect in size because gravity holds a thin layer of mostly nitrogen and oxygen gases just 50 miles above its surface. If Earth were smaller, such an atmosphere would be impossible, like the planet Mercury. If Earth were larger, its atmosphere would contain free hydrogen, like Jupiter. The right mixture of gases to sustain all plant, animal, and human life is found on Earth, the only known planet to be so equipped.[10]

"For thus saith the Lord that created the heavens; God himself that formed the earth and made it; he hath established it, he created it not in vain, he formed it to be inhabited" (Isaiah 45:18), and "he hath created his children that they should possess it" (1 Nephi 17:36). The Lord revealed to the Prophet Joseph Smith: "Yea, all things which come of the earth, in the season thereof, are made for the benefit and the use of man, both to please the eye and to gladden the heart; Yea, for food and for raiment, for taste and for smell, to strengthen the body and to enliven the soul" (D&C 59: 18-19).

Water. As we study the earth's complexities, perhaps the most important creation to sustain life is water, without which, no living thing could survive. Interestingly, about two-thirds of the human body is composed of water. Here are the miraculous properties and processes of this vital liquid.

a. Water carries throughout the body various substances including food, medicines, and minerals while leaving those substances unchanged.

b. Even though temperatures change, water enables our bodies to stay at 98.6 degrees.
c. Water is a universal solvent which enables various chemicals, minerals, and nutrients to make their way into the tiniest blood vessels.
d. Fish can continue to live during the winter because water freezes from the top down.
e. Through cohesive and adhesive properties, water in plants can flow upward against gravity, bringing moisture and nutrients to the tree tops.
f. Ninety-seven percent of the earth's water is in the oceans. An elaborate water cycle takes the ocean waters minus the salt, and forms clouds that are moved by the wind to disperse water over the land to sustain life for all living things.

Photosynthesis. The staggering organization and complexity evident in the process of photosynthesis—something man has yet to fully understand, let alone copy—screams of having been designed. This process by which plants, algae, and certain bacteria convert sunlight to chemical energy is one of nature's most elaborate biological machines. It converts light energy at unmatched efficiency at more than 95 percent compared to 10 to 15 percent in the current human-made solar technologies. The invisible machinery working behind the scenes to sustain the carbon cycle is astonishing.[11]

Photosynthesis is one of the most important chemical reactions on Earth because it allows plants to make their own food from sunlight and enables them to produce the oxygen essential to all air-breathing life. If we could duplicate it, photosynthesis would probably solve all the world's energy problems,[12] but even the most exceptional scientists have not been able to match the enormous usefulness of the common plant.

Uniform Laws of Nature

The fact that the universe operates under requisite, uniform laws of nature is perhaps the most striking evidence for God as creator. The universe is orderly, providing certainty day after day as to what we can expect in our physical world. Gravity, the seasons, light and dark, chemistry, mathematics, physics, all function by reason of natural law. They do not change and are elaborately fine-tuned to make life possible. Richard Feynman, a Nobel Prize winner for quantum electrodynamics, observed, "Why nature is mathematical is a mystery.... The fact that there are rules at all is a kind of miracle."[13]

Each new discovery about our origins seems to further ensconce some in the scientific community against a belief in God as creator. If science can explain it, they say, there is no need for God. But in this conclusion, they reject their own discoveries about the uniform laws of nature. The religious world believes that God created the laws of nature and maintains them in working order for the growth and survival of his children. Not only is nature bound by these laws, but so is he who created them. They are unchanging because they were created by the master biologist, astronomer, physicist, and chemist to operate perfectly and optimally for the good of humankind.

A case in point is the announcement by scientists on July 4, 2012, of the preliminary discovery of the Higgs boson, or "God Particle" that is considered the reason everything has mass. Without mass, there would be no structure or weight to anything such as trees, humans, and planets. Before this discovery scientists felt sure of the existence of this sub-atomic particle but were unable to find it. But when protons were shot at nearly the speed of light through the 17-mile long Large Hadron Collider, a particle accelerator in Switzerland, they found what they were looking for. Many feel this new discovery could explain how the universe works, where it came from, and where it is headed in the future.[14]

Time will tell what the discovery will teach us, but the reason for discussing it here is that atheistic big bang theorists feel the Higgs boson will help them track the laws of nature to the beginning of time, thus eliminating the need for God. They think just because they have knowledge of our physical world, they can close the book on all things spiritual. If they could open their minds further, as have many scientists who still maintain a belief in God, they would see the God Particle as evidence of a divine interconnectedness of all things. They would see that natural laws do not preclude

God in the grand scheme of things but actually support the argument for his existence. It's quite reasonable to say this discovery represents another incredible advancement in scientific knowledge for humankind as well as a moving appreciation for the intricacies of God's universe and evidence that he lives.

Elder Neal A. Maxwell said, "Since all truth comes from our Heavenly Father, when we celebrate truth in creative breakthroughs, whether in new understanding of molecular structure or in the beauty of new sculpture, painting, or poetry, we acknowledge the resplendent order in God's universe."[15]

Matter, Energy, and Spirit

The LDS Church is unique in its understanding of what exactly the human spirit or conscious is. Religion, in general, teaches that the spirit will live on after the death of the physical body, but it can't provide an understanding of its composition or origin.

Joseph Smith taught, "There is no such thing as immaterial matter. All spirit is matter, but it is more fine or pure, and can only be discerned by purer eyes; we cannot see it; but when our bodies are purified, we shall see that it is all matter" (D&C 131:7-8). He also said this spirit element has always existed and is co-eternal with God,[16] and is called "intelligence or the light of truth, which was not created or made, neither indeed can be" (D&C 93:29).

This religious truth that was revealed by a prophet of God is also corroborated through science. Relativity theory and laboratory experiments have proven that matter can disappear only to reappear again as energy. The nuclear bomb is a case in point. The transformation of uranium 235, or plutonium, into energy is manifested by the intense heat of the explosion. It is a literal change of matter into energy. It's important to note that the inverse process is also true: Energy can be changed into matter. Matter and energy are merely different forms of the same thing.[17]

Think of the religious implications this scientific fact provides. LDS doctrine says our spirit bodies are composed of a refined kind of matter [energy]. Because matter and energy are interchangeable, three very important religious facts are evident:

1. The spirit [consciousness] of man that resides within a physical body is real.
2. We all existed in a spirit form [refined matter] in a pre-existent state because matter has always existed.
3. The spirit will live on after physical death because it can't be destroyed.

Bruce R. McConkie wrote:

"The indestructibility of matter/energy is evidence of the doctrine of resurrection. Those natural or earthy substances of which the earth in all its parts is composed and which make up the physical or temporal bodies of all created things, are called elements. They are of the earth, earthy (1 Cor. 15:44-48); they are to be distinguished from the more pure and refined substances of which spirit matter is composed (D&C 131:6-7). 'The elements are eternal,' the Lord says; and when they are organized into a mortal body, those elements become the tabernacle of the eternal spirit that comes from pre-existence. In the resurrection 'spirit and element' are 'inseparably connected,' thus assuring immortality to the soul (D&C 93:33-35). It follows that elements which are mortal now are destined to become immortal elements hereafter."[18]

Think of how Joseph Smith taught that the word, *create* means *to organize*. He said, "We have already learned from science that element [matter] can never be destroyed, but it can be organized and reorganized. Like God, this element had no beginning and can have no end."[19]

In their efforts to explain the origins of the universe, secular scholars seem to land mainly in two camps: Those who reject a divine creator for the big bang that occurred from nothing [*ex nihilo*], and those who believe in a creator God who made the universe out of nothing. They just can't seem to let go of the "nothing" factor. There are, of course, in-betweeners, but these two camps should both consider the following logical line of reasoning.

If the universe truly did spring out of nothing as they claim, absolutely nothing at all, logic tells us there would still be nothing today as well as nothing forever. Because something [matter and energy] does exist now and we know that something could not come from nothing, it is logical to conclude that something [matter and energy] has always existed.

This concept was emphasized by Apostle James E. Talmage, a trained geologist, when he said, "Man's consciousness tells him of his own existence; his observation proves the existence of others of this kind and of uncounted orders of organized beings. From this we conclude that something must have existed always, for had there been a time of no existence, a period of nothingness, existence could have never begun, for from nothing, nothing can be derived."[20] Likewise, astronomer Hollis Johnson explained that "it is difficult to imagine that nothing exists anywhere. Creation from nothing is clearly a fantasy devised by certain theologians, perhaps in a misguided attempt to glorify God by making of him a fantastic magician."[21]

It should be noted that some people in the "no divine creator" camp get around the something/nothing argument by admitting that a "little something" did actually exist in order for the big bang to occur. Those in the other camp, while their main point of God as creator is correct, erroneously hold onto the illogical assumption that he created it from nothing. In this case, both camps have part of the answer but lack the full understanding that was given to us by Joseph Smith, as well as many renowned scientists, that matter has always existed and has no beginning or end. So God didn't create the universe out of nothing, but rather out of matter that already existed. Mormons should have no problem accepting the big bang as long as we don't exclude God from the process. Of course, it is still a theory, but it is certainly plausible that God used an explosive methodology under his omnipotent control to fashion our universe.

The Creative Period

Caught firmly in the middle of creation arguments between scientists and theologians, is the actual length of time it took to create the universe.

Discussion over the creative period recorded in Genesis usually entails three possibilities:

1. It actually took six 24-hour days.
2. It took 6,000 years with a day being equal to 1,000 years in God's time.
3. A day was used as an allegory for a much longer, undefined period of time.

Because of scriptural accounts of the creation in the Bible, the Pearl of Great Price, and the temple ceremony, Latter-day Saints have more understanding on the topic, although a full reckoning of the creation will probably not come forth until God makes all things known when the Savior returns (see D&C 101:32-34).

But in the meantime, science has provided some theoretical information that could actually be viewed in harmony with LDS doctrine. We know that science has estimated the universe to be approximately 15 billion years old and the earth, about 5 billion years old. There are many things that make the world appear old, but one of the most compelling items is the light coming from the stars. Some of the stars are so far away that it would take billions of years for their light to reach us.

We know that light travels at the rate of 186,282 miles per second, which means it takes sunlight 8.3 minutes to reach Earth. Even the closest star to Earth is so distant it takes 4.2 years for its light to reach us. Using this measurement of time, it would take 170,000 years for the light from the closest galaxy to reach our surface and a whopping 15 billion years for the light of the farthest galaxies to reach us.[22] Proponents of creation *ex nihilo* use this argument to negate the idea of a creator God who fashioned the universe in six days. But their logic is false.

BYU professors and scholars F. Kent Nielsen and Stephen D. Ricks, taught that the term 'day' [Hebrew *yom*] for the seven 'days' of creation is given as 'time.' This alternative word is acceptable in both Hebrew and English. The 'time' in which Adam should die after the Fall was after the

Lord's time, which Abraham said was after the time of Kolob [a great star nearest to the throne of God, whose revolution, we understand to be one thousand years, but is a day unto the Lord] (see Abraham 5:13; 3:2-4).[23] These professors further explained:

> "On the basis of the above passage, which clearly excludes the possibility of earthly twenty-four-hour days being the 'days' or 'times' of creation, some Latter-day Saint commentators have argued for one-thousand-year periods as the 'times' of creation as well as the 'time' of Adam's earthly life after the Fall; others have argued for indefinite periods of time, as long as it would take to accomplish the work involved. Abraham's account does contain the interesting passage, in connection with the 'organizing' of the lights in the 'expanse' of heaven: 'The Gods watched those things which they had ordered *until they obeyed*'" (Abraham 4:14-18).[24]

"Until they obeyed," suggests a certain amount of time was needed for the elements in the "organizing" process to be fully functioning as designed. This and all of the above scriptural passages help us conclude that periods of time for the creation of the universe were great and this information coupled with what science teaches points to millions, if not billions of years. Because these periods of time are indeterminate in length it appears that as one phase of the creation was finished, the next began. The only realistic conclusion to be drawn is that the age of the earth before Adam and Eve could have been immense.[25]

Brigham Young also had little problem with accepting an earth millions or perhaps billions of years old, and questioned the literalness of the Genesis account:

> "How long it [the earth] has been organized is not for me to say, and I do not care anything about it. As for the Bible account of creation, we may say that the Lord gave it

to Moses, or rather Moses obtained the history and traditions of the fathers, and from them picked out what he considered necessary, and that account has been handed down from age to age, and we have got it, no matter whether it is correct or not, and whether the Lord found the earth empty or void, whether he made it out of nothing or out of rude elements; or whether he made it in six days or in as many millions of years, is and will remain a matter of speculation in the minds of men unless He gives revelation on the subject."[26]

Worlds without End

Thanks to NASA's Kepler telescope, launched into orbit in 2009, we have learned that our galaxy is packed with planets. In fact, more than 2,200 of what appear to be planets have been discovered orbiting the Milky Way. Despite this new data showing how common planets are in the universe, we still don't know how many of them, if any, can support life. What we do know through Kepler is that about one in ten stars has a planet associated with it that appears to hold water, life's mandatory ingredient. Do the math and we find that more than 10 billion planets have the potential to support microbes, plants, or even intelligent beings like we humans. Some may be so close that we could use telescopes to detect signs of life in their atmospheres. The possibility that undiscovered Earths are hiding in every corner of our galaxy is completely reorienting the future of space science.[27]

This doctrine of worlds without end is not new to Mormons who have known about it since the Church's inception while science is just beginning to climb aboard. Brigham Young said there is no such thing as "empty space," lending to the idea that any space beyond this universe is occupied.[28] Apostle Orson Pratt said, "We can come to no other conclusion, but that worlds, and systems of worlds, and universes of worlds existed in the boundless heights and depths of immensity ...."[29] He also asked, "Can we get away from it? No; for it fills all the intermediate spaces between world and world, between one system and another, and between universe and universe; and there is no space in which there is no kingdom, and there is no kingdom in which there is no space."[30]

To get a little perspective on the immensity of God's statement that he created "worlds without number" (Moses 1:33), let's turn to the observations of LDS Scientist Rodney D. Griffin.

> "Astronomers and cosmologists estimate that our Milky Way Galaxy contains between 130 billion to 400 billion stars. To understand the magnitude of this number, imagine that you set out to count to 400 billion. Further suppose that you could count one number every second, no matter how large, and that you counted every second for 24 hours every day. At that rate you could count to 3600 in one hour and to 86,400 in one day. However, in 365 days—or one year—of counting, you would have only reached 31,536,000—a very tiny fraction of the projected number. In one lifetime—say 70 years—of counting, you would reach the respectable number of 2,207,520,000, but it would still take 181 such misspent lifetimes to reach the 400 billion mark."[31]

Mind boggling, right? Not when you put it in context with revealed truth. LDS doctrine teaches this earth was not the first of God's creations. Bruce R. McConkie said, "An infinite number of worlds have come rolling into existence at His command. Each is an earth; many are inhabited with his spirit children; each abides the particular law given to it; and each will play its part in the redemption, salvation, and exaltation of that infinite host of the children of an Almighty God. The Lord has said that his work and glory is to bring to pass immortality and eternal life for his children on all the inhabited worlds he has created" (Moses 1:27-40; 7:29-36; D&C 88:17-26).[32]

Christ, who created the earth under God's direction, created worlds without number. Enoch said, "And were it possible that man could number the particles of the earth, yea, millions of earths like this, it would not be a beginning to the number of thy creations" (Moses 7:30). This description sounds a lot like what scientists are telling us today as the tentacles of technology reach out ever farther into the abyss of space.

Because of the staggering distances and length of time it would take to reach even the closest star [hundreds of thousands of years], science has no way of ever truly proving life on other planets, let alone, in other galaxies. This is why, and is indeed the perfect example of the need for science to embrace theology and combine forces in searching for cosmological answers that science alone can't provide. And for those brave enough to study and accept the revelations of prophets on the topic, a wealth of knowledge is within their grasp such as the ones revealed to the Prophet Joseph Smith in June, 1830, of some earlier writings of Moses.

> "And calling upon the name of God, he [Moses] beheld his glory again, for it was upon him; and he heard a voice, saying: Blessed art thou, Moses, for I, the Almighty, have chosen thee, and thou shalt be made stronger than many waters; for they shall obey thy command as if thou wert God.
>
> "And it came to pass, as the voice was still speaking, Moses cast his eyes and beheld the earth, yea, even all of it; ...
>
> "And he beheld also the inhabitants thereof, ...
>
> "And he beheld many lands; and each land was called earth, and there were inhabitants on the face thereof.
>
> "And it came to pass that Moses called upon God, saying: Tell me, I pray thee, why these things are so, and by what thou madest them?
>
> "And behold, the glory of the Lord was upon Moses, so that Moses stood in the presence of God, and talked with him face to face. And the Lord God said unto Moses: For mine own purpose have I made these things. Here is wisdom and it remaineth in me.

"And by the word of my power, have I created them, which is mine Only Begotten Son, who is full of grace and truth.

"And worlds without number have I created; and I also created them for mine own purpose ....

"But only an account of this earth, and the inhabitants thereof, give I unto you. For behold, there are many worlds that have passed away by the word of my power. And there are many that now stand, and innumerable are they unto man; but all things are numbered unto me, for they are mine and I know them.

"And the Lord God spake unto Moses, saying: The heavens, they are many, and they cannot be numbered unto man; but they are numbered unto me, for they are mine.

"And as one earth shall pass away, and the heavens thereof even so shall another come; and there is no end to my works, neither to my words" (Moses 1:25, 27-33, 35, 37-38).

It's a stunning message! It so clearly and succinctly lays out the fact that other people are populating other worlds, many worlds, living the same sort of lives we are, at the same time we are. The apostle Paul also had knowledge of this. He said of God's son, "whom he hath appointed heir of all things," being the one "by whom also he made the worlds" (Hebrews 1:2).

The Expanding and Inflating Universe

Science has also discovered that the universe is expanding and that this expansion is accelerating over time. Confirmed by Edwin Hubble in 1929 using a 100-inch reflecting telescope, this discovery is seen as evidence of the big bang but can also serve as further evidence of God. Scientists say that since the time of creation, the universe has been expanding with galaxies continuing to move farther apart from each other as time goes on. There may be galaxies out there that we can't see any more because they have moved away so fast that their light has never reached Earth. Current researchers have even said they believe the universe may expand to eternity.[33] From a theological perspective, this phenomenon enhances LDS doctrine of the creation of worlds without number. This infinite stretching of the cosmos was even mentioned by the prophet Isaiah: "Thus saith God the Lord, he that created the heavens, and stretched them out ... " (Isaiah 42:5).

It also supports the revealed doctrine of eternal progression in that even as the universe stretches and expands so too do all of God's creations, including his children. Humans have been on a course of eternal progression since even before their creation on Earth. In fact, Church leaders have likened it to a three-act play: Our pre-mortal life being the first act, Earth life being the second, and our post-mortal life the third.[34] If we learn and accomplish all that is required on Earth, we receive exaltation and gain the fulness of the Father. By so doing, we will be privileged to continue to progress and become like God. (See Revelations 3:21; D&C 76:50; Romans 8:17; D&C 132:20). This, of course, is very much a process of evolution.

When discussing the expanding universe we learn that there are a number of questions the big bang simply can't answer, and so scholars have provided a tested and conclusive companion theory to help: Inflation theory. This theory proposes a period of extremely rapid [exponential] expansion of the universe during its first few moments. While the big bang theory suggests relatively gradual expansion throughout the history of the universe, inflation increased the linear size of the universe extensively in only a small fraction of a second. The two theories work together and maintain the basic paradigm of a standardized expanding universe.[35]

The models, equations, and general scientific jargon of this inflation theory go way beyond the scope of this book or this writer, but suffice it to say, it provides this astounding reality: Ours is not the only space-time universe that exists. This is important because it supports LDS doctrine of God's creation of worlds without number. John D. Barrow, research professor of Mathematical Sciences at the University of Cambridge observed,

". . . inflation has a tendency to be self-reproducing. Remarkably, it appears that the fluctuations that inflation produces have form that inevitably induces further inflation to occur from small sub-regions of the bubbles [universes] that are already inflating. Inflation appears to be a potentially unending, self-reproducing process: In short, it is an epidemic. Each bubble that it produces somewhere in space and time during this process can possess different values of many of its constants of nature, defining the form of the physical structures that can arise within it. The universe thus appears to be likely to be far, far more complicated in its historical development, as well as its spatial variation, than we had suspected."[36]

So what does all of this have to do with divine creation? Here's the answer. Inflation makes it clear that other universes existed prior to our own. This process of one universe originating as the offspring of another earlier universe coincides with LDS theology about eternity where there is no beginning or end. Blake T. Ostler, widely published author on Mormon philosophy, said it is possible that our own bubble universe has been preceded by an infinite number of prior universes that have come and passed away. "It is possible," he said, "that our universe arises out of the physical conditions obtained in a prior universe that had physical constants that were different and thus had different laws of nature than our own local universe!"[37]

The Multiverse and Eternal Progression

Some who doubt wonder how the doctrine of eternal progression can possibly fit into a paradigm of just one universe. Mormons believe in a plurality of gods where God, our Father, was once a man, who dwelt on an earth, became exalted to godhood and populated worlds of his own. He was one of an infinite chain of deities, all progressing eternally and creating innumerable worlds for their mortal children. Many of these mortal children also will become exalted as gods, continuing the process of creating and populating worlds in the same manner.[38]

The question arises how all of this eternal progression could be facilitated by our current single universe and, furthermore, does it even square with what revelation tells us about those who achieve godhood having their own dominions?[39] If each god shares this one common universe, then they would be relegated to only having dominion over a portion of it rather than one of their own. It seems untenable that an infinite number of gods and other eternal beings would share a small piece of one finite universe big enough to house worlds without number for all of them throughout the eternities. We know that Jesus Christ has dominion over the universe we occupy, but what is the domain of the other gods who are exalted beings?

It was revealed to Joseph Smith that Abraham, Isaac, and Jacob "have entered into their exaltation, according to the promises, and sit upon thrones, and are not angels but are gods" (D&C 132:37). The same godhood is promised to all who abide by "the new and everlasting covenant," for "then shall they be gods, because they have no end; therefore shall they be from everlasting to everlasting, because they continue; then shall they be above all, because all things are subject unto them. Then shall they be gods, because they have all power, and the angels are subject unto them" (D&C 132:19-20).

As mentioned earlier, inflation theory and other cosmological data in the field of quantum mechanics, marry up quite nicely with the doctrine of eternal progression. This information is not presented here as concrete evidence of God but only as a possibility in the burgeoning relationship between science and theology.

Scores of physicists believe we live in a multiverse instead of a single universe. For many years, scientists held firm to a belief in three dimensions that they felt described our universe: Superstring theory, hyperspace, and dark matter. When they realized these were no longer sufficient as sole explanations of our origins, these scholars concluded that our universe is simply one of infinitely many. The term, multiverse, was defined in 1960, by Andy Nimmo, the vice chair of the Scottish Branch of the British Interplanetary

Society, as "an apparent universe, a multiplicity of which goes to make up the whole universe."[40] Today, cosmologists and astronomers have run with the idea and suggest that our universe may be part of an ensemble of universes.

British cosmologist and astrophysicist Martin Rees explained it this way: "Our entire universe may be just one element—one atom, as it were,—in an infinite ensemble: a cosmic archipelago. Each universe starts with its own big bang, acquires a distinctive imprint [and its individual physical laws] as it cools, and traces out its own cosmic cycle. The big bang that triggered our entire universe is, in this grander perspective, an infinitesimal part of an elaborate structure."[41]

Science has learned that a universe is born, lives, and eventually dies, but the multiverse continues because of the constant adding of new universes within it. The idea of a multiverse cosmology is exquisitely portrayed in the Lord's avowal to Moses: "And as one earth shall pass away, and the heavens thereof even so shall another come; and there is no end to my works, neither to my words" (Moses 1:38). Dr. Kirk D. Hagen, author and professor of mechanical engineering technology and pre-engineering at Weber State University, wrote:

> "In a Mormon multiverse, a being who progresses to godhood brings about a universe for which that god has dominion. To provide suitable worlds for their children, the gods endow their universes with the required physical properties [constants of physics] to sustain life. In Mormon theology, gods exist 'simultaneously,' so separate universes coexist in the eternal multiverse. Each universe in the ensemble of universes becomes an extension and continuation of the creativity of every 'ancestral god' in an eternal family of deities. The creativity and glory of each god increases exponentially with the production of new universes. In this cosmology, the multiverse is a hallmark and witness of the infinite work and glory of God and the dwelling place for an infinite number of eternal progressing beings."[42]

There is obviously no way to prove that other universes exist unless we can observe them, something that has not yet and may never happen. But the hypothesis of the multiverse certainly helps explain eternal progression and the concept that some kind of eternal domain for all exalted beings must exist. It provides indirect evidence of God and his plan, and for some, can help to strengthen faith.

Conclusion

These and many other complex systems of our material world show compelling evidence of divine creation. I have only attempted to provide an appetizer in a veritable feast of information that puts science and Mormon theology side by side. Many should be strengthened when they see how well the two harmonize. Anyone who leans solely with science for their answers needs to look beyond the theories and textbooks of man and realize science alone will never solve every riddle about life. But when science is coupled with revelation, the mysteries of the universe seem less and less mysterious, and Godly answers seem more and more real. Both science and the restored gospel are continuously growing through new laboratory and/or revelatory information. Both scientists and prophets will continue to learn and share what they receive with the world as God sees fit to reveal it to them.

All of us—faithful believers, hardcore scientists, committed atheists, and everybody in between—must go through the dance of searching out the answers for enlightenment about God. Sometimes all we get are fleeting moments, flashes of eternity exhibited sporadically within our beautiful and wondrously intricate world. We can deny these moments and rationalize them as some mechanism of the brain, or we can internalize them as Godly revelation from a loving Heavenly Father.

Even scientists can be sincerely troubled, even menaced by the possibility that God is real. Famous astrophysicist Robert Jastrow, the founding director of NASA's Goddard Institute for Space Studies, wrote about this genuine tug-of-war.

"I think part of the answer is that scientists cannot bear the thought of a natural phenomenon which cannot be explained, even with unlimited time and money. There is a kind of religion in science, it is the religion of a person who believes there is order and harmony in the universe and every effect must have its cause .... This religious faith of the scientist is violated by the discovery that the world had a beginning under conditions in which the known laws of physics are not valid, and as a product of forces or circumstances we cannot discover. When that happens, the scientist has lost control. If he really examined the implications, he would be traumatized. As usual when faced with trauma, the mind reacts by ignoring the implications—in science this is known as "refusing to speculate"—or trivializing the origin of the world by calling it the big bang, as if the universe were a firecracker.

"Consider the enormity of the problem. Science has proven that the universe exploded into being at a certain moment. It asks, 'what cause produced this effect?' 'Who or what put the matter and energy into the universe?' 'Was the universe created out of nothing, or was it gathered together out of pre-existing materials?' And science cannot answer these questions .... For the scientist who has lived by his faith in the power of reason, the story ends like a bad dream. He has scaled the mountain of ignorance; he is about to conquer the highest peak; as he pulls himself over the final rock, he is greeted by a band of theologians who have been sitting there for centuries."[43]

CHAPTER TWO

The Origin of Life

Charles Darwin's theory of evolution, introduced in his 1859 book, *On the Origin of Species,* has been hotly contested in both science and religious groups for more than 150 years. While it does not answer every question about the origin of humans, it does provide enormous demonstrable data that points unequivocally to evolutionary processes. But some in the Church may be inclined to sidestep the issue for fear it is not in keeping with LDS precepts. The purpose of this chapter is to provide a broader point of view on evolution and related matters within the construct of LDS theology. It is my hope that it will help members who lean toward evolution find some level of comfort if they choose to accept what science has to say about the origin of life.

For some in the Church, it's a question that presents no concern whatsoever as their faith is sufficient without it. For others, it's a question that doggedly festers moving them to find answers that will augment and clarify in ways that help strengthen their faith. Our doctrine tells us *why* and *by whom* mankind found a home on this planet, but it doesn't tell us *how* it was done. Did we evolve through a process of natural selection, as Darwin asserts? Was it all a matter of cosmic chance or did God have a hand in it? Did God just plop Adam and Eve in Eden full grown or were they born like the rest of us? So many questions without concrete answers can be frustrating to truth seekers and lead to all kinds of speculation that may or may not be helpful.

Opinions vary greatly throughout the world about the theory of evolution despite what we know or don't know through science. In a 2012 Gallup poll, Americans were asked which of three statements came closest to their views on the origin and development of human beings. Responses are listed as percentages in parentheses.

1. (32 percent) Human beings have developed over millions of years from less advanced forms of life, but God guided the process.
2. (15 percent) Human beings have developed over millions of years from less advanced forms of life, but God had no part in the process.
3. (46 percent) God created human beings pretty much in their present form at one time within the last 10,000 years or so.[1]

So what is the theory of evolution? Succinctly put, the theory posits that all species of organisms arise and develop through the natural selection of small, inherited variations that increase the individual's ability to compete, survive, and reproduce. Broadly put, the theory suggests that over a three billion year period protoplasm could evolve into a corporate banker. There is an abundance of tested study and scholarly debate among scientists and theologians that continue to leave the topic of evolution versus divine design in dispute. Did evolution start and progress all on its own or did God have a hand in it?

The fundamentalist view of Genesis, where God literally created the earth and all things on it in six days, is where the controversy arises. This view suggests that God created nothing else after the creation of Adam and Eve and that all of his creations are exactly the same today as they were on the day of their creation. This is at total odds with scientific evolution, which places the appearance of single celled aquatic organisms at approximately 2.5 billion years ago, with humans eventually evolving from there.

Another school of thought, known as theistic evolution combines elements essential to both evolutionary theory and creationism. Theistic evolution accepts the basic axiom of evolution but contends that God is directing it. The three schools of thought include:

Evolution
- Mother Nature as creator
- Unicellular life sprang from the ocean.
- Species evolved by chance and natural selection.
- Humans developed over billions of years.

Creationism
- God as creator.
- God created all life exactly as described in Genesis.
- Species are fixed and do not change over time.
- Adam and Eve were first humans placed in Garden of Eden on the 6th day of creation.

Theistic Evolution
- God as creator by means of evolution.
- Evolution from unicellular life was set in motion by God.
- God created species which evolved sequentially over time.
- Humans evolved over eons until they became the crowning work of God.

While several other Christian denominations have declared their allegiance to a particular argument, the LDS Church has not taken an official stand on the topic. President David O. McKay once said, "We do not know enough of the facts to take a definite position on evolution, but the concept is certainly not incompatible with faith. After all, the process of creation is going on continuously. . . ."² But a variety of Church leaders and scholars over the years have provided their opinions to lend credence to theistic evolution. They say evolution and Mormonism do not contradict each other, however, Darwinism—that life evolved randomly by chance without any assistance from God—is a philosophy of man. Evolution [that life evolved] is a fact of science that has amassed enough evidence to merit our attention.

But the statement referred to most often in the Church on the topic was made in 1925, by the First Presidency under President Heber J. Grant. It came forth about the time of the famous Scopes trial where the right to teach evolution in Tennessee schools was debated. It reads in part:

> "'God created man in his own image, in the image of God created he him; male and female created he them' (Genesis 1:27). In these plain and pointed words the inspired author of the book Genesis made known to the world the truth concerning the origin of the human family. Moses, the prophet historian, who was 'learned' we are told, 'in all the wisdom of the Egyptians,' when making this important announcement, was not voicing mere opinion. He was speaking as the mouthpiece of God, and his solemn declaration was for all time and for all people. No subsequent revelator of the truth has contradicted the great leader and lawgiver of Israel. All who have since spoken by divine authority upon this theme have confirmed his simple and sublime proclamation. Nor could it be otherwise. Truth has but one source, and all revelations from heaven are harmonious one with the other.
>
> "Jesus Christ, the Son of God, is 'the express image' of His Father's person (Hebrew 1:3). He walked the earth as a human being, as a perfect man, and said, in answer to a question put to him: 'He that hath seen me hath seen the Father' (John 14:9). This alone ought to solve the problem to the satisfaction of every thoughtful, reverent mind. It was in this form that the Father and Son, as two distinct personages,

appeared to Joseph Smith, when, as a boy of fourteen years, he received his first vision. . .

". . . The Church of Jesus Christ of Latter-day Saints, basing its belief on divine revelation, ancient and modern, proclaims man to be the direct and lineal offspring of Deity. By His Almighty power God organized the earth, and all that it contains, from spirit and element, which exist co-eternally with Himself.

"Man is the child of God, formed in the divine image and endowed with divine attributes, and even as the infant son of an earthly father and mother is capable in due time of becoming a man, so the undeveloped offspring of celestial parentage is capable, by experience through ages and eons, of evolving into a God."[3]

In this statement, the First Presidency chose not to go beyond current revelation, leaving ancillary issues still open for debate. Over the years, some Church leaders have provided their own views on the topic but have continued to leave room for a variety of ideas among members.

Although no LDS Church president has ever denied evolution as an explanation of the origin of man, historically, many members feel as though they were taught from childhood that evolution is not true. This is mainly because of the teachings of Apostle Joseph Fielding Smith [before he became prophet] and Apostle Bruce R. McConkie, who both emphatically called evolution false. Their opinions, however, did not represent the Church but were nevertheless viewed as doctrine among the general membership. Joseph Fielding Smith's book, *Man: His Origin and Destiny*, took on a literalist view claiming Adam was made out of dust or clay, Eve was made literally out of Adam's rib, the Garden of Eden was located on our physical Earth with no death occurring anywhere before the Fall, no humans or evolving humans lived prior to Adam and Eve, and the earth was only 12,000 years old—6,000 years to create it and 6,000 years since Adam to the present.[4]

But as more and more scientific evidence has come forth, some Church members have felt concern over what is actually true. This is a perfect example of where they must implement the Church's teaching that the opinions of its leaders and actual revelation from God through them are two different things. What we must remember when reading the writings and statements of apostles and prophets is that there is a difference between what they say as "special witnesses" and what they say as regular members. The calling of an Apostle is to be a special witness of the name of Jesus Christ throughout the world, particularly of his divinity and of his bodily resurrection from the dead (see Acts 1: 22; D&C 107: 23). That directive as a special witness of Christ does not extend to the formulation of doctrine not expressly received from God through revelation. There is a line they are generally careful not to cross, but from time to time do cross because of human error in not making clear the source of their commentary—God or themselves. We also know that there must be a consensus among the apostles before any tenet can be released to Church members as doctrine.

This is made clear through the teachings of Apostle D. Todd Christofferson who said, "not every statement made by a Church leader past or present necessarily constitutes doctrine. It is commonly understood in the Church that a statement made by one leader on a single occasion often represents a personal, though well considered, opinion not meant to be official or binding for the whole Church. The Prophet Joseph Smith taught that a prophet is a prophet only when he is acting as such."[5]

Apostle Neil L. Anderson concurred by saying, "The leaders of the Church are honest but imperfect men. Remember the words of Moroni: 'Condemn me not because of mine imperfection, neither my father … but rather give thanks unto God that he hath made manifest unto you our imperfections, that ye may learn to be more wise than we have been'" (Mormon 9:31).[6]

Neither Elder Smith nor Elder McConkie ever described their teachings on evolution as being revealed doctrine, but because there were so many inquiries about Elder Smith's book, President David O. McKay made it clear through written responses to members that "this book is not an approved publication of the Church. The author alone is responsible for the theories therein expressed."[7] In a subsequent letter dated February 3, 1959, President

McKay also included Elder McConkie's *Mormon Doctrine* as not being an official publication of the Church.[8]

How LDS Educators Approach Evolution

As we compile statements of doctrine and opinion from Church leaders on the origin of man, we learn two important factors: One, tenets of the restored gospel are in contrast with much of orthodox Christian theology, and two, LDS tenets are more in sync with science. Yet official statements about the topic have been few, whereas personal opinion among the brethren has been substantial, leaving the average member to wonder what is considered doctrine and what is not. How to navigate these tricky waters can be found among educators at the various Church campuses who must teach the findings of science coupled with the doctrines of the Church. They have needed to come up with some sort of standard that gives balance to both.

In a presentation to the Natural Science Division and Religion Department in 1974, Kenneth J. Brown, then department chair of religion at Ricks College, introduced a standard for identifying doctrine. He said, "Doctrine may be identified as a principle, tenet, or teaching having religious or Church significance which has universal acceptance among the orthodox Latter-day Saints as being in *harmony* with revealed truth." He said because the prophets are the most representative body of the orthodox, anything that has universal acceptance among them as being doctrine is doctrine for us today.[9]

He said one of the biggest problems among academics as well as the Church membership at large is when someone teaches dogmatically as doctrine those things which have not been established as such. Brown's formula for identifying false doctrine is "a principle, tenet, or teaching having religious significance which has universal acceptance among the orthodox as being *contrary* to revealed truth." BYU educators can't simply refrain from discussing concepts not considered official doctrine because it would be like putting their heads in the sand to questions of real import to students. The teaching of only official doctrine would essentially push students, and by extension members in general, who need reasonable answers on these topics, to look elsewhere in the world, possibly outside the faith.[10]

Looking for alternatives, possibilities, and tentative answers where official doctrine does not exist is fully acceptable in the Church. Theologians such as B. H. Roberts, Orson Pratt, James E. Talmage, Joseph Fielding Smith, and others all dived deeply into tentative answers to gospel questions.

The Church, itself, even published an official statement in the April, 1910, *Improvement Era,* delineating the various possibilities for explaining the creation of man's physical body. The statement read, "Whether the mortal bodies of man evolved in natural processes to present perfection, thru the direction and power of God; whether the first parents of our generations, Adam and Eve, were transplanted from another sphere, with immortal tabernacles, which became corrupted thru sin and the partaking of natural foods, in the process of time; whether they were born here in mortality, as other mortals have been, are questions not fully answered in the revealed word of God."[11]

Here we have three possible options for the creation of our physical bodies offered by the Church, further suggesting the appropriateness of members aligning themselves with tentative answers where there is no doctrine. Of course, this has sometimes led to differences among members and leaders, but such is part of the learning and growth process of our second estate, even for apostles and prophets. Even with official doctrine we are encouraged to study it out in our minds and to pray for a personal conviction of the information received (see D&C 9:8). The obtaining of inspiration about theological possibilities should also be pursued until we arrive at a place that brings us peace of mind about the topic.

Brown offered insight on how BYU educators teach concepts about the creation of man's physical body. Through review of the scriptures, writings of Church leaders, official statements, and the temple endowment ceremony, he provided three minimal teachings, which he felt one must accept to be an orthodox Latter-day Saint.

1. Man came into being as an act of God. Whatever else may be said of man, he is foremost physically and spiritually of divine origin.
2. Adam, the father of the human race and first mortal man, was a civilized, intelligent being who was made in the image of God and who could comprehend the gospel. He was not sub-human in any way.
3. There was no birth, and consequently no death, of man prior to Adam because Adam fell, and mortal death was a consequence of the Fall.

He concluded his presentation by saying, "As long as one accepts these three basic doctrines all other alternatives are open to him. Whatever fits his rationale, makes sense to him, is congruent with other doctrinal points, helps to strengthen his faith, ought to be perfectly permissible. He can be as eclectic as he wants to."[12]

In 2013, BYU Dean of Religious Education Terry Ball, concurred with Brown's formula for teaching the origin of man and said it is as current today as it was in 1974. He also stated, "While the Church has no official position on evolution, our doctrine is very clear about the origin of man—that man was created in the image of God and has the potential to become like God. To put it in scientific terms—God and man are the same species. Many not of our faith are uncomfortable with that doctrine, often feeling it makes too much of man or too little of God, but it is foundational to our faith."[13]

Latter-day Saints, who didn't attend a Church college, may have lived their whole lives never realizing that not only is what we understood about evolution from the Smith/McConkie writings not Church doctrine, but also we are free to find our own alternatives where there is none stated. We are still members in good standing if we personally interpret the findings and theories of science such as evolution, in ways that make sense to us and increase our faith, even if other Church members see it another way.

Divinely Guided Evolution

With that in mind, let's take a serious look at evolution and the theological questions surrounding it. We must first establish that evolution has amassed so much physical evidence over the years that it has moved from a mere theory into a fully accepted certainty. It is widely recognized and taught among all fields of science, and where it was once considered intolerable among religious people, is now embraced and viewed by many theologians as harmonious with religion.

Geologists tell us the earth went through ages of preparation involving generations and varieties of plants and animals, that with their passing, helped develop the strata [parallel layers] we see today in rock formations. Within these strata are some of the oldest fossils of once living organisms, both plants and animals. Moreover, chemical activity and compression of certain plants anciently left vegetable matter that is found in the coal strata. Chalk deposits and limestone beneath the ocean contain the fossils of animals that lived and died through the ages until the earth could be fit for human life.

The most primitive species found in the oldest rocks reveal only the simplest of aquatic organisms. Some of them continue to exist today though changed because of their changed environment. Then, over time these simple forms developed into more complex bodies, advancing from a single-celled protozoan to the most complicated of plants and animals. The earth's crust is a veritable cornucopia of inscriptions in the earth's book of life as it formed and prepared itself for the benefit and use of man. When man finally entered the scene, he became the crowning work of God, who is the master scientist and creator of all. God left us with the task of translating the record in the rocks for ourselves, but he provided divine guidance to help us understand that portion of the creation needed for our salvation.

Juxtaposing what we know in both science and religion, it seems reasonable that divinely guided evolution would find a place in LDS thinking. Just as God is involved in many areas of organic and inorganic science, he is also a factor in the evolution of eternal man. It takes slow and steady growth involving learning and trial and error for humans to become like

God, so too, a slow and steady process was needed in the physical creation of life and the universe. Latter-day Saints should include God in any possibility of creation they choose to accept rather than the idea of pure chance. Even when studying randomness in science, when God is involved, it is anything but chance.

The Predictability of Chance

Let's talk about this idea of chance. People who discredit evolution often argue that random chance in the fluctuation of gene frequencies [genetic drift] is what makes evolution so hard to swallow. To be clear, genetic drift is defined as "random fluctuations in the frequency of the appearance of a gene in a small isolated population, presumably owing to chance rather than natural selection."[14] Skeptics say such randomness is akin to tossing up a deck of cards and expecting the wind to put them back in perfect order, or expecting an explosion in a print shop to produce a book. While these comparisons are colorful, they are not really proper comparisons at all.

Experts in the fields of mathematics, probability, and, statistics have a better comparison for random processes in evolution: When two dice are tossed and the total is counted, a sum of seven will randomly occur twice as often as four. The basis for this reality is there are regularities in the occurrences of events whose outcomes are not certain.[15] Another example is in the statement, "average life of 1,000 hours" on a package of light bulbs. This phrase is acceptable to us because we acknowledge that the actual life of a light bulb is uncertain but statistically predictable.

In biology, for example, a description of the random behavior of molecules would reflect some predictability rather than haphazardness as the average person might expect. Because random processes are predictable to a very high degree, their end product could be identified, foreseen, and employed by God. When the Creators of the primeval earth left matter to act for itself, even though it acted randomly, it would still be expected and foreseeable.[16] The same is true of chance and random processes in the evolution of life.

William S. Bradshaw, retired BYU professor of molecular biology, said,

> "Given a set of elements from which to construct molecules, cells, tissues, and organisms, and given air, water, and rock as environments in which organisms can live, evolution will fashion lungs and gills—wings, fins, and feet. Living things reflect both the properties of their raw matter and their environment. Thus the assembly of life, even a self-assembly, could not be totally capricious. I expect that if we were able to go elsewhere in the universe and study the history of life on other planets with conditions similar to Earth's, we would find evidence for sets of organisms remarkably similar to those that have inhabited this planet. Evolution will have mainly achieved there what it has here."[17]

Clearly living cells operate randomly with molecules moving and reacting in various ways influenced arbitrarily by the environment. But with God at the helm, the human body is not at risk because the body's chemistry will behave predictably and follow the laws he set that govern life. The human cell is so incredibly complex, divinely guided natural selection is reliably the only explanation for its ability to invent the chemical code for millions of sequences in every cell. The odds of a single protein molecule forming by chance, is 1 in 10^{243} [that is a 1 followed by 243 zeros]. A single cell is comprised of millions of protein molecules.[18]

Latter-day Saints should realize evolutionary mechanisms for such incredible processes could be accomplished through the hand of God. If this process of the forming of humans has occurred for eternity on countless earth-like planets in infinitesimal universes, the system has obviously been perfected and so becomes quite fathomable under God's direction. The intricacies of it all are testament alone to the need for God in the equation.

Medical and Biology Experts Weigh In

According to experts in the field of medicine, including Apostle Russell M. Nelson, who is an internationally renowned cardiothoracic surgeon, the body itself, is a testament to the existence of God.

"Each organ of your body is a wondrous gift from God. Each eye has an auto focusing lens. Nerves and muscles control two eyes to make a single three-dimensional image. The eyes are connected to the brain, which records the sights seen. Your heart is an incredible pump. It has four delicate valves that control the direction of blood flow. These valves open and close more than 100,000 times a day—36 million times a year. Yet, unless altered by disease, they are able to withstand such stress almost indefinitely.

"Think of the body's defense system. To protect it from harm, it perceives pain. In response to infection, it generates antibodies. The skin provides protection. It warns against injury that excessive heat or cold might cause. The body renews its own outdated cells and regulates the levels of its own vital ingredients. The body heals its cuts, bruises, and broken bones. Its capacity for reproduction is another sacred gift from God ....

"Anyone who studies the workings of the human body has surely seen God moving in his majesty and power. Because the body is governed by divine law, any healing comes by obedience to the law upon which that blessing is predicated. Despite a litany of evidences to the contrary, some people erroneously think these marvelous physical attributes happened by chance."[19]

Other LDS physicians, scientists, and scholars have added their expertise in this union of science and theology over evolution. In a letter from Gary A. Strobel, an LDS plant pathology scientist at Montana State University, to Elder Boyd K. Packer in 1984, Strobel outlines some of what he had discovered about evolutionary processes in the laboratory. As a biologist, he provides a peek at some of the scientific data being gathered in support of evolution.

"I have studied these matters for years and have personally, literally constructed new life forms by gene manipulation.

The literature is replete with examples of men being born with tails, fully covered with hair, and with extra digits on their hands—in other words reversion to an ancestral form. In my lab we have made non-pathogenic bacteria behave in a manner in which they are pathogenic, by placing a new piece of DNA in them. About nine years ago we regenerated plants from single leaf cell protoplasts and at least 10% of the new plants did not resemble either the parents.

"In my view, the scriptures do not state how the Lord created life or man. I prefer to think that He used evolutionary processes to ultimately reach this purpose, but other alternatives exist. It may have meant that pre-man forms lived [i.e. ape-like creatures]. Such a creature became man upon receiving the spirit. This seems logical and in complete agreement with the scriptures as well as compelling scientific arguments. There are too many lines of evidence in favor of evolution to dispel it. Especially to those in the LDS community who will be the life scientists and scholars of the next generation.

"I prefer to think of matters of this type as Bro. H. Eyring used to tell me—'Gary, you are required to accept nothing but the truth.' I consider evolution as a serious process that the Lord uses to develop life. He is not likely to wave a wand and make life appear, but this certainly is an alternative. It seems to me, if we are to become like Him we must not only learn His commandments, but also His creative ways. This makes life fun."[20]

Fixity of Species

Fixity of species is a belief held tenaciously by some who subscribe to the literalist view of scriptural accounts of the creation of man. It theorizes that all species have remained unchanged throughout Earth's history. Science has learned that the appearance of living things has changed over time, but despite these changes, their genealogy can be traced to common ancestors. For example, 50 million years ago whales had legs, having evolved from land mammals.[21] When literalists point out that living things were designed to reproduce "after their kind" (Moses 2:25) they are out of sync with what we know about heredity: Offspring inherit genes from their parents and look like them. There is nothing in evolution that requires fixity of species because genes can be inherited generationally and still allow for chance mutations over eons of time.

Unfortunately, theologians jumped the gun on the idea that "kind" (Genesis 1:24-25) in scripture meant "species" because of the research that was done in the 17th century by John Ray (1627-1705) and Carl Linne (1707-1778). Linne, in particular, was passionate about cataloguing organisms for proper naming and classification and during the process declared fixity of species didn't change from its original genesis in Eden. Later Linne realized there was no fixity of species but by then the concept had caught on with the world and there was no turning back. Theologians determined that "kind" meant "species," but as Linne discovered, there were just too many species to be explained so simply—too many distributions, too many intermediate grades, too many hybridizations to fit neatly into his little creation box.[22]

Eventually, science self-corrected, adopting Darwin's theory of natural selection, but theology has been much slower to catch up. Today, most commentators consider "kind" to represent a geological grouping at the family level of taxonomy. Very few try to equate it with "species."[23]

Decay and Death

The second law of thermodynamics, or universal law of decay, is a good argument for the process of evolution being guided by the hand of God. Some evolution naysayers erroneously believe this law is another reason evolution is not feasible. Basically, the law of decay is the reason material things ultimately fall apart and disintegrate over time, such as clothing that becomes faded and threadbare, wood that weakens and decays, and food that becomes rotten. After enough time and usage, everything eventually returns to dust. Even death is a manifestation of this law.[24]

Admittedly, as we observe our world, this law does hold true, but it does not negate the theory of evolution in any way. Here's why: Since evolution requires an upward development, with physical laws and atoms organized into increasingly complex, orderly, and beneficial systems that propel natural selection, it would take divine orchestration to overcome decay. Things in our world can both decay and evolve—the two are not mutually exclusive. It's not difficult to see how things evolve until they reach a certain point when the growth cycle concludes and decay begins.

Brigham Young found little difficulty harmonizing Mormonism and the second law of thermodynamics. He said, "The elements form and develop, and continue to do so until they mature, and then they commence to decay and become disorganized. The mountains around us were formed in this way. By and by, when they shall have reached their maturity, the work of disintegration and decay will commence. It has been so from all eternity, and will continue to be so until they are made celestial."[25]

Unique Abilities of Humans

Because humans are literally a part of the earth and all things in it, we feel an aesthetic appreciation and reverence for the earth. Nature is often the means for rekindling our reverence of God and helping us build up the spiritual part of who we are. It makes us look to him to give our moral compass direction and helps us better distinguish between good and evil. Despite our evolution from lower organisms, humans have unique abilities that are found in no other species of living thing. These include the processes of creativity, consciousness, and abstract thinking. No other species can design and appreciate art and literature. No other species has a brain that receives the unique experience of consciousness, exhibits intricate personality traits, or can form abstract thoughts beyond what they can see.[26]

Unless a person purposefully destroys that inner light or moral compass that dictates his or her actions, conscience is a uniquely human condition.

Conscience affirms the reality of the Spirit of Christ in man with sensitivities not found in other species. It affirms, as well, the reality of good and evil, justice, mercy, honor, courage, faith, love, and virtue, as well as their necessary opposites, hatred, greed, brutality, and jealousy (2 Nephi 2:11, 16). Such values, though intangible, respond to laws, with cause and effect relationships as certain as any resulting from physical laws.[27]

Furthermore, humans possess a spirit that allows us to experience Deity directly. No other animal species can do that, again suggesting it's the inclusion of man's spirit within the body that makes him human and far removed from animals. It seems reasonable that if God did create us, then he would also create the ability for us to feel and communicate with him. Within that spirit is also the ability to make moral judgments and display special skills in social awareness, perception, reasoning, and judgment. These are Godlike qualities, which are further evidence that we were created in his image as his literal offspring. Evolutionary theory must, of necessity, go hand in hand with divine guidance in the process to achieve the ultimate abode and creation of the children of God. Even seemingly random mutations that provided survival advantage are directed through Godly science.

Making Sense of the Origin of Man

Those who struggle to believe in the gospel of Christ but who accept evolution will likely have questions about the biblical account of man's origin, questions that will require alternatives and tentative answers with which they can live. Many have trouble with the literalist viewpoint as recorded in Genesis because so much of it simply defies reason and leaves far too many gaps in the narrative. Allowing for alternatives as taught by BYU professors, brings us to the topic of pre-Adamites living on the earth prior to the Garden of Eden. This is a question that many have wondered about and tried to dismiss in light of what they thought was Church doctrine [Smith/McConkie texts].

The Origin of Life

Because of Joseph Smith's revelation in the Book of Moses that says Adam was "the first man" (Moses 3:7) upon the earth, we should fully understand what the word "man" actually means. When Moses used this term, he was "learned in all the wisdom of the Egyptians," (Acts 7:22), who like many of the ancients, thought they were the only true "men." Egyptologist Barbara Mertz wrote, "Like the Greeks and others, the Egyptians called themselves, 'the people.' Other men were not people, they were only barbarians."[28]

Protestant Bible scholar Arthur C. Custance shed some light when he wrote,

> "Among most primitive people the habit is to refer to themselves as 'true men,' referring to all others by some term which clearly denies to them the right of manhood at all. Thus the Naskapi call themselves *Neneot*, which means *real people*. The Chuckchee say that their name means *real men*. The Hottentots [of South Africa] refer to themselves as Khoi-Khoi; which means *Men of Men*. The Yahgan of Tierra del Fuego (of all places) say that their name means *men par excellence*. The Andamese [of the Indian Ocean], a people who appear to lack the rudiments of law, refer to themselves as *Ong*, meaning *Men*. All these people reserve these terms only for themselves."[29]

Evidence suggests that ancient Hebrews were no different, and when they said Adam was "the first man," they meant the first one of their particular race.

Some Church leaders also have indicated a belief in pre-Adamites. Early Church Apostle Orson Hyde said in the 1854 General Conference, "The world was peopled before the days of Adam as much so as it was before the days of Noah."[30]

Apostle James E. Talmage said in 1935 in the Salt Lake City Tabernacle: "Geologists and anthropologists say that if the beginning of Adamic history dates back but 6000 years or less, there must have been races of human sort upon the earth long before that time—without denying, however, that

Adamic history may be correct, if it be regarded solely as the history of the *Adamic* race." Elder Talmage's talk was published under the Church's name as a pamphlet and distributed to Latter-day Saints throughout the Church. Elder Talmage strongly suggested in the tract that pre-Adamites existed, and that Adam and Eve were the parents of a *new* race of men; not the first human beings on Earth.[31]

Also in 1935, B. H. Roberts, a Seventy, was writing a Church manual called *The Truth, The Way, The Life,* in which Roberts wrote that pre-Adamites existed. It was never published as a Church manual because of concerns from Joseph Fielding Smith, prompting the First Presidency to withdraw the work and issue this statement: "The statement made by Elder Smith that the existence of pre-Adamites is not a doctrine of the Church is true. It is just as true that the statement: 'There were not pre-Adamites upon the earth' is not a doctrine of the Church. Neither side of the controversy has been accepted as a doctrine at all."[32]

Elder Smith's reasoning against pre-Adamites was that since Adam could not have brought death on pre-Adamite life [the Fall], they could not have been partakers of the resurrection, which the Lord said would come to all things partaking of the Fall of Adam.[33] His reasoning seemed to be that there was no death prior to the Fall [despite the mountain of physical evidence in the fossil record] so Christ's atonement could not be extended to these people as is promised to all God's children. Therefore, they could not have existed. "As in Adam all die, so in Christ all shall be made alive" (1 Corinthians 15:22). But he was assuming a literal interpretation of the Fall which simply does not equate with what we know in anthropology. Among others, there are two intriguing possibilities that could provide an answer to this concern.

Possibility #1. The Fall of Adam could have occurred in the spirit world where all Mormons believe is the location of Paradise. This would eliminate concern about no death on the earth prior to the Fall. A spiritual Fall could have occurred long before Adam and Eve were actually placed on the earth.

"And every plant of the field before it was in the earth, and every herb of the field before it grew. For I, the Lord God, created all things, of which

I have spoken, spiritually, before they were naturally upon the face of the earth" (Moses 3:4-5).

"Each creation "remaineth in the sphere in which I, God, created it" (Moses 3:9).

"That which is spiritual being in the likeness of that which is temporal; and that which is temporal being in the likeness of that which is spiritual; the spirit of man being in the likeness of his person, as also the spirit of the beast, and every other creature which God has created" (D&C 77:2).

Elder Russell M. Nelson said, "Adam and Eve were first created with bodies of flesh and spirit, without blood, and were unable to die or beget children. Thus, we might describe this as a paradisiacal creation."[34]

Jesus' comment to the thief on the cross, "Today shalt thou be with me in Paradise" (Luke 23:43), referred to the spirit world where we lived prior to our physical birth and where we go after mortality. They are both called Paradise. It makes sense that it is where all spiritual creation takes place, including the Fall of Adam.

Possibility #2. The Fall took place in an earthly Garden of Eden, but it was an exclusive area set apart from the rest of the physical world and was not subject to death. Paradisiacal conditions existed in the garden such that the citation of 'no death' referred to only those forms of life that existed there. Death, however, was occurring in the rest of the temporal world. We know this temporal world already existed because Adam and Eve were cast out of the garden into the lone and dreary world where various forms of life already existed. As previously noted, Elders Talmage and Widstoe taught this concept.

They also taught that Adam was not the first human on the earth, but the first of a new type of human. He was the first of the Adamic race of humans, with other races being much older.

Dr. Hugh Nibley, a prolific author and former BYU professor of biblical and Mormon scripture, taught:

> "Do not begrudge existence to creatures that looked like
> men long, long ago, nor deny them a place in God's affection

or even a right to exaltation—for our scriptures allow them such. Nor am I overly concerned as to just when they might have lived, for their world is not our world.... God assigned them their proper times and functions, as he has given me mine—a full-time job that admonishes me to remember his words to the overly eager Moses: 'For mine own purpose have I made these things. Here is wisdom and it remaineth in me' (Moses 1:31). It is Adam as my own parent who concerns me. When he walks onto the stage, then and only then the play begins."[35]

Of course, the play to which he is referring is the populating of the Adamic race that received the priesthood of God, eternal covenants, and the plan of salvation. Ancient humans may have existed outside the Garden of Eden, but the human race from which we sprang and with which we are concerned began with Adam and Eve.

Garden Story Meanings

The evolution of our physical bodies as well as our spiritual salvation, both ultimately can be traced back to the doorstep of Eden. Because of its significance to all human life, we should grasp the imagery and deeper meanings it embodies. Even a look at certain words in their original form brings more clarity to the Eden story.

For instance, in Hebrew, Adam means "mankind,"[36] indicating that Adam is representative of all human beings. If you add the Hebrew feminine ending *ah* to the word Adam, you have *adamah*, which means "earth." Continuing with the symbolic meanings of these important names, the Hebrew word for Eve is *chavvah*, which is a feminine adjective that means "living."[37] Given the root meaning of these names, we see that both Adam and Eve together symbolize *mankind living* on *earth*. God taught Moses, "In the image of his own body, male and female, created he them and blessed them, and called *their* name Adam" (Moses 6:9).

When studied from a symbolic perspective, the creation story of our first parents brings a deeper meaning than if taken as purely literal. It teaches us that the creation of mankind is not just about biology but is about the greater goal of salvation and how to achieve it. When we couple the physical evidence of how we came to be with the multi-layered spiritual elements derived through imagery, a more brilliant interpretation unfolds.

BYU Professor of Church History and Doctrine Alonzo L. Gaskill asked,

> "Why all of the Adamic parallels? Because Adam and Eve are our pattern. Their story is ours. Noah, Abraham, covenant Israel, and you and I are to consider ourselves as if we were Adam and Eve. We are to see the story of the Fall as the story of our fall. Thus, so much of our lives—and so much of the lives of the ancient patriarchs and prophets—seems saturated in symbols of the paradise that was willingly given up in the hopes of obtaining an inheritance in the celestial kingdom.
>
> "The fact of the matter is that the story of the Fall—as told in scripture and the temple—is intended to give us more detail regarding our personal falls [as weak and sinful mortals] than about the Fall of historical figures, Adam and Eve. Each of the inspired, authorized accounts have been couched in such a way as to serve as a message about *our* need for obedience, the consequences of *our* sins, and *our* desperate need for a Savior to redeem us from *our* fallen condition. To misunderstand this is to misunderstand the Fall."[38]

The Fall is inseparably connected with the Atonement of Christ because mankind could not be redeemed without it. And like Adam and Eve who were taught all aspects of the plan of salvation once their bodies changed from immortal to mortal, we too, have received the same vital information to help with our earthly sojourn. The value of the journey will be greatest if we clear the brush from the road that leads us back to God. We do that when we make every effort to understand who we are and how his plan works in our lives.

Conclusion

President Gordon B. Hinckley once said, "What the Church requires is only belief 'that Adam was the first man of what we would call the human race.'" He added that scientists can speculate on the rest. He recalled his own study of anthropology and geology, saying, "Studied all about it. Didn't worry me then. Doesn't worry me now."[40]

For Mormons who worry that adopting evolutionary biology would be going against their faith, please know there is no scientific data requiring the absence of God in the evolutionary process of living things. There is nothing in evolution that should cause a person to leave the Church or denounce its teachings. Many solid Church members accept evolution as God's vehicle for the creation of life. In an article on the topic, retired BYU professor William S. Bradshaw shared the feelings of two university students after they completed a study of evolutionary biology.

One student said, "I have, for the most part, resolved the conflict I had with evolution and my religious beliefs. I believe God could and may have used evolutionary means to develop the organisms on the earth. I do not believe He would make the earth appear in a 'zap,' but rather would use scientific devices. The same goes for the organisms He created. I believe the evidence for the evolution of other creatures is valid and do not believe He would change His method to make man. The thing He did differently is to give man a soul and the ability to use free agency in order to return back to Him."[41]

Another student expressed it this way: "I find the theory of evolution to be a beautiful explanation of the creative process. The idea that the organisms here on the earth, including man, have evolved from "lower forms" and are genetically related is to me a remarkable concept—a concept that increases my belief in a Supreme Being who has governed this wonderful process. Indeed, I feel there need be no conflict between the theory of evolution and LDS theology."[42]

I too, add my own testimony that the evolutionary process of our physical life on Earth is but a mirror conceptually of the evolutionary process we go through to become celestial beings. It fits with science and it fits with theology. Still, it is difficult for many to accept the unknown when we so desperately want to know it all. But that too is part of the evolutionary process—waiting upon God to reveal what he knows we need, when we need it. While my presentation here by no means answers every question on the topic, it provides a point of view that for me makes sense and strengthens my faith. And for now, that is enough.

In the meantime, the words of President Harold B. Lee can help keep this quest for evidence of God in perspective.

> "Would it be wonderful if, when there are questions which are unanswered because the Lord hasn't seen fit to reveal the answers as yet, all could say, 'I accept all I read in the scriptures that I can understand, and accept the rest on faith. How comforting it would be to those who are restless in the intellectual world, when such questions arise as to ... how man came to be, if they would answer as did an eminent scientist and devoted Church member. A sister had asked: 'Why didn't the Lord tell us plainly about these things?' The scientist answered: 'It is likely we would not understand if He did. It might be like trying to explain the theory of atomic energy to an eight-year-old child.'"[43]

CHAPTER THREE

Spiritual Communication

As a child I would try to imagine how God could possibly answer the vast number of prayers that were coming in to him at any given time. I would conjure up a massive hot air balloon with God standing in the basket surrounded by a bank of telephones. Each prayer would come through one of the phones, which God would answer, provide soothing information, then hang up and go on to the next call. There were no cell phones at that time, so I'm not sure how my child's mind reconciled the incredible lengths of cable that would be needed for such a scenario, but hey, this was God after all, who could accomplish all things.

In some ways I'm still trying to figure out how he does it, ever the searcher for practical answers that can be intellectually fused to my faith and testimony. Some might say my quest for tangible answers shows a lack of faith. However, as has been already established, the seeking of truth wherever it can be found is the ensign of true religion. So let's take a look at how God really communicates with his children.

Henry Eyring, a noted scientist, scholar, and LDS Church leader, once wrote,

> "In our everyday world, we use units of feet and seconds. In the chemical world of molecules and atoms, the electrons

complete their revolutions in a hundred million millionths of a second, while a hundred million atoms side by side extend only a distance of one inch. Inside the nucleus of the atom, we enter a third world, where events happen a million times faster still, and distances are a thousand times smaller than in the atom. In the fourth world, the astronomers measure revolutions of the planets in years, and the unit of distance, the light year, is about ten thousand million miles. Finally, we come to the spiritual world where time is measured in eternities and space is limitless. Thus, in thought we can travel from the almost infinitesimally small to the infinitely large."[1]

It is thought—consciousness and spirituality—that has always been the biggest puzzlement to science. But understanding human thought, like a needle on a compass, always points true north to the science of God, despite scholarly efforts to change its direction. That's because a look at the spiritual aspect of humans opens up a profusion of information about who we are that would not be available if we limited our study to just the physical. Researching our physical bodies will only bring half the answers leaving us with half the truth, and that's because humans are dual beings. "For man is spirit. The elements are eternal, and spirit and element, inseparably connected, receive a fulness of joy" (D&C 93:33). One of science's greatest weaknesses is the exclusion of spiritual, metaphysical realities like consciousness, pre-mortal and post-mortal life, and the idea of God, himself.

Even those who doubt God generally agree there is a definite spiritual world around us. Scholars, scientists, theologians, and truth seekers of all kinds must acknowledge and study it as passionately as any other examination of time and space in our physical world. Those who deny the existence of God must grapple with how consciousness managed to arise in a world full of physicality. They are left to figure out how humans developed above all things physical to become endowed with a consciousness that receives and emits spiritual energy. That level of spirit consciousness gives people the ability unique among God's creatures to feel, show empathy, make moral judgments, and ultimately communicate with him. No other living thing can do that. Spirit touching spirit from God to man gives the sweet assurance that we are not alone and that a divine creator, the Father of us all, cares about each one of us in a way that is as infinite as he is.

All people, religious or not, communicate on a spiritual level with each other and with Deity in a number of ways. This spirituality may not be acknowledged as such by some, but it's an undeniable part of being human. From a religious perspective most people feel God communicates in the following ways:

1. Still, small voice of the Holy Ghost (Acts 11:12; Acts 13:2; Acts 16:67, 1 Kings 19:12; Isaiah 30: 19-21)
2. Audible voice of God (Acts 9:45, Revelation 4:1; Enos 1)
3. Dreams (Matthew 1:20-21; Genesis 28:11-18)
4. Visions (Acts 10:9-18)
5. Angels (Luke 1: 26-38; Mosiah 27:8-37)
6. Prophets (Proverbs 12:15)
7. Scripture (2 Timothy 3:16; Psalms 119:11, 105)

The actual mechanism for these communications may be little more than conjecture on the part of we mortals, but there are some interesting evidences in science that can give us pause.

From a religious perspective we know that God created the universe to operate using fixed laws of nature. So, it is not a big leap to suggest that he, himself, utilizes those same laws to conduct business with his children on Earth. It's not inconceivable that a simple answer to prayer may be communicated using energy akin to such natural phenomena as electricity, radar, and radio waves but obviously in an infinitely more advanced way. Physicists have told us that matter and energy never travel faster than the speed of light, so God would also have a vastly superior knowledge of this law of nature and use it in his communications with us. Again, this is all simply an idea, but it makes some sense in our quest for answers about our world and our Creator.

Others have suggested, such as Henry Eyring, that "we cannot understand exactly 'how' God communicates, but that He has methods of communication which travel by other means and at speeds unknown and perhaps unknowable to mortal man. They feel the actual mechanism used to communicate transcends the laws of physics as we know them, but that this should not seem strange when you think of all the marvels in communication we enjoy today that were unimaginable" a century ago.[2]

Even the miracles performed by Jesus—walking on water, changing water into wine, healing the sick—would either have to be manifestations of a superior understanding and use of natural laws or simply be laws of physics as yet undiscovered by humankind. I suspect our understanding of *how* he communicates is of less importance to God than the fact that he *does* communicate, and yet it is in our nature to continually dig for the answers. It is in the process of digging that rewards of enlightenment come, both in science and in spirituality, and so let us turn over the next searching shovel and see what we can find.

Spiritual Phenomena are Part of Being Human

It's interesting that for all the scientific theories construed to negate a Godly connection to spirituality and consciousness, people are still holding firm in their religious beliefs. Often, their tenacity is based on the personal spiritual experiences they're having. Even when science claims that spirituality is simply a product of brain activity, people of all cultures, ages, religions, and beliefs, continue to have phenomenal spiritual encounters that give them reason to believe there's more to it than that.

In a June, 2002 Gallup Survey, U.S. respondents were asked to rate the statement, "I have had a profound religious experience or awakening that changed the direction of my life." Their responses were placed on a scale from 0 to 5, with 0 standing for "does not apply at all" and 5 for "applies completely." Forty-one percent of Americans—which projected to about 80 million adults nationwide—said the statement *completely* applies to them.[3]

Of note are some 6,000 accounts of written religious experiences housed at the library of the University of Wales at Lampeter, home to the Religious Experience Research Centre (RERC). Founded in 1969 by British scientist and biology professor Alister Hardy, the center continues to be a bastion for the study of spiritual experiences today. It receives and archives letters and e-mails several times a month from people who believe they had a spiritual or religious experience or felt a presence or power different from their everyday life. Here are two examples of these accounts:

"It was an absolutely still day, flooded with sunshine. In the garden everything was shining, breathless, as if waiting expectant. Quite suddenly I felt convinced of the existence of God; as if I had only to put out my hand to touch Him. And at the same time there came the intensest joy and indescribable longing, as if in exile, perhaps, for home. It seemed as if my heart were struggling to leap out of my body."[4]

In the second account, a six-year-old boy from a twice yearly active Christian family answered a researcher's questions about his religious beliefs: "Well once I went um... in the night and I saw this bishopy kind of alien. I said, 'Who are you?' And he said, 'I am the Holy Spirit.' I did think he was the Holy Spirit."

The boy called for his mother and explained his experience, but she rejected his story suggesting that the Holy Spirit looks like a ball of fire. While he accepted his mother's explanation he told the researcher, "But I often felt the Holy Spirit in me."[5]

Since Hardy's passing in 1985, there has been a steadily growing amount of research into spiritual phenomena. Surveys indicate that between one third and one half of British people claim to have had direct personal awareness of "a power or presence different from everyday life." Much depends on exactly what question is asked, but the figure seems to be going up. A study in 2001 by David Hay, a lecturer at the University of Nottingham, found that 76% of the British population claimed experience with a transcendent reality.[6]

And it's not just happening in the western world. Similar results were found in a 2006 survey of nearly 3,200 people in China from 10 different areas of the country. Among the more interesting findings was that only

8.7% of Chinese described themselves as "religious," 28.6% felt comforted or empowered through prayer and worship, and 56.7% experienced the influence of "a kind of power that people cannot control or explain clearly." They identified this power with a religious being or force. Only 4.4% claimed to be Buddhist and 2.8% claimed Christianity, further emphasizing the universal nature of spiritual experiences.[7]

The sheer numbers of experiences with the divine among all peoples should count for something in our quest for evidence of God. Of course, not all accounts may be true as people may fabricate stories for whatever reasons or simply mistake actual encounters with the Spirit for their own thoughts and feelings. But because so many people are having these occurrences, we should give reasonable consideration to their claims.

The Brain as a Conduit

As we accept that God indeed communicates with humankind, it helps to understand how. A look at the human brain is a good place to start. The brain, with a weight of only three pounds, is the most organized matter on Earth—organized as the most advanced, powerful, data-processing system in the cosmos.

Here's a snapshot of how it works. Brain cells called neurons communicate to each other through electrical and chemical impulses along thin fibers called axons. At the end of each axon is a synapse, which through the use of neurotransmitter molecules and chemical receptor molecules, sends the signal on to another neuron. Each synapse has different receptor proteins that affect the firing pattern of a neuron. This amazing communication system is how the brain sends millions of messages throughout the nervous system to control various functions of the body.

The kicker is that the adult human brain contains billions of neurons and up to 500 trillion synapses. There are more synapses in the human brain than there are stars in the known universe.[8] If we compare the brain to a computer, we learn that each of these billions of neurons emits more than

1,000 instructions per second, which is about 100 more than the 103 million instructions per second of a modern microprocessor.[9]

With such an incredible super computer for a brain, one would think we could harness it to solve for the common denominator between science and spirituality. Dr. Andrew Newberg, a radiologist at the University Pennsylvania Hospital, is one such thinker. He has spent a lifetime studying the coupling of modern technology with religion, spirituality, and faith. While there are many approaches in the study of neurotheology—the relationship between brain, religion, and spiritual experiences—old fashioned behavioral studies are fading away in place of brain scans. With brain scan technology researchers can watch the brain directly and record indications of spiritual activity.

It's a fascinating field, and because we know a lot about how the brain works, we also know how religious metaphysical phenomena such as prayer, visions, dreams, voices, and images are manifested in the brain. Newberg has used neuroimaging devices such as MRI's or SPECT scans to test a wide range of spirituality. He has tested simple spiritual experiences such as someone watching a sunset, all the way to Tibetan Buddhists in profound states of consciousness after years of meditation.

But hard as Newberg and others like him have tried to find answers in this new field of study, the conclusions they draw are limited solely to the physical world. They can only tell us how the brain creates or reacts to religious experiences, not where they came from.[10]

Because consciousness is the other half of being human, we all experience spiritual phenomena—believers and doubters alike. Think of the "coincidences" in our lives that may not be coincidences at all. Have you ever been thinking of a person only to have them suddenly call or drop by? Maybe you've had a brief encounter with someone new who impacted your life deeply from something they said or did. Maybe you've had a premonition or dream that warned you about something or someone you love that turned out to be true. Think of the circumstances involved in the notable events of your life and the spiritual aspects of how they came to be. Perhaps you've had those "ah ha" moments when light bulbs go on in your head illuminating answers derived from something as simple as a beautiful melody or cascading waterfall. All are surely instances of Godly intercession to bring us peace and joy and to help us navigate our way in the world.

If we fail to acknowledge this spiritual world where time is measured in eternities and space is limitless,[11] then we deny a full half of who we are as human beings. Even scientists understand this, which is why they work tirelessly for answers to this aspect of the human condition. When we put God in the equation, we learn that it is this spiritual aspect of man that is our Creator's sphere of influence. Through the Holy Ghost, he transmits personal revelation, regardless of religion, to every individual who attempts to live by a moral compass. Because God is no respecter of persons, he will pour out his Spirit unto all who have faith in him (see D&C 8:1-3; 46:7; Matthew 7:7-8; James. 1:5).

All of this suggests the spiritual part of human beings cannot be explained away as mere fabrications of the brain. We can blindly accept this explanation or take in the bigger picture and ask, isn't brain activity another testament of God using his own laws of nature to help us receive, feel, and experience the workings of the spirit? Isn't brain activity the most reasonable way for God to reach our conscious selves through the tabernacle of our physical bodies? He uses the workings of our bodies as conduits to our spirits to provide comfort, answers, warnings, and enlightenment to help in our everyday lives. We are also told that as our faith and commitment grows, so too, will the level of revelation we receive.

Nephi wrote: "For behold, thus saith the Lord God: I will give unto the children of men line upon line, precept upon precept, here a little and there a little; and blessed are those who hearken unto my precepts, and lend an ear unto my counsel, for they shall learn wisdom; for unto him that receiveth I will give more; and from them that shall say, We have enough, from them shall be taken away even that which they have" (2 Nephi 28:29-30).

In addition to personal helps, we are promised through our faithfulness that God will reveal to us

> "all mysteries, yea, all the hidden mysteries of my kingdom from days of old, and for ages to come, will I make

known unto them the good pleasure of my will concerning all things pertaining to my kingdom. Yea, even the wonders of eternity shall they know, and things to come will I show them, even the things of many generations. And their wisdom shall be great and their understanding reach to heaven; and before them the wisdom of the wise shall perish, and the understanding of the prudent shall come to naught. For by my Spirit will I enlighten them, and by my power will I make known unto them the secrets of my will—yea, even those things which eye has not seen, nor ear heard, nor yet entered into the heart of man" (D&C. 76:5-10).

Such blessings of wisdom and enlightenment are what mankind has sought since the beginning. They are why we study science and theology, why we seek a connection between the two, and why we hold tenaciously to our personal experiences with the cosmos to define our belief systems. As we come to more fully understand how God uses spiritual and physical processes to communicate with us, we will grow in our testimonies that he lives.

Communication through Dreams

Dreaming is a universal part of being human and is one of the basic connectors of spirituality among most world faiths throughout history. For example, dream interpretation is found in the Talmud, a collection of Jewish religious teachings compiled from 200 BC to AD 300; descriptions of dreaming is in the Upanishads, the sacred Hindu texts that reach back to the seventh century BC; it shows up among the writings of tribal shamans among the Diegueno, a Native American people from what is now Southern California; and we find dream analysis in the treatise *On Dreams*, written by Synesios, a Christian bishop of Ptolemais in the early fifth century AD.[12] It's also found in the Bible and Book of Mormon (see 1 Nephi 1:16; 8:2; Isaiah 29:17; Daniel 2; 7; Alma 30:28; Genesis 28:10-22; 1 Kings 3:5, Ether 9:3).

The very act of dreaming is a testament in and of itself that humans have a spirit distinct from the body. Dreams give us the experience of traveling to other dimensions of time and space, interacting with people in surreal surroundings apart from our physical world while the body lies dormant in bed. As we look at the sensation of dreaming, the conscious seems to separate from the body. Then, when dreams also include departed friends and relatives, one might begin to see the possibility of the soul actually surviving physical death.

Some in science would have us believe that dreams are merely by-products of a partially activated brain during sleep that manufactures bizarre, fleeting images stemming solely from biophysical activity in the brain and body.[13] So they study and experiment using sophisticated neuroimaging devices to record brain activity and interpret what they find. And they know a lot. Dozens of neuropsychological and neuroimaging studies have conclusively shown that REM [rapid eye movement] sleep, which is most reliably linked with vivid dreams, is associated with a very particular brain activation pattern centered on the amygdala in the limbic system. Portions of the anterior area of the brain are consistently activated during REM sleep while other brain areas and systems are de-activated. The product of this unique design of activations and de-activations in the brain is, inescapably, dreams.[14]

That's the purely physical explanation of dreaming, but studies also look at it from other angles. Some research focuses on the biophysiology of dreaming and sleep and what influences these processes, while other research looks into the content of dreams. Experts also look at why we dream and the functions that dreams serve, producing a variety of theories. The more popular theories include to:

- Restore our body and mind.
- Help with learning and memory.
- Keep the brain at the right level of awareness/rest during sleep.
- Allow the mind to handle disturbances in the night without waking up.
- Keep our sense of self and wholeness through sleep.

- Allow ourselves some time to explore new and unusual areas of ourselves.
- Resolve conflicts which occur during the day.
- Contextualize emotions from waking.
- Practice dealing with threats.[15]

While most dreams seem of little value on a day-to-day basis, very few would argue against how amazingly helpful some dreams can be. They can provide all of us with a potpourri of benefits such as prophetic insight, flashes of creativity, and elevated self-awareness. So far, there is nothing here to negate what religion would have us know about dreams as a vehicle for communication with Deity. While the brain creates or facilitates the dreaming process that goes on in the human conscious, it also acts as the conduit for the reception of spiritual messages or messengers. It is once again God using the laws of nature, in this case, brain activity during sleep, to interact with his children.

Dreams Connect Us with God

As stated in the preface of this book, I have sometimes doubted, questioned, and sought answers about God and the universe throughout my life. As a practicing member of the Church, I have always envied those who have gifts of the spirit with regard to faith—knowing by revelation, testimony, and the discerning of spirits—(see D&C 46:11-26; Moroni 10) because those things never come easily to me. Yes, I have had a few awe inspiring spiritual experiences that I hold near and dear, and yes, I have felt the Comforter bring peace on occasions when I needed it. But because I'm never quite sure if those feelings are from God or just something my own conscious self manufactures, I have spent much of my life feeling a step behind or out of touch in many areas of spirituality. Sad as this is, I know I'm not alone in experiencing this challenge.

If you're like me, I hope you'll benefit from a few of the things I've learned. First, remember that sometimes you can be so sure you lack spiritual discernment you overlook the still, small voice or the subtle messages of the Spirit all around. You gloss over certain spiritual encounters as nothing special when, in fact, they may contain glimpses of the divine for which you yearn. Sometimes this lack of self-confidence keeps you from giving these experiences the sufficient weight they deserve. Then over time, they fade and get swept under the carpet of life's constant foot traffic and you lose what might have been a meaningful spiritual gain.

When you do receive a special encounter of the Spirit, capture it, ponder it, and catalog it in your repertoire of life's experiences that bring meaning. Don't brush it aside as nothing and don't ever forget about it. The more significance you give it, the more it will influence your life and serve as an answer to your questions. With that in mind, let me share a dream I had many years ago that made an incredible impression on me, especially considering my natural tendency to doubt.

The dream began with me and one of my best friends sitting on a bench outside the office of our bishop, apparently waiting to go in for interviews. As we sat there we began to discuss my intense desire to glimpse beyond the veil and witness, for myself, that life did indeed go on after death and that what I had been taught all my life in the Church was true. My friend listened caringly and then said out of the blue, "I can take you there." I responded with incredulity but was assured that she could take me through the veil into the spirit world right then and there. When I excitedly agreed, the image in my dream showed us instantaneously leaving one realm and finding ourselves in another. I understood this place to be the spirit world where the spirits of those who have died reside prior to the resurrection and judgment.

The portion of this world in which we found ourselves looked very much like the inside of a big high school or college campus. There were roomy open areas like cafeterias and outside courtyards that were filled with people in small and large groups in the process of learning. Group leaders or teachers were instructing these souls in what I sensed were principles of eternal progression. I say "sensed" because I never actually heard anything audible, although I could hear my friend as she conducted the tour. I asked her if I could get all my questions answered in this place, and she assured me that I could. Needing clarification I asked a second time, "Do you mean that every question I've ever had about life and the universe I can ask and find answers to right now?" She responded positively again and I was immediately overcome with joy and amazement, the likes of which I'd never felt before in my entire life. At long last, I could find answers.

The feeling stayed with me as I awoke, bringing sensations of weightlessness and a tingling sensation throughout my body and spirit. I endeavored to hang on to all that I had seen and felt knowing how fleeting dreams could be. For me, this was no ordinary dream. It was a gift from God, a glimpse of eternity that he knew I needed to bolster my faith. The dream ended with us back on that bench outside the bishop's office without having had an opportunity to ask questions while in the spirit world. Surprisingly, I remember feeling no disappointment after waking at not having asked any of my burning questions. It seemed to be enough that my glimpse of the divine gave me a secure assurance that this life was not the end and that everything I longed to understand would someday be within my grasp.

Everyone dreams but some are filled with messages about religious matters and spiritual awakenings from beyond the veil that seem to cry out that there is a God. They provide sacred solace and enlightenment, even a foretaste of eternity, and are produced and directed especially for a particular individual, at a particular time, for a particular purpose.

While revelatory dreams all come from God, often his messages are conveyed through other people. Richard G. Scott, of the Quorum of Twelve Apostles, said of dreams:

> "Revelation can also be given in a dream when there is an almost imperceptible transition from sleep to wakefulness. If you strive to capture the content immediately, you can record great detail, but otherwise it fades rapidly. Inspired communication in the night is generally accompanied by a sacred feeling for the entire experience. The Lord uses individuals for whom we have great respect to teach us truths in a dream because we trust them and will listen to their counsel. It is the Lord doing the teaching through the Holy

Ghost. However, He may in a dream make it both easier to understand and more likely to touch our hearts by teaching us through someone we love and respect."[16]

For example, Church member Martins Enyiche described in the *Ensign* how he quit going to Church because of a disagreement with his stake president. After his wife counseled him to pray about it before making such a drastic withdrawal, he took her advice and knelt in prayer. That night, he had a dream in which his grandfather appeared to him and rebuked him for his inability to follow his priesthood leader. After awaking and not being able to go back to sleep, he spent the night pondering his dream. This prompted him the next day to go to the stake president, apologize, and return to Church activity. He said he felt this experience was in preparation for what happened shortly thereafter. The company for which he worked sent him and his family to live in Nigeria where he was soon called as a branch president.[17]

Visitation dreams, where a departed relative is sent to console a bereaved spouse or to provide a message of some kind, are not uncommon. Renowned dream researcher and educator Patrick McNamara, Ph.D., provided some good information on the common elements of visitation dreams. Among them are the appearance of the deceased as they were in their healthy life rather than when ill. They often appear much younger too. The deceased reassured the dreamer telepathically or mentally that they were alright and still nearby. Visitation dreams are typically clear, vivid, and intense rather than disorganized or bizarre and are felt to be real visits when the dreamer awakens. The dreamer undergoes a marked change from the experience and describes a wider spiritual perspective and resolution in their grieving.[18]

Another example involves Lynda and her sister who both felt tremendous guilt over not being present when their mother died. Circumstances beyond their control kept them away at that important moment. But a few weeks after her mother's passing, Lynda had a dream that brought her peace. She saw herself standing behind a railing at the crest of a deep and narrow canyon. Her parents [her dad had died years earlier] were seated together on the patio of a restaurant in Mexico, where they had vacationed years before. When her mother saw her, she smiled and waved. Lynda knew she could not join her parents but was happy to see them together and to know her mother had made the transition okay.

A week later, Lynda discovered that her sister had received the same dream—with one variation. Her sister had scurried back and forth along the railing in an attempt to find a break in it so she could go to her parents. In addition to finding peace through these dreams, the sisters enjoyed a laugh because their mother would often say of Lynda's sister, "That girl just can't take no for an answer."[19]

Dreams can also provide divine warnings or messages that the dreamer needs to make changes in his or her life. Dr. McArthur Hill, a former abortion physician, describes what he called a recurring nightmare that eventually led him to stop doing abortions. "In my nightmares I would deliver a healthy newborn baby and I would hold it up, and I would face a jury of faceless people and ask them to tell me what to do with this baby. They would go thumbs-up or thumbs-down and if they made a thumbs-down indication then I was to drop the baby into a bucket of water which was present. I never did reach the point of dropping the baby into the bucket because I'd always wake up at that point. But it was clear to me that there was something subconsciously going on in my mind."[20]

Further examples of dream accounts are found throughout the scriptures. The subject matter of these dreams varies, demonstrating that God will send messages to touch and teach us according to his purposes and according to our needs. Some examples are:

1. The telling of future events (Genesis 37:5; 40:5, 8; 41:15)
2. Foretelling the appearance of the Savior (Genesis 28:10-22; 31:24; 1 Kings 3:5; 1 Nephi 2:1-2; 3:2)
3. Ministering of angels to the faithful (Genesis 31:11; Matthew 1:20; 2:13, 19)
4. Prophetic warnings (Ether 9:3)

5. The teaching of truth through symbolism (1 Nephi 8; 9; 10; 15:21)[21]

These scriptural accounts, along with all other revelatory dreams received by people every day, are testaments to a God who communicates to his mortal children. They serve as evidence that our brains were designed to be conduits for that communication and that our conscious selves are capable of transcending the physical. Dreams, like other forms of communication beyond this mortal veil, are further evidence of God.

Visions are Spiritual Gifts

The Church teaches that all inspired dreams are visions (1 Nephi 8:2) but all visions are not dreams. Visions that are not inspired dreams are received during wakefulness and are considered gifts of the Spirit (7th Article of Faith). Such visions take on some common characteristics as recorded in scripture:

1. *The appearance of actual personages*: Joseph Smith's First Vision of the Father and the Son (Joseph Smith 2:15-20); Abram's vision of the Lord who promised him seed (Genesis 15); Paul's vision of the risen Lord (Acts 9:1-9; 26:12-19); Moses and Elijah's appearance on the Mount of Transfiguration as seen by Peter, James, and John (Matthew 17:1-9); an angel's appearance to Amulek (Alma 8:20).
2. *Conversing with heavenly beings* in vision while not personally in their presence: Lehi was "overcome with the Spirit," and saw the heavens open where he thought he saw God and angels (1 Nephi 1:8); Stephen saw "the heavens opened, and the Son of man standing on the right hand of God" (Acts 7:56).
3. *Past, present, and future events*: The destruction of Jerusalem as seen by Nephi (2 Nephi 1:4); view by Moroni of the Hill

Cumorah where the golden plates lay hidden (Joseph Smith 2:42); the vastness of the Lord's creations as seen by Abraham and Moses (Moses 1; 2; 3; Abraham, 3; 4; 5); Ezekiel's vision of the last days (Ezekiel 37-39); the brother of Jared's vision of all the inhabitants of the earth (Ether 3:25).

4. *Symbolisms that teach gospel truths*: The tree of life, the iron rod, and the straight and narrow path shown in vision to Lehi and Nephi (1 Nephi 8; 11); Peter's understanding that the gospel was to go to the Gentiles after a vision he received about unclean animals he needed to kill and eat (Acts 10:9-48; 11:1-18).[22]

As with dreams, science has pinpointed the regions of the brain that "produce" visions. There is a visual-association area in the brain that interprets what the eyes see and connects images to emotions and memories. When a religious symbol or inspiring story triggers a sense of spiritual awe, it is because this visual-association area has learned to link those images to that feeling. Visions that arise during prayer or ritual are also generated in the association area. Electrical stimulation of the temporal lobes [which nestle along the sides of the head and house the circuits responsible for language, conceptual thinking, and associations] "produces" or is the conduit for visions.[23]

Again, as with dreams, just because spiritual experiences have distinct neural patterns does not mean they are mere neurological illusions. Newberg insists, "It's no safer to say that spiritual urges and sensations are caused by brain activity than it is to say that the neurological changes through which we experience the pleasure of eating an apple cause the apple to exist. There is no way to determine whether the neurological changes associated with spiritual experience mean that the brain is causing those experiences ... or is instead perceiving a spiritual reality."[24]

No matter how you decide to look at it, people are having profound metaphysical visions through what they consider to be God, his messengers, and the afterlife in ways that simply can't be explained by medical science.

Some studies have tried to suggest that those who claim to have had visions are really having psychotic delusions like the mentally ill who see things and hear voices that aren't there. But other research by psychologists indicate that the vast majority of people claiming visions are normal and sane and are often reluctant to share their stories for fear of being labeled delusional.

Those who would fix such a label and claim it all as lunacy forget that some of the biggest religions of the world often started as a result of a vision. Allah is said to have appeared to Muhammad in a cave on Jabal al-Nour. Krishna reportedly revealed himself to Arjuna who was in a chariot on a battlefield. Guru Nanak, the founder of Sikhism, said he found himself in the presence of God while bathing in a river.[25] Suffice it to say, such phenomena are widespread in all cultures and have been throughout history. Massive numbers of people have accepted as true these religious leaders and their visions. Are they all lunatics too? People have visions. It happens. What is needed in order to find truth in these various theologies is an understanding of the proper source of those visions and/or the correct interpretation of them. More will be presented on the topic of other religions in chapter six.

For Mormons, the most miraculous vision of all was the appearance of God the Father and his Son, Jesus Christ, in 1820, to the 14-year-old boy prophet, Joseph Smith. He said, "I saw a pillar of light exactly over my head, above the brightness of the sun, which descended gradually until it fell upon me …. When the light rested upon me I saw two Personages, whose brightness and glory defy all description, standing above me in the air. One of them spake unto me, calling me by name and said, pointing the other—'This is My Beloved Son. Hear Him'" (Joseph Smith 1:17).

This singularly astounding moment was destined to have the most profound effect on all that we know about science and religion. Born of this encounter is information that answers many of humankind's most salient questions about life and its meaning and yet people still call it delusional or just plain fabricated. And while this particular vision is in a class all by itself, it illustrates the ultimate pipeline that visions provide between God and his children.

There are no rules about who can receive visions, although the LDS Church teaches that people should not expect to receive revelations regarding matters beyond their own personal lives, stewardships, and families. Prophetic revelations for the Church as a whole must remain the stewardship of the Lord's chosen prophet. But beyond that, every human being is entitled to Godly communication with their Maker.

One example of a "normal" person's vision comes from Dr. Mary C. Neal, an orthopaedic surgeon who wrote a book about her near-death experience (NDE). As a sidebar to the actual NDE, Neal described an incident with a former patient's wife, who had a visitation from her deceased husband that she wanted to share with Neal.

The woman, who happened to be LDS, told Neal that in the time since her husband's death, his spirit would occasionally visit their home and give her guidance. During one visitation, her husband told her that Neal had been in a terrible accident and that he had asked God if he could be one of those sent to help save her. The woman did not know that Neal had already had a terrible boating accident resulting in an NDE and subsequent miraculous help by strangers who seemed to vanish after getting her to safety. When Neal told the woman about the details of her boating accident, she was taken aback at the woman's lack of surprise because her deceased husband had already shared those same details with her.[26]

In his book, *Echoes from Eternity*, Alvin Gibson tells about an experience LDS Church member Eloise Weaver had after a car accident she was in along with her husband and daughter. After the car quit rolling a number of times, she found herself fully awake but struggling to breathe because of what turned out to be a broken neck.

She recalled, "Looking into the window I saw two personages. Who they were, I don't know. I could see them from their shoulders up. One of them said to me, 'Pull your legs up to your chest, hold them tight, and breathe shallow and you will live.' Then they were gone. I think they were two men from the tone of the voice of the one, and they were dressed in white. The white was as bright as … it was as bright as the snow when the sun hits it. And there was a warm, calm, sweet feeling in that light. I did as they told me; I pulled my legs up and I held on tight. That action probably saved my life."

After more than a month in the hospital and another four months of painful recovery from broken vertebrae, a ruptured spleen, broken ribs, collapsed lungs, and multiple diaphragm breaks, Eloise made a full recovery. She insisted, "I know those people were there, and I know what they told me and what I did. Someday when I meet them again I'll know who they were."[27]

Still another vision experience was described by Elder Russell M. Nelson when he was at the Washington D.C. Temple dedication in 1974 with Elder Hugh B. Brown, a former member of the First Presidency. Elder Brown, who had some challenging responsibilities in the building of that temple, shared the following account as told by Elder Nelson:

> "On the morning of the temple dedication, President Brown greeted me with the news that he had been visited during the night by President Harold B. Lee. (President Lee, former LDS Church president, had died the year before)." Elder Brown "described it as a glorious visit, one that meant much to him, for President Lee had been aware of some of the difficulties encountered by President Brown in the decisions that led to the construction of the temple in Washington, D.C.
>
> "Later that morning, as we took President Brown to breakfast, Sister Harold B. (Freda Joan) Lee approached us. As we exchanged greetings, President Brown said to her, 'I had a glorious visit with Harold last night. He is just fine. It was so good to visit with him.' This was such a moving experience for us all. We felt the presence of President Lee's spirit in the temple through the witness of President Brown."[28]

After-death Communications

Otherworldly visitations from deceased loved ones via a person's visions or dreams have been examined through numerous studies. Those who study these after-death communications (ADC) seek to document the number and comparability of these occurrences. Researchers Karlis Osis and Erlunder Haraldsson studied ADCs in a number of different cultures and found that these experiences were nearly indistinguishable from one culture to another.[29] So not only do they occur frequently, they are virtually the same all over the world.

In the first complete research study in this field involving 2,000 people who lived in all 50 states and the ten Canadian provinces, some 3,300 firsthand accounts of (ADCs) were collected. The accounts were from people claiming direct communication from a deceased family member or friend without the involvement of psychics, mediums, or hypnotists. Based on this study of people in all social, educational, economic, occupational, and religious backgrounds, it was estimated that at least 50 million Americans, or 20% of the population, have had one or more ADC experiences. And this is a conservative estimate.[30]

According to this research, the purpose of these visits was to offer comfort, reassurance, and hope to those left behind. Those interviewed said the most frequent messages expressed by the deceased person, verbally or non-verbally, included:

> "I'm okay ... I'm fine ... Everything is okay ... Don't worry about me ... Don't grieve for me ... Please let me go ... I'm happy ... Everything will be all right ... Go on with your life ... Please forgive ... Thank you ... I'll always be there for you ... I'm watching over you ... I'll see you again ... I love you ... Good-bye ..."[31]

One such experience came to a man whose mother died when he was a preteen.

> "My father remained an incredible optimist his whole life, even when he was dying. I was busy trying to make sure

he was comfortable and pain-free, and at first didn't notice he had become very sad.

"He told me how much he was going to miss me once he was gone. And then he mentioned how much he was saying goodbye to his loved ones, his favorite foods, the sky, the outdoors, and a million other things of this world. He was overcome by sadness I could not [and would not] take away from him.

"My father was very down-hearted for the next few days. But then one morning he told me my mother, his wife, had come to him the night before. 'David, she was here for me,' he said with an excitement I had not seen in him in years. 'I was looking at all I was losing, and I'd forgotten that I was going to be with her again. I'm going to see her soon.' He looked at me as he realized I would still remain here. Then he added, 'we'll be there waiting for you.'

"Over the next two days, his demeanor changed dramatically. He had gone from a hopeless dying man with only death in front of him to a hopeful man who was going to be reunited with the love of his life. My father lived with hope and also died with it."[32]

Not everyone is blessed to pierce the veil and sometimes have difficulty with why their deceased loved one hasn't come to them. Often, conversations I have with my own mother include a distressing lament that my deceased father hasn't come to comfort her. To those like her with similar sadness, I can only hope that there is comfort in knowing they'll be together again based on the experiences of others, as well as their own faith.

Often people have stories that are shared within the generations of their families of visits by deceased relatives who came to escort a dying person through the veil into the spirit world. My mother has told us many times of an experience in 1935 that her grandmother, Cordelia, had just before she died. Cordelia's first husband, Edgar, to whom she was sealed in the temple, had died many years earlier. She later married again to a man the grandchildren referred to as "Brother Butler." On one occasion, Cordelia's daughter, Mary, spoke of an incident that occurred when her mother was very close to death. The dying Cordelia suddenly sat up in bed, focused intently on something in the room, and said, "But Edgar, I'm not ready to go yet." That was all she said before laying back down from what appeared to be an extraordinary visit from her first husband. She died the very next day.

After-death communications are further confirmed by Hospice and critical care hospital staff who often report how dying patients see visions of deceased loved ones. If these paranormal visions were simply hallucinations, how could countless patient stories match up with each other? Reports of dying patient visions are found all through Europe, Asia, and the United States with uncanny similarities. Aside from minor religious differences, the deathbed visions of these patients were consistent.[33]

One of the largest cross-cultural studies on deathbed visions in patient care settings was conducted in 1977 by Osis and Haraldsson, who examined the visions of approximately 440 terminally ill patients from the U.S. and India. Some 91 percent told their doctors or nurses they saw deceased relatives. In 140 cases patients reported seeing religious figures, usually described as an angel or God.[34]

In their 1993 book, *Final Gifts,* hospice nurses Maggie Callanan and Patricia Kelley reported how an elderly Chinese lady, terminally ill with cancer, had recurrent visions of her deceased husband asking her to join him. One day she saw her sister with her husband, and both were calling her to join them. Puzzled over this, she told the hospice nurse that her sister was still alive in China, and that it had been many years since they'd last seen each other. When the hospice nurse later related this conversation to the woman's daughter, the daughter stated that the patient's sister had in fact died two days earlier of the same kind of cancer. The family had decided not to tell the patient to avoid upsetting or frightening her.[35]

Caregivers in the family often tell of receiving visits from the very dying person for whom they are caring. After returning home from an exhausting day caring for her dying mother at the nursing home, one caregiver told this story:

> "My mother had been very ill for some time. After dinner with my husband and children, I went to bed. During the middle of the night, I awoke from a very deep sleep. I had dreamed my mother had come to visit me. In this dream, she was with my father who had passed 5 years ago. Both of them looked happy and healthy. My mother blew me a kiss. Then she and my father turned around and walked off, over a hill. When I awoke, tears filled my eyes, but I also felt a sense of peace. My parents had looked so joyful. I looked at the clock and noted it was 3 a.m., then lay back down and went to sleep. The next morning my brother called to tell me my mother had left us. When I asked him about the time of her death, he replied she had passed at 3 a.m."[36]

Although just a precious few of the thousands of religious metaphysical experiences recorded throughout the world are listed here, they send a message loud and clear that:

1. God lives,
2. Life continues after death, and
3. Science alone cannot explain human existence.

Conclusion

Revelatory dreams and visions and after-death communications with loved ones are truly fascinating. They offer verification of life beyond our physical world as well as communication with Deity. There is a reverent tranquility in this knowledge because it helps to build our faith and gives us hope that this gospel is, indeed, true. Some may question why they, too, aren't blessed with such vivid communications beyond the veil. After all, wouldn't such experiences more effectively turn one's faith into knowledge and bring true conversion?

The truth is that dazzling encounters with spirit messengers don't always have the staying power to help us overcome doubt and the natural man as some might think. They can be fleeting as time goes by until the distance between us and the experience becomes clouded, diffused, and nearly forgotten. As the vagaries of life close in and we've built our testimonies solely on a single visionary moment, no matter how amazing or life-changing at the time, we may find that it's simply not enough to keep our testimonies solid down the road. Some examples in scripture and in history make this point.

Cain, the son of Adam, knew the gospel and the plan of salvation. He even spoke personally with God (Moses 5; Genesis 4), and yet he eventually openly rebelled, worshipped Satan, and killed his brother, Abel, forever retaining the shameful distinction as the first son of Perdition. What an awful waste of human potential for Cain to actually have had a perfect knowledge of God, and then allow himself to be dragged down to the depths of Hell, by someone who cared nothing about him beyond his total destruction.

Laman and Lemuel in the Book of Mormon actually saw and heard an angel who rebuked them when they were being rebellious. Without so much as a blink of an eye, "after the angel had departed, Laman and Lemuel again began to murmur ...." (1 Nephi 3:31). While they reluctantly went forth anyway to accomplish the angel's instructions, the two brothers continued to live their lives in open rebellion against God. It's fair to say most of us, after seeing an angel, would be at least a little humbled and moved to repent and be more righteous. But the angel's appearance seemed to have little, if any, affect at all, on Nephi's older brothers. This is because "they knew not the dealings of that God who had created them" (1 Nephi 1:12; see also Mosiah 10:14), suggesting that it's the steady, sustained communion with God that brings true conversion and motivates us to choose the right.

Of course, we can't forget about the testimonies of Martin Harris, Oliver Cowdery, and David Whitmer, the three witnesses of the Book of Mormon.

They saw with their own eyes the gold plates and the angel of God who brought them. Their glorious experience was recorded on the introductory pages of every Book of Mormon ever printed, and yet, each one of them left the Church because they disagreed with some of Joseph Smith's policies.[37] Despite all of this, they never denied what they saw, and two of the three witnesses, Martin Harris and Oliver Cowdery, even returned to full fellowship before they died. All three witnesses continued throughout their lives to bear witness to the Book of Mormon and their vision of the angel and the plates. It is incredulous to active members that these specially selected men could have ever turned away from the Church. Imagine being part of one of the most momentous events in all of history and still finding that such a miraculous one-on-one was not enough to keep your faith intact. It's difficult to absorb but it serves well as an example of what actually builds testimony best.

While the Church teaches that personal revelation does come in the form of visions, dreams, and visitations by angels, most revelations to Church leaders, regular Mormons and non-Mormons alike, come through the whisperings of the Holy Ghost. Through visions and the ministration of angels, the Lord restored his gospel in the latter days, but it's through the less astounding, yet satisfying and sacred inspiration of the Spirit that we build eternal relationships with God and Christ. It is within the sanctity of those relationships that our conversion to the gospel has staying power.

"Quiet spiritual promptings may not seem as spectacular as visions or angelic visitations, but they are just as powerful and lasting and life changing," according to the Church's official website. "The witness of the Holy Ghost makes an impression on the soul that is more significant than anything we can see or hear. Through such revelations, we will receive lasting strength to stay true to the gospel and help others do the same."[38]

We are taught that God speaks to the mind and heart in a still, small voice. The Lord said, "I will tell you in your mind and in your heart, by the Holy Ghost, which shall come upon you and which shall dwell in your heart. Now, behold, this is the spirit of revelation" (D&C 8:2-3, 1 Kings 19:9-12;

Helaman 5:30; D&C 85:6). Joseph Smith said, "The Holy Ghost is a revelator" and, "no man can receive the Holy Ghost without receiving revelations."[39]

Because true conversion is not based on spectacular experiences, we'd be better off not to seek after them. President Spencer W. Kimball spoke of the many people who "have no ear for spiritual messages ... when they come in common dress .... Expecting the spectacular, one may not be fully alerted to the constant flow of revealed communication."[40]

Even Alma the younger told the people of Nephi that it wasn't the appearance of an angel that made him know "in the energy of my soul" (Alma 5:43), that God and his Son, Jesus Christ, were real. He said, "Behold, I say unto you they are made known unto me by the Holy Spirit of God. Behold, I have fasted and prayed many days that I might know these things of myself. And now I do know of myself that they are true; for the Lord God hath made them manifest unto me by his Holy Spirit; and this is the spirit of revelation which is in me" (Alma 5:46).

God communicates with us in a variety of situations and for a variety of reasons ensuring he is always doing his part to keep connected to us spiritually. It is incumbent upon us to do our part as well. Sometimes the personal revelations we receive are answers to prayers or they may be warnings about impending danger. Some come to us instantaneously in bursts of pure intelligence, while others come gradually, line upon line, like the growing light of the rising sun.

Apostle David A. Bednar explained,

> "I have talked with many individuals who question the strength of their personal testimony and underestimate their spiritual capacity because they do not receive frequent, miraculous, or strong impressions. Perhaps as we consider the experiences of Joseph in the Sacred Grove, of Saul on the road to Damascus, and of Alma the Younger, we come to believe something is wrong with or lacking in us if we fall short in our lives of these well-known and spiritually striking

examples. If you have had similar thoughts or doubts, please know that you are quite normal. Just keep pressing forward obediently and with faith in the Savior. As you do so, you 'cannot go amiss'" (D&C 80:3).[41]

CHAPTER FOUR

Near-death Experiences and the Afterlife

One of the most fascinating phenomena of our time is the near-death experience [NDE]. It has baffled science, in general, because it can't be tested in a laboratory, but has been the icing on the cake for people of religion who appreciate the added back-up to their faith. The research into NDEs is no longer just "fringe science" now that psychologists, neurologists, and theologians study it with great intensity. The scientific community, though at first reluctant to give the topic much credence, has decided it can no longer ignore NDEs because of the sheer numbers of people who report having them. Incidences seem to occur with increasing frequency because of improved survival rates due to modern resuscitation techniques.

This chapter will examine near-death experiences and use them as evidence that consciousness, or the spirit self, lives on after death. Detailed studies will show how frequently they occur throughout the world, and how many researchers, unable to find reasonable scientific explanations, have concluded that NDEs are real and serve as verification of God. Moreover, because various experiences described coincide with LDS doctrine, it is my hope that Mormons whose faith is weak, may be strengthened by what they read.

Perhaps the account of an LDS Apostle's NDE is a good place to start. Jedediah M. Grant once told fellow Apostle, Heber C. Kimball, about his experience visiting the spirit world. Both Presidents Grant and Kimball had served as counselors to LDS Prophet Brigham Young. So moving was this spirit world account, that Heber shared what he had been told with those who attended President Grant's funeral. The record of Heber's remarks reads:

> "Brother Grant said to me, Brother Heber, I have been into the spirit world two nights in succession, and, of all the dreads that ever came across me, the worst was to have to again return to my body, though I had to do it. But O, says he, the order and government that were there! When in the spirit world, I saw the order of righteous men and women; beheld them organized in their several grades, and there appeared to be no obstruction to my vision; I could see every man and woman in their grade and order. I looked to see whether there was any disorder there, but there was none; neither could I see any death nor any darkness, disorder or confusion. He said that the people he saw there were organized in family capacities; and when he looked at them he saw grade after grade, and all were organized and in perfect harmony. He would mention one item after another and say, 'Why, it is just as brother Brigham says it is; it is just as he has told us many a time.'
>
> "That is a testimony as to the truth of what brother Brigham teaches us, and I know it is true, from what little light I have.
>
> "He saw the righteous gathered together in the spirit world, and there were no wicked spirits among them. He saw his wife; she was the first person that came to him. He saw many that he knew, but did not have conversation with any except his wife Caroline. She came to him, and he said that she looked beautiful and had their little child, that died on the Plains, in her arms, and said, 'Mr. Grant, here is little Margaret; you know that the wolves ate her up, but it did not hurt her; here she is all right.'

"'To my astonishment,' he said, 'when I looked at families there was a deficiency in some, there was a lack, for I saw families that would not be permitted to come and dwell together, because they had not honored their calling here.'

"He asked his wife Caroline where Joseph and Hyrum and Father Smith and others were; she replied, 'they have gone away ahead, to perform and transact business for us.' The same as when brother Brigham and his brethren left Winter Quarters and came here to search out a home; they came to find a location for their brethren.

"He also spoke of the buildings he saw there, remarking that the Lord gave Solomon wisdom and poured gold and silver into his hands that he might display his skill and ability, and said that the temple erected by Solomon was much inferior to the most ordinary buildings he saw in the spirit world.

"In regard to gardens, says Brother Grant, 'I have seen good gardens on this earth, but I never saw any to compare with those that were there. I saw flowers of numerous kinds, and some with from fifty to a hundred different colored flowers growing upon one stalk.' We have many kinds of flowers on the earth, and I suppose those very articles came from heaven, or they would not be here.

"After mentioning the things that he had seen, he spoke of how much he disliked to return and resume his body, after having seen the beauty and glory of the spirit world, where the righteous spirits are gathered together."[1]

Presented on December 4, 1856, in the Salt Lake Tabernacle, this is one of the few recorded descriptive accounts of life beyond the veil from an LDS leader. Prophets and apostles treat these gateway experiences as very sacred and so rarely speak openly about the topic. In fact, there is no official statement from the Church on near-death experiences although there are some references and stories by Church leaders that illustrate the thinness of the veil.

References to NDEs are also mentioned in the Bible and Book of Mormon. For example, Jesus characterized an NDE in his parable of the rich man and Lazarus, when the beggar Lazarus died and was carried by angels into Paradise (Luke 16:22). Stephen, an early church leader who was stoned to death, saw the resurrected Jesus standing at the right hand of God at some point in the dying process (Acts 7:55-56). Paul described his visit to "the third heaven" during which he was unsure whether he was in or out of his body (2 Corinthians 12:1-5). Some researchers feel this event occurred when Paul was stoned and left for dead during his trip to Lystra (Acts 14:19-20). Descriptions in Acts 9:36-42, Acts 20:6-12, 1 Kings 17:17-24, and 2 Kings 4:18-37 record people who came back from the dead, establishing the plausibility of other NDE accounts.

Likewise, the Book of Mormon provides accounts of NDEs. In the book of Mosiah, we learn how Alma was "nigh unto death" for three days and nights, so astonished was he at his encounter with an angel (Mosiah 27:28). What he learned during his NDE is described in Alma 40:11-14. In another account, King Lamoni "fell unto the earth, as if he were dead" (Alma 18:42), then rose on the third day to prophesy, which then prompted a similar experience for his wife (Alma 19:1–34). A comparable event in the court of Lamoni's father is detailed in Alma 22:18-22.

Reports of near-death experiences date back to the Ice Age. There are cave paintings in France and Spain that depict possible after-life scenes related to NDEs.[2] Plato's *Republic* presents an NDE in the story of a Greek soldier named Er. In this account, the soldier is killed in battle and his body is placed on a funeral pyre. Just before he is to be cremated, he awakens and tells a story of leaving his body and traveling with others to a place where they were all to be judged.[3]

The occurrence of NDEs in antiquity and in scripture is sizeable and merges neatly with spirit world experiences reported today. In the last 50 years or so, mostly since Raymond Moody's book, *Life After Life*, in 1975, the topic and study of NDEs has exploded. As a psychologist and medical doctor, Moody spent 40 years of his life researching and writing about this intriguing phenomenon because of the large number of his own patients who reported them.

After a near lifetime of NDE investigation, he acknowledged, "I don't mind saying that after talking with over a thousand people who have had these experiences, and having experienced many times some of the really baffling and unusual features of these experiences, it has given me great confidence that there is a life after death. As a matter of fact, I must confess to you in all honesty, I have absolutely no doubt, on the basis of what my patients have told me, that they did get a glimpse of the beyond."[4]

Beginning with such an expert testimony of the veracity of NDEs, the next step in our examination is grasping what an NDE actually is. Moody defined a near-death experience as a conscious occurrence in which the individual undergoes a sense of being detached from the physical world during the process of physiological dying. He and other researchers identified some common elements experienced by people claiming NDEs. Not every element is experienced by every person every time, but some elements occur in all NDEs. They include:

- Hearing sounds such as buzzing
- A feeling of peace and painlessness
- Having an out-of-body experience
- A feeling of traveling through a tunnel
- Seeing an intense light beyond the tunnel
- A feeling of rising into the heavens
- Seeing and being greeted by people, often deceased relatives
- Meeting a deity such as Jesus
- Viewing vibrantly colorful scenery
- Observing people in classroom or educational settings
- Being presented with a review of one's life
- Feeling a reluctance to return to mortality

With each examined case containing all or some of these elements, one thing is becoming increasingly clear: Humans are dual beings, i.e., they have a physical as well as a conscious component to life. We are learning that while the physical body does seem to need the spirit to survive in mortality, the spirit appears able to exist independently of the body. Consciousness is not necessarily localized in the brain. Once we understand and accept this premise, we can begin to savor the reality of who we are and the boundlessness of what we can accomplish.

This analogy may help: Consciousness is like a television signal in the air waves. The signal is managed by a television set [the brain] to create pictures on the screen [brain chemistry] representing a television show [a near-death experience]. Some in science claim that the NDE, or the television show, is manufactured by the television set. But this is clearly incorrect because it is the signal operating with the TV that generates the show, not the TV, itself. Death is the end of consciousness, according to science, just like hitting the off button on the TV set is the end of the signal out there in the air waves. Again, this is not true. Shutting off the television set has nothing to do with the existence of television signals in the atmosphere; they still exist even if every television set in the world were shut off. Using this analogy, it seems clear that death is not the end of consciousness.[5]

A look at some reported accounts of NDEs in this chapter will add greatly to the growing body of evidence, as a whole, that God is real and that our conscious or spirit selves live on after physical death.

Out-of-Body Experiences

What many consider to be the most profound aspect of NDEs is how dying people observe themselves from outside their bodies. They often report floating above their bodies while they watch people work to resuscitate them at the scene of an accident or in a hospital. They even find themselves in other locations away from their bodies observing activities that are later verified by people who were there. This exceptional event is called an out-of-body experience (OBE) or "veridical perception." These accounts are about as close as we can get to scientific proof that consciousness survives bodily death. At the very least, they qualify as very powerful circumstantial and anecdotal evidence of life after death. The following are examples of veridical NDEs documented by Raymond Moody:

Example 1. One patient told Moody, "After it was all over the doctor told me that I had a really bad time, and I said, 'Yeah, I know.' He said, 'Well, how do you know?' and I said, 'I can tell you everything that happened.' He didn't believe me, so I told him the whole story, from the time I stopped breathing until the time I was kind of coming around. He was really shocked to know that I knew everything that had happened. He didn't know quite what to say, but he came in several times to ask me different things about it."

Example 2. A woman with a heart condition was dying at the same time her sister was in a diabetic coma in another part of the same hospital. The woman reported having a conversation with her sister as both of them hovered near the ceiling watching the medical team work on her body below. When the woman awoke, she told the doctor that her sister had died while her own resuscitation was taking place. The doctor denied it, but when she insisted, he had a nurse check on it. The sister had, in fact, died during the time in question.[6]

In a rare occurrence, prominent LDS researcher Arvin Gibson, documented the testimony of an entire group of elite Mormon firefighters called the Hotshots, who succumbed to the flames while fighting a fire in 1989, only to return with a shared NDE. They all saw each other outside their lifeless bodies after the forest fire they were fighting engulfed them. Remarkably, they were each promised by who they interpreted to be God, that upon returning to mortality, their bodies would not be burned. When they all revived, remarkably, none were burned though the mountainside where they had been working was completely destroyed.[7]

Accounts like these are exceedingly convincing. Still, some researchers hold tenaciously to their belief that physiological explanations, alone, are what account for these out-of-body experiences. However, such explanations can't account for the veridical perception aspect of NDEs. For example, NDE researcher Susan Blackmore attributes veridical NDEs to a combination of "prior knowledge, fantasy, lucky guesses, and the remaining operating senses of hearing and touch."[8] The best way to test Blackmore's theory is through a control group of people who did not have an NDE, but who had similar experiences and medical knowledge as those who did have one. This control group should be asked to describe what they would have expected to see during resuscitation procedures performed on them.

In 2006, Penny Sartori, a Ph.D. and long time intensive care nurse, did exactly this when she studied heart attack patients in hospitals. Sartori caught the attention of the world with her published findings. She reported that about 25% of the patients studied said they had NDEs and were able to describe accurately the procedures used during resuscitation attempts. The remaining 75% without an NDE had no idea what went on during resuscitation and could not even venture a correct guess.

Children have NDEs

Accounts from children reporting NDEs are particularly touching and lend credibility to NDEs, in general, because children may not have had time to embrace the same socio-religious beliefs about death as adults or developed any particular fear of death.

About 85% of children who survive cardiac arrest have NDEs, according to P.M.H. Atwater, Ph.D., who has studied more than 270 children who reported NDEs. She found that very young children, just barely able to speak, could recall NDEs they had as infants or in the process of being born. She found that:

- 76% reported a comforting "initial" experience. Such reports involved up to three elements, such as a loving nothingness, a friendly voice, a visitation by a loving being, an out-of-body experience, and/or the peacefulness of either a safe light or safe dark place.
- 19% reported a pleasurable or heaven-like experience.
- 3% reported a distressing or hell-like experience.
- 2% had a "transcendent" experience in which they felt they acquired special knowledge.[9]

Similar to adults, children have reported being taken on tours of heaven where they saw angels, colorful geometric patterns, and deceased relatives and pets. These amazing stories involving children are surely testaments to life after death, and by extension, the existence of God.

One interesting case was reported in 1995 by K.M. Dale, M.D. The account involved a 9-year-old boy, whose fever went on for nearly 36 hours before it broke in the hospital. As soon as he opened his eyes, at 3 a.m., the boy urgently told his parents, who had been keeping vigil, that he had been to heaven and had seen his deceased grandpa, aunt, and uncle. As startling as that was, he went on to say that he also saw his 19-year-old sister, a student away at college at the time, who told him he had to go back. Because of the boy's story, his parents phoned the college where the sister had been attending and were told that she had been killed in a car accident just after midnight. College officials had tried unsuccessfully to reach the family at their home to let them know the tragic news.[10]

In another account, Clara, now an adult, described how at age 10, she began to have extreme pain in her lower right side while at school. She was eventually rushed to the hospital when the pain intensified and later described in great detail her experience while under sedation. Clara remembered fighting the ether mask one moment, and then the next, was falling down a dark hole as if in a well. She then described being up by the ceiling looking down on herself watching a nurse, one of several in the room, wheel in a big green machine the doctor used to work on her. She described a feeling of being spread out all over the room like a vapor or cloud.

Suddenly, she found herself standing in a room with large, heavy doors. She was greeted by a man who led her down a tunnel where she heard the sounds of children playing and laughing, which helped her feel calm. Another man appeared and explained it wasn't her time to be there yet but nevertheless, led her up a sidewalk to a large building with large doors. Inside were people busy with activities. She describes moving into a huge iridescent white room and being asked to sit down on some steps that led up to a large white chair, and wait there for someone who would come. Soon a man dressed in a white, long-sleeved, floor-length robe with a wide gold band around the mid-section sat in the chair. No words were spoken, as they communicated with their thoughts. He told her what she needed to accomplish in her life and allowed her to glimpse her future. Clara said she believed the man was Jesus Christ.

"When I revived," recalled Clara, "a nurse was sitting beside my bed and she said, 'Thank God you finally woke up.' I told the doctor that I had watched him work on me and the color of the machine brought into the surgery room. He didn't know what to say."[11]

In his book, *Parting Visions*, Dr. Melvin Morse, described an 8-year-old patient, Chris, who had nearly drowned when his family's car plunged over a bridge and into the freezing waters of a river near Seattle, Washington. His father died in the accident but his mother and brother managed to swim out. After a very long time in the water, Chris was finally rescued by a passerby and flown by helicopter to a nearby hospital. He ultimately survived but described afterward his experience beyond the veil.

He said, "First the car filled up with water, and everything went all blank. Then I died. I went into a huge noodle. It wasn't like a spiral noodle, but it was very straight. When I told my Mom about it, I told her it was a noodle, but it must have been a tunnel, because it had a rainbow in it. Noodles don't have rainbows in them. I was pushed along by wind, and I could float. I saw two tunnels in front of me, a human tunnel and an animal tunnel. First, I went in the animal tunnel, and a bee gave me honey. Then I saw the human heaven. It was like a castle, not all broken down, just a regular castle."

Dr. Diane Komp, a pediatric oncologist at Yale, was transformed by hearing children's NDE accounts, such as that of an 8-year-old with cancer envisioning a school bus driven by Jesus, or a 7-year-old leukemia patient who sat up in bed just before dying and cried, "The angels—they're so beautiful! Mommy, can you see them? Do you hear their singing? I've never heard such beautiful singing!" Dr. Komp put it this way: "I was an atheist and it changed my view of spiritual matters. Call it a conversion. I came away convinced that these are real spiritual experiences."[12]

The Blind Can See

Even the blind can see in NDEs. Dr. Kenneth Ring, professor of psychology at the University of Connecticut, who has done major research on the topic, investigated 31 blind people claiming NDEs who had flat-lined with cardiac arrest. He found that 80% of the respondents claimed they were able to see when out of their bodies, even those who were blind from birth. The congenitally blind have no concept of sight and dream only in audio.[13] Five of the 31 saw things that could be verified independently.

Those who were blind from birth reported having difficulty relating to what they were seeing, whereas those who lost sight later in life immediately recognized the return of vision. Many of these patients also experienced veridical perception and were able to describe the surgery room, the hospital, and other environmental factors in the room, which a blind person could not know. They also reported seeing specific relatives in the waiting room, which they could not have known were there at the time.[14]

One of the people in this study was Vicky Umipeg, a 45-year-old woman, blind from birth, who described floating above her body in the ER after a car accident. She watched as the doctor and nurse worked to repair the damage to her body. She described being taken up a tunnel-like structure toward light culminating in a world where she "saw" trees, birds, and flowers, and encountered deceased friends and relatives who were "made of light." She said, "This was the only time I could ever relate to seeing and to what light was, because I experienced it."[15]

Other accounts of the blind actually receiving their vision during NDEs are remarkable. For example, Vickie Noratuk was blind from birth because of excess oxygen given to her in a faulty hospital air lock incubator in 1950. She was 22 weeks old, weighing just three pounds at birth. "Since then," she said, "I have seen no light, no shadows, nothing, the optic nerves to my eyes having been destroyed. When I dream, I dream with the same sensations I experience when I'm awake. There is no visual data, just other sensations such as touch and sound. But I have seen as you see. Twice I nearly died, and on those occasions, for the first time in my life, I saw. I left my body and saw."[16]

Moody told of a 70-year-old woman, blind since the age of 18, who related in vivid detail the scene of doctors resuscitating her after a heart attack. She was able to describe the instruments being used and even what color they were. Wrote Moody: "The most amazing thing about this to me was that most of these instruments weren't even thought of over 50 years ago when she could last see. On top of all this, she was even able to tell the doctor that he was wearing a blue suit when he began the resuscitation."[17]

Atheists have NDEs

The majority of recorded claims link NDEs to feelings of joy and comfort. One statistician calculated that 69% of the thousands of cases he investigated reported a feeling of overwhelming love. When he broke his subjects down by belief [Christian, religious but non-Christian, non-religious, New Age, etc.], he found 100% of people calling themselves atheists had experienced "tremendous ecstasy" during their NDEs. Some 63% of these atheists reported the life review experience.[18]

In his research, Ring learned that NDEs are "no respecter of persons" and occur in all races, cultures, ages, education, social class, and religions. Even those who describe themselves as atheist have them. Most atheists who have this experience are convinced they had been in the presence of some supreme power or being and glimpsed a bit of life after death. Almost all atheists who experienced an NDE said their lives were transformed, which included an increased inclination to love and serve others.[19]

Even A.J. Ayer, a famous atheist who founded the philosophy of positivism [that anything not verifiable by the senses is nonsense], had a life-changing NDE. It seems that later in life, he choked on a piece of smoked salmon that stopped his heart for at least four minutes. During that time he said he saw "a red light for governing the universe" and some barrier he crossed, "like the River Styx." He said the experience "weakened my conviction that death would be the end of me, though I continue to hope it will be."

After seeing and hearing things in his NDE he had spent a lifetime denying, Ayer wrote a dismayed account of his other-worldly experience. He found it difficult to admit what he saw in the spirit world though he did provide some reluctant descriptions. It was actually the doctor who attended him after the choking event, who finally came out and said that Ayer, himself, "told me he saw the Supreme Being." No further explanation was given. The physician said simply that when Ayer recovered, "he told me he saw the Supreme Being."[20]

NDE Elements and LDS Beliefs

Many NDE elements tie in well with Mormon theology. It's even plainly laid out in Alma's NDE after an angel rebuked him for seeking to destroy the church of God (Mosiah 27:10-32). The profound nature of Alma's teachings to the Nephites throughout his life was a direct result of the things he learned during that experience. Notice the similarities in Alma's account with common elements found in other documented NDEs.

1. *He experienced both positive and negative events*: When he finally rose after three days "nigh unto death," he told the crowd: "My soul hath been redeemed from the gall of bitterness and the bonds of iniquity. I was in the darkest abyss; but now I behold the marvelous light of God. My soul was racked with eternal torment; but I am snatched, and my soul is pained no more" (Mosiah 27:29; cf. Alma 38).
2. *He underwent a life review*: "Yea, I did *remember* all my sins and iniquities ... yea, I *saw* that I had rebelled against my God ... I was harrowed up by the *memory* of my many sins" (Alma 36:13, 17). NDErs often say they judge themselves during the life review. Alma learned similarly, "for behold, they are their own judges, whether to do good or evil" (Alma 41:7).
3. *He experienced timelessness*: "All is as one day with God, and time only is measured unto men" (Alma 40:8). And like NDErs who are often told it is not their "time" to leave

mortality, Alma said, "God knoweth all the times which are appointed unto man" (Alma 40:10).

4. *He became less materialistic and more spiritual*: NDErs often seek for a religion that speaks to their experience and become frustrated when all they find is hypocrisy. Alma demonstrates this characteristic when he became appalled by the hypocrisy and materialism of the Zoromites (Alma 31:17-35).[21]

Alma's account and others in scripture help give added value to modern-day reports of NDEs, especially within the Church. Interestingly, LDS researchers Craig Lundahl, Ph.D., and Harold A. Widdison, Ph.D., found that Mormons report very detailed and rich NDE accounts, more so than most non-Mormon accounts. For instance, Church members who reported visiting a "City of Light" also described a variety of encounters consistent with their religious beliefs. These included continued roles, rights and obligations of families, beautiful vistas and gardens, a hierarchy of authority, genealogical work, missionary work, and school and teaching settings.[22]

The social activities observed in Latter-day Saint NDEs can be classified into seven categories: 1. Gaining knowledge and understanding; 2. Assisting those on earth who need help; 3. Preparing for future events; 4. Teaching; 5. Developing musical skills; 6. Researching family records; 7. Accomplishing routine as well as major tasks.[23]

One LDS near-death experience was that of Betty Eadie, who recorded her story in the book, *Embraced by the Light*. A convert to the Church prior to her NDE, who went inactive for a time and then reactivated after and because of her experience, Eadie provides a thorough dissertation on many aspects of life after death. Unlike other NDE accounts which can be somewhat vague, hers included such things as meeting several beings including Jesus Christ, and a memory of her pre-existence. Her account of the spirit world is filled with Mormon doctrine.

Spencer, another member of the Church, described in his book, *Visions of Glory*, how he had an NDE during a hospital procedure for his kidneys.

When a code blue was called, his spirit immediately left his body and he discovered he had a number of remarkable abilities as a spirit.[24]

Detailed renditions by Mormon NDErs are often welcomed within the Church community. This is because the Church, according to researchers, is one of few religious or social groups to provide an atmosphere that encourages people to relate their near-death and other spiritual experiences. Often NDErs are afraid to share for fear of disbelief or ridicule. But what LDS experiencers report affirms doctrines of the Church and its belief in an afterlife, something that is not as clearly defined in conventional Christianity. The following are some elements in many NDE accounts that support LDS beliefs.

Heaven and Hell. Moody reported that in all his interviews with NDErs, he never heard of any account of heaven or hell even close to the generally accepted ideas of society and religions. One woman NDEr reported: "I had always heard that when you die you see both heaven and hell, but I didn't see either one." Another NDEr said, "The strange thing was that I had always been taught in my religious upbringing that the minute you died you would be right at these beautiful gates, pearly gates. But there I was hovering around my own physical body, and that was it! I was just baffled."[25]

One of the more oft mentioned NDE elements is of a divide or divisions people see in the spirit world based on the amount of love possessed by the inhabitants. In his NDE, George Ritchie saw spirits in hell who were totally devoid of love, others in an area who were stuck in the physical and worldly desires they had developed on earth, and still others who abided in a realm where good and honorable people loved others more than themselves.[26]

This coincides with LDS teachings of two major divisions in the spirit world—spirit paradise and spirit prison. Paradise is for righteous spirits awaiting their resurrection. It is "a state of happiness ... a state of rest, a state of peace, where they shall rest from all their troubles and from all care, and sorrow" (Alma 40:11-14; 4 Nephi 14; Moroni 10:34; D&C 77:2, 5). Spirit prison is reserved for the wicked and disobedient who reject the truth and can no longer progress until they accept it. This is also illustrated in the Bible when Abraham told the rich man in hell that between him and Lazarus [who was in paradise] there was "a great gulf fixed; so that they which would pass from hence to you cannot; neither can they pass to us, that would come from thence" (Luke 16:19-26).

Gospel Taught to Spirits in Prison. Many NDErs describe how they saw masses of people in classroom settings in the process of being taught. They don't always report any specific teachings going on, but it is clear from the number of accounts that learning is an important part of the spirit world. Eighteenth-century philosopher and theologian Emanuel Swedenborg, in his famed treatise on his visit to the spirit world, described in detail the preaching of the gospel to those who were without such knowledge on Earth. No other church in his day ascribed to such doctrine, making his account all the more remarkable.[27]

Mormons believe that righteous spirits teach the gospel to those imprisoned by sin and false traditions.[28] Once they accept the gospel and overcome the obstacles of sin, they can dwell with the righteous in paradise (D&C 138:29-31). NDEs that verify this tenet are often troublesome to evangelical Christians who believe people must accept Christ in this life to go to "heaven." But the LDS Church teaches that because death is not the final judgment, there is space for a loving Heavenly Father to give his children every chance to come unto him.

Guardian Angels. Many NDEs contain references to guardian angels or ministering angels they learned were helping them on Earth. Moody reported that "one man was told by such a spirit that, 'I have helped you through this stage of your existence, but now I am going to turn you over to others.' A woman told me that as she was leaving her body, she detected the presence of two other spiritual beings there, and that they identified themselves as her 'spiritual helpers.'"[29]

A moving example involves Lance Richardson, a Mormon NDEr who was in a medically induced coma when his deceased cousin, Randy, visited him. According to Lance, Randy told him, "I had suffered so long that it was a welcomed rest to leave my bodily pain, but, oh how I missed my family at first. I wonder if it was right for me to have died. Then I was shown what is about to happen in your world. And it was explained to me that certain members of each family chose, long ago, before this life, to die and come to this realm that they might better help their families endure what is about to happen."

During his NDE, Lance said Randy reverently explained that many people die so they can better help their families navigate their mortal lives. Randy told Lance of several instances where he had helped Lance come through some difficult moments. Lance recalled,

> "Each was a time I could remember, and I became deeply thankful to God, to know He had sent someone whom I loved so much to help in those times when I had needed help so desperately. And again, I gained a greater appreciation for family and its eternal function .... I was deeply moved. I had never understood nor thought of how God delivers assistance to us. With billions of children, what more perfect plan could He use than through righteous family members? It made me think about how often I may have been given inspiration from God through ministering *family* servants of God. I could believe it was truth. And once again I felt that burning warmth inside, testifying to me that it was."[30]

The Church teaches that whether it's a guardian angel or a deceased friend or family member assigned by a caring Heavenly Father to help us from time to time, it is real. The Lord promised, "I will go before your face. I will be on your right hand and on your left, and my Spirit shall be in your hearts, and mine angels round about you, to bear you up" (D&C 84:88).

Eternal Families. A common element is the sense of order to family organization throughout generations experienced by NDErs. Non-LDS

NDErs often don't understand the significance, but for Church members, it is central to their beliefs. President Ezra Taft Benson said, "They are organized according to priesthood order in family organizations as we are here; only there they exist in a more perfect order. This was revealed to the Prophet Joseph."[31] This family organization started on Earth, continues in the spirit world, and goes on for eternity for all who are completely obedient to gospel or celestial law (see D&C 88:16-32).

This is verified time and time again as NDErs are greeted by deceased family members, sometimes from past generations, or from those not known to them on Earth. For example, in 1989, a man named Stuart had an out-of-body experience in which a woman who lived 100 years earlier appeared to him. He perceived her to be an ancestor. He also saw two deceased grandfathers, two deceased grandmothers, and many others whose visits with him were like a "big reunion."[32]

Children as Adults. Although many NDEs involve seeing children beyond the veil, Moody reported that "a surprising number of them say they are adults during the episode, although they can't say how they know this." One woman reported looking back on her experience and realizing that she was fully mature when she was in the presence of the being who met with her. She recalled, "I was only seven, but I know I was an adult."[33] When another woman, Luella Child Wilkes Blacker, became gravely ill, she was visited by her deceased husband and younger son. She saw her son "as a full grown man, although he had died at the age of 10." She didn't recognize him at first until he smiled and said "Mother," before disappearing.[34]

Joseph F. Smith clarified this phenomenon when he said, "The spirits of our children are immortal before they come to us, and their spirits, after bodily death, are like they were before they came. They are as they would have appeared if they had lived in the flesh, to grow to maturity, or to develop their physical bodies to the full stature of their spirits. If you see one of your children that has passed away it may appear to you in the form in which you would recognize it, the form of childhood; but if it came to you as a messenger bearing some important truth, it would perhaps come... in the stature of full-grown manhood..."[35]

Physical Handicaps Gone. Many people with physical handicaps find those disabilities are gone in the spiritual realm. Dr. Elisabeth Kubler-Ross, a noted psychiatrist and author who is also a pioneer in near-death studies, once observed, "In a near-death experience, the body becomes perfect again. Quadriplegics are no longer paralyzed, multiple sclerosis patients who have been in wheelchairs for years, say that when they were out of their bodies, they were able to sing and dance."[36] One man, who fell from a billboard onto some high-voltage wires and lost his legs and part of one arm from the burns, had an out-of-body experience in the operating room. "He didn't even recognize the body on the table as being his own. When he finally realized that badly damaged body was his, he noticed something else peculiar: His spiritual body was not handicapped in anyway."[37]

In the previously mentioned account of Mormon firefighters who had a shared NDE after succumbing to a forest fire they were fighting, Jake, one of the firefighters, reported seeing the spirits of other fire-fighters standing above their bodies in the air. He noticed that one of his fellow crew members, who had a defective foot from birth, no longer had that affliction. As he came out of his body, Jake looked at him and said: "Look, Jose, your foot is straight."[38]

Again, these experiences coincide perfectly with Mormon tenets. In the Church's official statement, *The Origin of Man,* we learn that "God created man in His own image. This is just as true of the spirit as it is of the body, which is only the clothing of the spirit, its complement; the two together constituting the soul. The spirit of man is in the form of man, and the spirits of all creatures are in the likeness of their bodies."[39] Elder Orson Pratt, an apostle to Joseph Smith, said, "Of course there may be deformities existing in connection with the outward tabernacle which do not exist in connection with the spirit that inhabits it. These tabernacles become deformed by accident in various ways, sometimes at birth, but this may not altogether or in any degree deform the spirits that dwell within them ...."[40]

What Research Studies Reveal

There have been an enormous number of studies conducted on various aspects of NDEs since Moody's first research was published. Some show the huge numbers of people claiming to have had one, such as a 1991 Gallup poll in the United States which estimated 13 million Americans, or 5% of the population, had experienced an NDE.[41]

In 1988, a group of researchers in the Netherlands conducted a study of 344 survivors of cardiac arrest in Dutch hospitals. These patients were chosen because medically, it is not possible to experience consciousness during a cardiac arrest, when circulation and breathing have ceased. In this study, the depth of the experience was measured based on the number of elements occurring in the NDE. As the number of elements increased so did the person's score, with the higher score considered to represent a deeper experience.

The results: 62 patients [18%] had NDEs at varying depths, leaving 282 patients [82%] with no recollection of the cardiac arrest at all.[42] The study found that about 50% of the patients with an NDE reported awareness of being dead, or had positive emotions, 30% reported moving through a tunnel, had an observation of a celestial landscape, or had a meeting with deceased relatives. About 25% of the patients with an NDE had an out-of-body experience, communicated with "the light" or observed bright colors, 13% experienced a life review, and 8% experienced a border or gulf.[43]

Some researchers conducted their studies after having NDEs themselves and indicated their utter amazement at what they found. Many such researchers joined their patients as witnesses that these experiences are real. But because NDEs cannot be tested and measured using the scientific method, science has generally dismissed them as chemical or neurological reactions in the brain.[44] The fact that science is investigating NDEs at all is a good sign it is taking the phenomenon seriously, but much of what it is claiming just doesn't add up. Let's take a look at some of the theories science proposes.

Dying Brain Theory. This argument theorizes that upon clinical death, the brain is slowly starved of oxygen and creates a vivid hallucination that is later remembered as an NDE. Ironically, this explanation negates science's own medical assertions that when the heart stops there is no brain activity at all, including consciousness. So how could a person in this condition have hallucinations? And yet, time and time again, patients who have completely EEG flat-lined report after coming back, a clear consciousness, in which cognitive functioning, emotion, sense of identity, or memory from early childhood occurred.[45]

The Dying Brain Theory also is unable to explain why only 18% of patients in the Netherlands study who survived clinical death had an NDE, while the other 82% did not, even under the exact same conditions. According to Dr. Pim Van Lommel, the study's lead architect, "Our most striking finding was that near-death experiences do not have a physical or medical root. After all, 100 percent of the patients suffered a shortage of oxygen, 100 percent were given morphine-like medications, 100 percent were victims of severe stress, so those are plainly not the reasons why 18 percent had near-death experiences and 82 percent didn't. If they had been triggered by any one of those things, everyone would have had near-death experiences."[46]

DMT Chemicals. DMT [Dimethyltryptamine] is a powerful hallucinogen that occurs throughout the plant and animal kingdom and is produced by humans in their pituitary glands. It is released in the brain as soon as the brain realizes it is dying, such as in heart attacks and car accidents. Efforts by science to focus on the effects of DMT or other drugs as a medical explanation for NDEs, is insufficient. That's because it doesn't account for veridical perception or the fact that when brain waves go flat, it's impossible for the brain to produce images of any kind. DMT may act as an initial NDE trigger, but cannot make up for the entire experience.[47] The most reasonable explanation is that the images occurring in the NDE must be coming from a consciousness that lives outside the body.

Navy Airmen Stress Test. These studies used U. S. Navy Airmen in G-Force stress tests that caused the blood in their heads to drain, inducing something akin to a simulated clinical death. During these tests, NDEs were reported by these airmen, offering the medical community ammunition for NDEs being purely physiological since they could be simulated. But in reality, there is no conflict here because these airmen were essentially put into a state of clinical death because of the conditions to which they were subjected. It's reasonable to predict some might have an NDE. Of note is that like Van Lommel's findings in his study of cardiac arrest survivors, it only occurred in 18% of the airmen.[48]

The Tunnel. The neural-noise theory posits that the tunnel effect is because there are more nerve cells within the visual cortex representing the retina core than there are representing the periphery of the retina. A computer simulation of increasing neural noise in the visual cortex induced by drugs or disease, revealed a blob of white light gradually increasing in size, which, when viewed on a screen, gave viewers the sensation of moving down a tunnel toward a bright light and finally being enveloped by the light.[49]

This explanation is interesting but doesn't account for the fact that people can see the light and the confines of the tunnel while at the same time seeing other things around them. They wouldn't be able to see peripherally under the neural-noise theory.[50] Also, there are NDE accounts that refute this theory such as the woman who was born blind, having had her optic nerve severed in her incubator at birth. She still visually saw a tunnel during her NDE and out-of-body experience.[51]

Temporal Lobe – The God Spot. Medical researchers opine that seizures in the limbic and temporal lobes of the brain may be responsible for NDEs. Because they say this is where feelings of spirituality are generated, this part of the brain has been dubbed "The God Spot." People with abnormal function in this area of the brain, such as those who suffer from epilepsy, have certain types of hallucinations which appear to share some elements of an NDE. But if NDEs occur because of these seizures in the limbic and temporal areas of the brain, one would also expect to see other features associated with these abnormal brain functions in NDEs, such as loss of memory, unconscious spontaneous behaviors, and déjà vu experiences. These, however, do not occur in the NDE accounts studied by researchers.[52]

Other explanations offered by the medical community for NDEs include psychological avoidance of death, normal shutting down of brain activity, sleep disorders, and hallucinations. All such medical explanations, even peripherally, have a disconnection with what NDErs report. Take hallucinations, for example. Hallucinations tend to produce confusion and fuzzy memories, exactly the opposite of near-death experiences, which tend to be remembered vividly for decades and are described as "real" occurrences.[53] After decades of investigation, researcher and psychiatrist Bruce Greyson, MD, stated, "No one physiological or psychological model by itself explains all the common features of NDE."[54]

As some in science continue to seek physiological explanations for NDEs, people everywhere are continuing to have them. Often, a skeptics' biggest argument is that the person wasn't really dead. But it appears to be the dying process, not just death that triggers the NDE. A very good case in point is the NDE account of noted neurosurgeon Dr. Eben Alexander.

This physician's NDE provides a resolute account of someone who lost all function of the part of the brain that makes us human. In a coma for seven days with spontaneous E. coli meningitis where his spinal fluid and the outer portion of his brain were filled with pus, Alexander's condition was a 1-in-10 million rarity, with similar statistics on his chance for survival. Medical experts say conditions such as head trauma, stroke, brain hemorrhages, or brain tumors are not able to completely damage the entire surface of the neocortex, where "higher functions" occur such as sensory perception, generation of motor commands, spatial reasoning, conscious thought, and language. But bacterial meningitis is arguably the best disease for mimicking human death without actually bringing it about. Alexander's was a technically near-impeccable conduit for a near-death experience.

As a physician familiar with NDEs, Alexander was always a skeptic before his own experience. Since then, he has shared his journey beyond death in his book, *Proof of Heaven*, where he details his encounter with an angelic guide who escorted him into the deepest parts of the spirit world. He tells a riveting story that includes speaking with what he calls "the divine source of the universe itself."[55]

Interpreting the Experiences

Near-death experiences have been recorded in folklore, religious, and social writings across the globe. Reports are recorded among Native Americans, as well as in Tibet, Japan, Melanesia, Micronesia, Egypt, China, India, Africa, Australia, Europe, and the United States.[56] Researchers say there does not appear to be any relationship between an individual's religion or level of spirituality and the likelihood of having an NDE.[57] But it does appear that the way NDErs interpret their experience may be related to personal convictions, social conditioning, and religious beliefs. Religious diversity may also explain differences reported in the NDE setting, encounters with spiritual beings, and the various elements included in the experience. Most accounts appear to support the experiencer's own religious beliefs such as communion with spiritual beings and various levels of good and bad, heaven and hell.[58]

The following are examples from various books and web sites that illustrate some of these variations in the NDE. One person reported traveling throughout the universe. Another toured a "temple of knowledge." Another was shown the future by 13 light beings. A guided tour of the afterlife was provided by an experiencer's deceased dog. One viewed the earth from way out in outer space. One traveled in time to see the crucifixion of Christ. Another was told she would be reincarnated if she committed suicide. Meeting a future, yet unborn child was another person's experience. Someone else was liberated by Christ after being in hell. One man encountered a "God of wrath" followed by a "God of love." Another woman identified the Being of Light as the basic pattern behind the atom and all things in the universe. One man saw the Being of Light changing into various personalities such as Jesus, Buddha, Krishna, and Mohammed. Another saw her higher self as the Being of Light.[59]

What a potpourri of differing and sometimes strange experiences found in NDEs—and these are just a smattering of examples. One cross-cultural study found that on the whole, NDErs saw beings that represented their earthly belief system. Christians tended to see what they believed were angels,

Jesus, or the Virgin Mary. Hindus would usually see Yama, who is the god of death, one of his messengers, Krishna, or some other deity.[60]

At first glance, this might be cause for concern among LDS members who believe in one true Church. The Doubting Thomas might well ask, if there is indeed life after death and it is all orchestrated by one God, then shouldn't each experience be more in line with the same religious teachings? Good question. A closer look will show there is room for validation of all NDEs, Mormon and non-Mormon alike. The following are a few considerations to help us understand:

Consideration #1. LDS researcher Carol Zalesk's book, *Otherworld Journeys,* provides a cross-cultural view of the NDE. She suggests that NDEs are "socially conditioned, imaginative, and yet nonetheless real and revelatory."[61] Because we see culturally specific symbols in the dreams and visions of prophets in scripture, we can understand how such symbols would also hold true in NDEs. Nephi explained that we can't properly understand Isaiah without some knowledge of the Hebrew culture (2 Nephi 25:5). We also learn from the Book of Mormon and Doctrine and Covenants that revelation is given to people "in their weakness, according to their language and understanding" (2 Nephi 31:3). Joseph Smith taught that God adapted his teachings to a people's ability to understand.[62]

For example, a Catholic priest saw his father during a 1909 NDE "looking exactly as he had in the last few years of his life," wearing the "last suit of clothes he had owned."[63] Father Tucker wrote, "I knew that the clothes father wore were assumed because they were familiar to me, so that I might feel no strangeness in seeing him, and that to some lesser extent, his appearance was assumed also."[64]

Consideration #2. It's important to note that those beings who appear to the experiencer generally don't introduce themselves nor do they try to dissuade the NDEr from their perceptions of who they're seeing. The identity of these beings is completely left to the interpretation of the person having the NDE. Researchers surmise that people experience these glimpses of the spirit world as they "need" them to appear to give them a frame of reference that will ease them through the transition of death. For instance, Ring noticed some of his NDErs leaned toward the idea of reincarnation, not because of anything in their experience, but because of how they saw life afterwards. He also said these people had "a sense of homecoming" in the experience. If reincarnation is the only familiar concept that accommodates this "sense of homecoming" or "premortal existence" then it's understandable for them to lean in that direction.[65]

Consideration #3. This variety of religious interpretation in NDEs also provides an opportunity for education, which is after all, consistent with the purpose of life. It appears the initial phase of the death experience is a kind of introductory phase that helps prepare people to face their misconceptions and begin to learn from them. We all accumulate an abundance of false ideas, illusions, and misjudgments in our lifetimes, but we learn from our mistakes, grow and progress, and then continue in that vein when our conscious selves live on. The learning process in the spirit world may be quick or long depending on the incorrect ideas and biases a person brings with them. Their perception is literally their reality.[66] Fitting here is the scripture, "As a man thinketh in his heart, so is he" (Proverbs 23:7).

Consideration #4. Researchers report that NDErs often say a person's denomination doesn't seem to matter in the spirit world. All appear to be loved and accepted upon their arrival no matter their earthly belief structures. The Book of Mormon, in part, provides some agreement where our relationship with God is concerned. Nephi tells us that God "inviteth them all to come unto him and partake of his goodness; and he denieth none that come unto him, black and white, bond and free, male and female; and he remembereth the heathen; and all are alike unto God, both Jew and Gentile" (2 Nephi 26:33).

All the Standard Works underscore personal worthiness or righteousness (D&C 1:30–34) rather than membership as being most important—for now. Having God's Church on the earth helps to teach truth, build testimony, provide service, perform ordinances, and exercise priesthood power to aid us in our sojourn toward future exaltation. In the case of ordinance work, for example, these symbolic outward manifestations of an inward commitment are part of God's requirements for Earth life. This is manifested in the Church's vicarious temple work for the dead.

But until the gospel reaches everyone, it's what we do with our opportunities to improve ourselves in this life according to the light that we have that will be the ultimate yardstick for judging our eternal futures (see Alma 9:14–24). There is a big difference between inward spirituality and outward observance of a religion, as these NDErs discovered. A great example is how the Savior condemned the scribes and Pharisees for being hypocritical in the way they lived the letter of the law while totally missing the spirit of it. What everyone must ultimately find is true doctrine along with true conversion, which won't happen for the majority of God's children until the next life.

Because Mormons possess greater knowledge of God's plan, they will be held to a higher accountability. They are also required to share what they know, i.e. where "much is given, much is required" (D&C 82:3). Continued growth throughout eternity opens doors to limitless opportunities for all of God's children, and those who have received more in this life are simply expected to reach out to those who have not, so all may be partakers in the fulness of God's plan.

Consideration #5. Few NDErs are told by the Being of Light or other messengers in their experience that "The LDS Church is the only true Church." Instead, what they seem to be given is symbolic information. It appears the NDEr must work to ascertain the meaning of it once back in their physical bodies. They, like all of us, must still exercise faith and put forth the work required for increased knowledge and testimony. Moreover, it's possible many NDErs simply don't ask which Church is right.

Elane Durham asked. She was dying and given last rites when she had an NDE after suffering a stroke at age 32. She describes the answer she received from her spirit guide when she asked which church was true. "He let me know that when I found the church here on earth that believed in the history of the people as described in the King James version of the Bible and believed that there was additional history that had been found—and that there was still more to be revealed—I would recognize that church by the same spirit I felt there with him. He also told me that the church had apostles and prophets but that they weren't accepted any more today than they had been in ancient times when Christ was here. He told me that fifteen or twenty years in the future I would come upon a new people, and I would find them on my own."[67] Elane did find the LDS Church and is an active member.

William Sillyman, another Mormon NDEr who joined the Church after his experience beyond the veil, said during his NDE, it became known to him that the religion in which he was raised wasn't right. He explained that he knew this because, "it wasn't what was said, but a deeper understanding ... that I would know the truth when I heard it. Little did I realize that less than a year after that experience I did hear the truth of what belief was right. I felt that 'familiar' spirit from my NDE, yet I didn't know what an NDE was at that time. The moment I heard the first word of the true Church, it was like every fiber of my body jumped. I didn't get goose bumps; it felt like warm welts on my skin. I knew to the cellular level and the spirit confirmed it to me."[68]

Consideration #6. The deceased friends and family who guide NDErs through the experience may not mention the LDS Church because they don't know the true Church yet either. They may be still learning themselves in this otherworldly setting along with countless others who must be taught the truth. In addition, not all of us were appointed in the preexistence to receive the gospel in this life. We don't know the reasons why, but if that's the case, each person must continue to "work out their own salvation" (Mormon 9:27), if not in this life, then in the life to come where everyone will be given a chance.[69]

Conclusion

Near-death experiences are eye-opening evidence of God's existence because they testify of an afterlife with him and of an open door to eternal opportunities. In addition, they help to confirm the truth of the LDS Church because they provide a welcoming background for all the visions of Joseph Smith. The fact that people are so plugged into the literature on NDEs, and that science is now studying them in earnest, may give space for, and credibility to, the visions of Mormon prophets in the minds of the general public. Although Joseph Smith was snubbed and persecuted as a liar or delusional in his day, today's growing interest in NDEs, may make people more open to hearing and believing his sacred testimony. It appears likely that these growing afterlife occurrences are actually part of God's blueprint for opening doors during the accelerated missionary work planned for the latter-days.

The conversion of souls doesn't stop with new members; it also includes the conversion and reconversion of Church members who struggle with their own testimonies. These remarkable accounts can at least provide a supporting role in that conversion process. While this presentation is not meant to be an exhaustive treatise on NDEs, it contains enough information to give the reader pause in his or her search for evidence of God and his Church.

We must never forget Joseph Smith's instruction that we are "to receive truth, let it come from whence it may."[70] Such truth could very well include near-death experiences and what we learn from them. The stark reality is they happen. They have occurred to generations of people in all walks of life. One could certainly argue that people may be fabricating these stories, but evidence suggests that there are too many for all of them to be made up. Taken at face value, these experiences teach us about God's universal love for all his children and the importance of changing our lives to exhibit that love to each other without judgment or prejudice. They also reinforce the fact that Earth life is but a tiny point in time in the context of eternity and that there is, indeed, a chance for continued growth and learning beyond the veil.

A good summation comes from a non-LDS NDEr, Dr. Mary C. Neal: "The absolute knowledge that God is real, that He has a plan for each of us, and that there really is life after death changes the way I experience each day. I do not fear death, and that also changes the way I experience the death of others, even my own son. I know that every day really does matter and that

I need to be about God's business every day. I also know that God loves all people deeply and unconditionally... even those people whom I may not like or agree with. It motivates me to try to see the beauty in them that God sees."[71]

CHAPTER FIVE

Avenues to Miracles

*M*iracles are further evidence of God. Sometimes they happen without warning or effort on our part, because God has reasons for intervening when we need help beyond our own abilities. Sometimes they happen as a result of the avenues we take that channel us toward these divine manifestations. Those avenues—faith, prayer, and revelation—can be prerequisites to miracles, conduits to miracles, or the actual miracles, themselves. They create awe and wonder and often are the means for turning hearts toward God. Exploring these avenues will help us better understand how each principle works, how to apply them effectively in our lives, and how they will ultimately connect us to Deity. When we fully utilize faith, prayer, and revelation, miracles occur.

The Power of Faith

Robert McMinn, who wrote *Grey's Anatomy* and other popular medical books on the human body, provided some insight about faith and science. He said,

"Although the existence of atoms is considered an undisputed scientific truth today, it has not always been so. In the early history of man's search for physical knowledge, some believed in atoms and some did not. But what can the current proof of the existence of atoms tell us about the existence of God ....

"I had to see the atoms, it seems, before I really believed they existed. My co-workers did not. They had proven to themselves the existence of atoms long before they could see them. How could they do this? Because things that are unseen may often be made known by things that are seen. One may have faith in the unseen on that basis. Then, when one finally sees what has previously been unseen, one's faith is confirmed by sight. This is why the existence of atoms has become a scientifically accepted truth. Scientists were willing to believe in the unseen atom because of its specific effects on what they could see, long before they could actually see an image of the atom itself."[1]

Sounds like even science must rely on faith. But those who doubt often wonder "why all the hoopla about faith?" Why, they may ask, is it so important to believe in things we can't see? Why can't more extensive information about God and his Church be revealed now so that conversion to the gospel is more easily achieved? Moreover, how can mankind have faith in things they don't know about or have little knowledge of? Doesn't it take a certain amount of knowledge and exposure to truth, first, to give people something in which to have faith?

Joseph Smith had a good answer for these questions. "The God of heaven, understanding most perfectly the constitution of human nature, and the weakness of men, knew what was necessary to be revealed, and what ideas must be planted in their minds in order that they might be enabled to exercise faith in him unto eternal life."[2]

So it appears that the kind and amount of information God chose to give us in order to help us progress through life and acquire faith was a bit of a balancing act. He wanted to give us enough to help us understand that he exists and has a plan for us, but not so much that we bypass faith altogether and move toward a perfect knowledge we haven't earned. And he, being God, was perfectly equipped to provide that exact balance leaving us, of necessity, to once again acquaint ourselves with that sometimes elusive principle—faith.

A more in depth look at faith can yield some perspective. Too often Christians, including Mormons, don't fully understand the supremacy and power embodied in the principle of faith. It is more than just a belief in an idea or a person or a deity; it is a living, breathing force that creates and propels literally every good thing. "Now faith is the substance of things hoped for, the evidence of things not seen" (Hebrews 11:1). Joseph Smith said from this scripture,

> "we learn that faith is the assurance which men have of the existence of things which they have not seen, and the principle of action in all intelligent beings." He said further, "Faith is ... the moving cause of all action in ... intelligent beings. And as faith is the moving cause of all action in temporal concerns, so it is in spiritual .... But faith is not only the principle of action, but of power also, in all intelligent beings, whether in heaven or on Earth .... *Faith, then, is the first great governing principle which has power, dominion, and authority over all things; by it they exist, by it they are upheld, by it they are changed, or by it they remain, agreeable to the will of God.* Without it there is no power, and without power there could be no creation, nor existence .... How would you define faith in its most unlimited sense? It is the first great governing principle which has power, dominion, and authority over all things."[3]

This is powerful because it teaches that God is the embodiment of faith, and while our limited knowledge gives us the faith to do some things, God's limitless knowledge gives him the faith to do all things. Faith is literally the power he used to create all things and to govern all things both temporal and spiritual. It is more than just a belief in God and Christ, it is the power to create, the source of all intelligence, the instrument of omnipotence.

Joseph Smith also explained that "the whole visible creation, as it now exists, is the effect of faith. It was faith by which it was framed, and it is by the power of faith that it continues in its organized form, and by which the planets move round their orbits and sparkle forth their glory. So, then, faith is truly the first principle in the science of theology."[4]

So how does the doubter, who is beginning to understand how faith works and why he needs it, actually acquire it? The answer: Faith is harnessed by the thoughts we think and subsequently, by the associated actions we take. Our thoughts can propel us to the highest heights spiritually or conversely to the lowest lows depending on what we choose to nurture. Sometimes doubters hate to hear it because receiving a sign of some sort seems so much easier and more palatable, but the truth is, the more we study and learn about God and his plan of salvation the more we feed thoughts that build faith. The more we take action to live a Christ like life, the more our conscious selves embrace the effects of righteous living, thereby increasing our faith. But it starts with our thoughts.

There are positive and negative energies in the conscious world in which we live, which we attract by the kind of energy, or thoughts, we give out. Positive attracts positive and negative attracts negative. Light cleaves to light and darkness loves darkness. Simply by thinking positive thoughts and speaking positive words we attract positive energy. In our thoughts and words we create our own weaknesses and strengths. If we overdose ourselves with negative thoughts and words, we do nothing more than attract more negative energy until we become completely overwhelmed. Sometimes we beat ourselves up with the thoughts we think.

We also beat other people up with our thoughts. Thoughts of envy or harsh judgment end up surrounding us with negative energy. Eventually, our hearts become laden with darkness and our desires become anything but righteous. If we understood the power of our thoughts, we would guard them more closely. Until we develop the fine art of positive thinking we are doomed to fail in many of our goals, including the development of faith. There is a great lesson in "the little engine that thought he could." There is also a great lesson in the adage, "if you think you can or you think you can't, you're right." And let's not forget the lesson within the scripture "For as he thinketh in his heart, so is he ..." (Proverbs 23:7).

Optimism Builds Faith

Researchers call positive thinking "dispositional optimism" and have linked it to everything from decreased feelings of loneliness to increased pain tolerance. Optimism is associated with better health of patients recovering from an illness or disease because they have better coping strategies, are problem solvers, and tend to accept reality and move on when things don't go their way. For instance, a 1994 study found that dispositional optimism was a significant predictor of early mortality among young patients with recurrent cancer.[5] Also, the Mayo Clinic reported a number of health benefits associated with optimism, including a reduced risk of death from cardiovascular problems, less depression, and an increased lifespan.[6]

The power of faith is derived from our thoughts. The two are interconnected, cemented together by an eternal bonding agent that stipulates one could not exist without the other. A common element in near-death experiences is when a person merely thinks of some other place and is instantly transported there. Another common NDE element is that the experiencer doesn't communicate with others through verbal exchanges, but through mental telepathy. Thoughts are central to events that take place in the spirit world, and so by extension, are central to the temporal world as well.

There is something else I think we should consider. Behavioral science teaches that there are two things that motivate us to do or not do something: To receive pleasure or to avoid pain. If we're more afraid of the pain that may come with failure than we are of the pleasure that accompanies success, we will be stymied in our efforts to achieve. On the other hand, people who are more motivated by the pleasure or rewards of success than the fear of pain are those who will achieve their desires and even fulfill their dreams. Positive thinking will help eliminate the fear, and perseverance will help us keep putting one foot in front of the other in our quest to develop faith in God.

Sometimes doubters, because they doubt, aren't willing to put in the work required to develop faith. They may have tried from time to time to experiment upon the words of Alma (Alma 32) by planting the seed of faith in their bosoms, nurturing it a bit here and there through Church attendance and prayer, but because they didn't receive immediate results, they let doubt take over again. They probably have spent most of their lives with one foot in and one foot out of the Church doors because they simply couldn't sustain the needed effort to acquire and maintain faith. They were looking for a quicker fix or maybe even a miraculous intervention.

As we come to understand the sheer power that is faith, we more fully discern why we absolutely need to have it. We cannot ever hope to believe in God, let alone share in his power through our own growth and progression, until we have faith. It is good and helpful to study our world and seek answers through science, but we are limiting ourselves if we stop there because science, as we know it, is incomplete. God is not.

President Harold B. Lee once told BYU students that "learning by faith is no task for a lazy man. Someone has said, in effect, that 'such a process requires the bending of the whole soul, the calling up from the depths of the human mind and linking the person with God. The right connection must be formed; then only comes knowledge by faith, a kind of knowledge that goes beyond secular learning, that reaches into the realms of the unknown and makes those who follow that course great in the sight of the Lord.'"[7]

So here's where the Doubting Thomas just feels helpless. He really could use a sign, he feels, to give his faith a kick start, but is told first he must have faith and signs will follow. "Faith cometh not by signs, but signs follow those that believe. Yea, signs come by faith, not by the will of men, nor as they please, but by the will of God. Yea, signs come by faith, unto mighty works, for without faith no man pleaseth God" (D&C 63:9-11). But when a person seeks for signs to bolster faith without fully living gospel principles, that person basically is trying to circumvent the "trial of our faith" process.

Learning and growth line upon line, precept upon precept (D&C 128:21)—the building blocks of faith—is paramount to obtaining a perfect knowledge. Miracles and signs alone would constitute a short cut, and there are no short cuts in becoming like God. We must do the hard work of hope in God and his plan, followed by faithful and righteous actions before we are rewarded with a spiritual confirmation.

Righteous Actions Required

Anyone truly converted to the gospel of Jesus Christ has followed this formula, and stories abound to testify that it works. Inspiring personal accounts that range from budding testimonies to unwavering conversion, some recorded in this book, serve as shining examples that teach and motivate. In keeping with that design, I'd like to share my own story as an example of how hope in things not seen, coupled with action in planting the seed, can result in faith, the fossil fuel of gospel testimony.

During my late teen and young adult years in the late 1960s and early 1970s, I completely left the Church, having been drawn by peers to the excitement going on among the youth of that day. And while I received a powerful education about things of the world that provided first-hand knowledge of how easily we can be deceived, I was also blessed with a never-give-up mother who eventually found a way to reach me.

Over the years I spent exercising my agency in Los Angeles, California, she would constantly send me Church books, pamphlets, or articles in the hopes I would read them and be moved to change my life. Instead, I would promptly file them in the kitchen trash can without so much as bending a page. Eventually, however, time and circumstances united to create a realization in me that there was more to life than the way I was living. A desire to make a change began to grow within me, but I wasn't sure how to go about it.

Miraculously, as if right on cue, I received a book in the mail from my mother—*A Time to Choose*, by Neal A. Maxwell. This time the book did not go into the trash. This time I sat down immediately and read the entire book, or maybe a better description would be, I absorbed the entire book so remarkable and timely was its message. Being the vagabond that I was anyway, I packed up my meager belongings in the trunk of my 1966 Ford Mustang and drove from L.A. to Northern California where I had grown up in the Church. My parents had since moved to Utah, but I had friends in the area I thought might lend a hand of fellowship.

Suffice it to say, these old friends did welcome me back into their midst and helped me begin the arduous journey of building faith that would lead to repentance. I say arduous, because the fact that one realizes they're on the wrong path and needs to make a change doesn't mean the change happens over night. And I call it a journey because it literally took step after step after step of continuous effort to find answers about God and his Church sufficient to give me the staying power I needed.

After finding a job and an apartment, I made an appointment with a member of the stake presidency whom I remembered fondly from my youth. I had devised a list of 21 theological questions to which I needed answers before I could even begin to build my faith. This kindly man spent over four hours with me one night going over every single question. While he did a good job planting seeds of faith because of that visit, I was still a long way from being convinced that the LDS Church was indeed the Kingdom of God on Earth.

The next thing I did was read the Book of Mormon with the intention of kneeling in prayer afterward to test Moroni's promise that God would reveal its truthfulness to me if I asked with a sincere heart. I still remembered a thing or two from my early morning seminary days and so knew what to do. I read the entire book in three weeks in the evenings after work and was touched by a lot of what I read, though much of it was also over my head. Upon finishing it, I took a deep breath feeling somewhat confident that an answer would come, knelt by my bed, and asked God if the Book of Mormon was true. Nothing happened. I continued praying for some time, pouring out my heart with the hope that I'd feel something, anything that signaled I was being heard. Still nothing came.

Undaunted, I began attending Church and associating with others in the Young Adult program, whose own personal testimonies helped me keep going. But I wanted my own testimony based on my own spiritual experiences and answer to prayer so that I'd never waver again. Every night I continued to study the Book of Mormon and every night my prayers continued to go unanswered. This went on for some time, so I concluded that I must not be doing enough. I wanted to show God that I was worthy of his time; that I was worthy of his sacred assurance regarding gospel truths. So I took a long look in the proverbial mirror and discovered there were still some things I could do to show him that I was serious.

The next thing I did was to lower all the hems on my skirts and dresses, no easy sacrifice for a young person living in the mini-skirt generation, but one that needed to be made. I just knew this would please God, but once again when I knelt to pray that night, my efforts were met with silence from the heavens. Disappointed but not completely discouraged, I took another self assessment and decided to get rid of my zodiac key chain and a psychedelic poster of Jimmy Hendrix I had on the wall. I was also now attending two separate sacrament meetings, reading multiple Church books, and fasting along with some of my prayers. Still, my prayers yielded no concrete experience with the Spirit. It was beginning to affect my morale as I was not looking for a bolt of lightning or some other miraculous sign, I merely wanted some small spiritual connection with God that would confirm for me the faith I so desperately wanted to acquire.

Another self check revealed yet one more thing, however small, I could do to show Heavenly Father I wanted back in the fold. I took a knife and scraped off a peace sign sticker that was on the back bumper of my car. A peace sign, in and of itself, was not exactly a tool of the devil, but I thought it might be emblematic of a lifestyle not in keeping with the gospel of Jesus Christ and removing it seemed to me an appropriate gesture. After doing so, I once again retired to my bedroom and began to pray feeling sure I would finally make a spiritual connection. After all, what else was there left for me to do? But once again nothing happened.

Tears of anguish streamed down my face as I pleaded with God to love me again. I told him I was sorry for my bad choices and that I had learned from my mistakes and wanted to feel him in my life again. Why was he keeping his distance? Was there more I needed to do? Or was it all just simply not true? In the very depth of my despair I looked up toward heaven and cried out in sorrow, "Heavenly Father, don't you want me back?"

And then, it happened. My whole body began to tremble, as it were, in sensations of pure repose. It felt like I was bathing in the tepid, undulating waters of divine love. I literally felt levitated from my kneeling position as if I were lighter than air, all the while continuing to be consumed in warmth that enveloped every inch of my inner and outer being. I felt completely wrapped up in the arms of a Heavenly Father whose very presence in the room brought reassurance that I was indeed forgiven, that he was real, and that the Church was true.

The experience lasted for a long time, such that I began to feel weak and finally crawled upon my bed to rest until the feeling eventually subsided. I'm not sure what I was expecting by way of answer to my prayer, but it wasn't that. This experience came with undeniable power from a source beyond anything I'd known in the physical world. It had to be from God. There was no other explanation. His inexplicable effort to reach out to little ol' me in such a powerfully moving way not only sealed for me a knowledge of his incredible love for each of his children, but also became a compelling foundation of faith for which I had longed and worked to achieve.

I learned that faith to work miracles, like answer to prayer, does not come until after a trial of our faith. If we start with a desire to believe followed by actions commensurate with faith, we are promised an understanding of things beyond our earthly capacity. We can commune with God and receive all that he has, even unto a perfect knowledge. We must first do the work through our thoughts and actions, and then we will reap the rewards we seek. It is the only way.

I also learned that God responds in his own way and time table to ensure the kind of growth each individual requires. Elder Richard G. Scott said it well: "God will not always reward you immediately according to your desires. Rather, God will respond with what in His eternal plan is best for you, when it will yield the greatest advantage. Be thankful that sometimes

God lets you struggle for a long time before that answer comes. That causes your faith to increase and your character to grow."[8]

Prayer, the Ultimate Conduit

Once we have developed sufficient faith in God, we become naturally desirous of communicating with him on a regular basis. But those whose faith is lacking also have trouble with prayer, because they find it difficult to pray to someone they're not even sure exists. Again, a little evidence through scientific research in the efficacy of prayer might lend a hand. This evidence is not meant to bypass the bedrock spiritual aspects of prayer to a Heavenly Father anxious to respond to his children. Rather, it is offered as an interesting avenue that unifies the spiritual elements of life with the temporal world in which we live.

Because there is a seeming lack of spiritual/temporal unification in the space-time continuum as it relates to prayer, it can be a real problem for some people. For instance, even if we allow that prayer travels at the speed of light, it doesn't explain how God can receive our messages instantaneously. Believers may have trouble understanding why this is even an issue since God can do all things, but for doubters, it's a valid concern.

Instantaneous communication. Let's take a look at how the occurrence of separate events can affect each other. Causal events are generally seen as happening linearly, that is, one event must travel through space and time in order to influence another event elsewhere. An example would be the shooting of an arrow from point A to pop a balloon fastened to a target at point B. This linear sequence of events is called locality. Critics of theology would say that because prayer is supposed to involve a type of instantaneous, non-local communication with God, it couldn't possibly be true because it doesn't follow the principle of locality.[9]

However, recent discoveries in quantum mechanics challenge this idea suggesting that regardless of the distance separating two events in space, they can still simultaneously occur. Studies of the spin characteristics of twin photons [subatomic electromagnetic particles] spinning in opposite directions at a distance from each other, demonstrated that the measurement of one photon's spin instantly influenced the spin of its twin. It shows that individual photons have an interconnectedness that makes them part of the same system despite the distance between them.[10]

This instantaneous linking of events through non-locality discovered by physicists is a perfect temporal explanation of prayer. When we pray here on Earth, our words and thoughts travel instantly through time and space to be heard by God where he resides. His answers to us follow the same immediate course (see 3 Nephi 1:11-13). How can this be? The scriptures tell us that the light of Christ "fills the immensity of space," thus making it possible for us to connect with him instantaneously (D&C 88:6-13). Furthermore, these same non-local processes also make possible the instantaneous interstellar appearance of angels and departed beings that are in one place while we're in another.[11]

Healing. It is one thing to understand how prayer operates in a finite world, but the more pressing question is, does it work? A powerful witness can be found in the area of healing. Archaeological evidence and studies of primitive cultures have shown that human beings have always looked to a supernatural power for worship and healing. Researcher Carol Osman Brown wrote in *HealthLinks* magazine, "The origins of prayer are lost in antiquity, but there is no known culture that does not use prayer in some form. In numerous world cultures healers, whether physicians, medicine men, or psychic healers, all use some form of prayerful intervention in their work."[12]

Dating back thousands of years, early medical practitioners understood the connection between the human spirit and physical health and used both to provide positive results for their patients. But somewhere along the way, practitioners departed from the spiritual part of patient care while their patients continued to use it. Every day people continued to use prayer to aid in their own recovery. The fact that prayer has been utilized for so long by so many is reason enough to believe in its efficacy. It seems the practice would have been discarded long ago if it didn't work.

Historically, faith healing through prayer has been a part of most cultures and religions and is still very much a part of the belief system of people today. The extent of America's belief in prayer for healing was shown in 1996 in a poll reported in *Time* magazine. The poll found that 82% of adult Americans believed in the healing power of personal prayer, 73% believed praying for someone can help cure their illness, and 64% believed doctors should pray with patients if requested to.[13]

Even more striking is a poll of 296 physicians in 1996 that showed 99% felt that religious beliefs can heal, and 75% believed that prayers from friends and family could help a patient to heal.[14] These physicians were keenly aware of the huge body of scientific evidence that support the merging of medicine and prayer.

Of note is a landmark study in 1984 by cardiologist Dr. Randolph Byrd on how prayer heals. Some 393 coronary patients at San Francisco General Hospital were either assigned to a control group or to a group who were prayed for daily by people in home prayer groups. The selection for the two groups was done randomly and no one knew who was in which group. Here is what was discovered about those in the prayed for group:

1. They were five times less likely to require antibiotics.
2. They were three times less likely to develop pulmonary edema, a condition where the lungs fill with fluid.
3. None of those prayed for required endotracheal intubation, the insertion of an artificial airway in the throat, compared with 12 in the control group who required the treatment.
4. They experienced fewer cases of pneumonia and cardiopulmonary arrests.
5. Fewer patients died.[15]

Since Byrd's study, many similar experiments were conducted with similar results, enough so that 90% of the country's medical schools now include spirituality education in their curricula.[16]

Reginald Cherry, M.D., who is not LDS, has been a firsthand witness to the power of prayer to heal, and so he not only prescribes prayer for his patients but also prays with them. In his book, *Healing Prayer*, Dr. Cherry provided several case histories of patients who had miraculous cures through prayer.

Case One: Gloria was diagnosed with atrial fibrillation, a potentially serious cause of stroke. She immediately began to include her medical condition in her prayers. She was encouraged by Dr. Cherry to see a cardiologist who told her she had the condition for a long time, which makes it even more difficult to solve. When Gloria was told the only way to correct her condition was electrical shock to her heart, she was afraid but reluctantly consented. But prior to her return visit, she earnestly prayed to be healed and when she saw the cardiologist two weeks later, he was amazed that her atrial fibrillation had completely moved back to a normal rhythm.[17]

Case Two: Harold had contracted hepatitis C, a viral infection that attacks the liver and can lead to chronic hepatitis, cirrhosis of the liver, and liver cancer. Through prayer, he and Dr. Cherry determined that because traditional treatment only worked in a minority of cases, they needed Harold's own immune system to recognize, seek out, and destroy the virus in his body. Daily prayer led Dr. Cherry to an herb known as milk thistle, which can help regenerate liver cells and strengthen liver function. After being on this herb for several weeks, Harold's liver enzyme count had dropped dramatically, and eventually it became completely normal and stayed that way.[18]

Priesthood power. So prayer alone is a powerful tool in faith healing, but when you couple prayer and faith with the priesthood, the old adage "miracles never cease," takes on a whole new meaning. When a worthy priesthood holder lays his hands upon a person in need, he becomes a channel for God's healing power as if God, himself, were standing there giving the blessing. The combination of that power and the faith of all involved becomes the perfect recipe for incredible outcomes. Of course, we are encouraged to take advantage of medical help and not rely solely on priesthood blessings. Generally speaking, we try to exhaust all efforts simultaneously.

Many have experienced occasions when a healing did not occur and wondered if they lacked sufficient faith. But the truth is, despite our best efforts, if the healing is not according to God's will for reasons known only to him, it will not happen. During those times, we must have the faith to accept the outcome knowing there are reasons beyond our understanding. It may simply be one of the trials which we must undergo as part of Earth life. In that case, our faith in God's ability to comfort and sustain us will be activated to provide the needed blessings of endurance.

Such was the case several years ago involving a young father who had been active in the Church as a boy but left it as an adult. After serving in the military, he married and started a family. One day the couple's four-year-old daughter became critically ill and was hospitalized. It had been many years since the father felt a need to pray, but desperation over his daughter's life brought him to his knees. He asked that her life be spared, but instead, her condition worsened. Gradually, this father realized his little girl would die and so his prayers began to change from pleadings for healing to understanding and acceptance.

When the young girl slipped into a coma, the father and mother, who were now fortified with understanding, trust, and power beyond their own, prayed again, this time for the opportunity to hold her close once more while she was awake. "The daughter's eyes opened, and her frail arms reached out to her parents for one final embrace. And then she was gone. This father knew their prayers had been answered—a kind, compassionate Father in Heaven had comforted their hearts. God's will had been done, and they had gained understanding."[19]

An acceptance of God's will can be difficult for any of us, but all too often, doubters see it as proof that prayer doesn't work because there is no God. They often want to believe, but need to have personal experiences of their own with prayer and the influence of the Holy Ghost. The problem many have is that they tried to pray, came up empty handed, and so gave up on it altogether. But they gave up too soon. We know that answer to prayer may not be instantaneous, but will come in God's time when it will have the biggest impact on our lives. Also, the person may just need to put more work into it or come at it from a different angle.

Our prophet, President Thomas S. Monson, has counseled us to pray always and that "there is no finer hour to begin than now. William Cowper declared, 'Satan trembles, when he sees the weakest saint upon his knees.' Those who feel that prayer might denote a physical or intellectual weakness should remember that a man never stands taller than when he is upon his knees. We cannot know what faith is if we have never had it, and we cannot obtain it as long as we deny it. Faith and doubt cannot exist in the same mind at the same time, for one will dispel the other."[20]

Prayer is found in homes of all religions and is often such a common element of life that people sometimes forget what an enormous privilege and blessing it is. As the ultimate conduit to God, prayer will yield its greatest benefits when used daily. Perhaps the stories of others will serve as motivation for doubters to take to their knees in pursuit of their own experiences.

Church member Marcos Walker shared an experience with prayer he used to help resolve a dispute between his 10 and 12-year-old sons. When Brother Walker intervened, the younger son responded inappropriately with yelling, crying, and generally being out of control. The tirade was beginning to stretch the nerves of this father who realized he needed to help his son find a calming solution. The need for prayer came into his mind so he took his son into a room and closed the door. He solemnly asked the boy to kneel with him in prayer.

"We both knelt down as his cries of fury continued. I prayed with the objective of trying to help my son. In the middle of the prayer I noticed that his sobs were dying down. The tears rolling down his cheeks were now tears of repentance." When the prayer concluded the boy raised his head and asked, 'Dad, can you forgive me?' We embraced, and I was not able to contain my own tears. Feelings of peace and love filled my soul. [My son] said nothing more, but I knew that he had experienced the restoring power of prayer and that the Holy Ghost had penetrated his heart. Now he not only knew about the power of prayer, but he had gained a testimony of it."[21]

In another story, a married couple met together with their two young children to eat sandwiches brought from home in a college dining room while they discussed their bleak financial situation. Their money was used up for the month and they had a week until payday. They were faithful tithe payers and had prayed mightily for help so they wouldn't have to go to their families or incur credit card debt. Suddenly, a man sitting several tables away who had been watching them walked up to the family and with a smile handed a folded piece of paper to the husband saying, "It looks like you've got your hands full."

The man promptly left the room and the father opened the paper which read, "Good luck! It looks like you're doing a good job so far." Inside was enough money to get them through the next week and more. With tears in their eyes, they knew this was an answer to prayer.[22]

A third story I'll share comes from Elder Hartman Rector Jr. of the Seventy. He described how a man who was taught the gospel by the missionaries and believed it to be true couldn't join because he couldn't stop smoking. Elder Rector encouraged the man, his wife who was a member, the missionaries, and himself to fast and pray about it. After two days of fasting they all met, knelt together, and prayed one by one that the man would have strength to quit smoking. Being the last to pray, the man poured out his heart with words of sincerity. When he concluded his prayer he jumped to his feet and said with amazement, that his desire to smoke was gone. And from that moment he never smoked again.[23]

In its purest form, prayer is a gift to be utilized whenever we need to connect with a loving Heavenly Father who is ever ready to provide answers, comfort, and even miracles. He cares not whether we're rich or poor, learned or uninformed, famous or ordinary. We can find peace in knowing that for all the numberless worlds he has created, we are so important to him that we can speak with him personally, and he will answer.

Personal and Prophetic Revelation

Some may wonder why we need the priesthood if God hears and answers all prayers, sends his angels to attend us, and provides miracles regardless of our religious convictions. The answer is because the priesthood, while it embodies power to act for the well being of God's children, which may include prayers, blessings, and miracles, is also there to govern the kingdom of God on Earth. Priesthood holders can be authorized to preach the gospel and administer the ordinances of salvation as well as preside within the organizational structure of the Church.

On one hand, it has a managerial component since God's house is a house of order (D&C 88:119), but on the other, it has real power to function at a far deeper level than individual spiritual experiences. Joseph Smith said, "It is the channel for obtaining revelation, the channel through which God reveals himself and his glory, his intents and his purposes, to mankind: The priesthood holds 'the key of the mysteries of the kingdom, even the key of the knowledge of God'" (D&C 84:19-20).[24] It conveys the mind and will of God; and when his servants use it to accomplish his work, it functions as if by the Lord's own mouth and hand (see D&C 1:38).

Priesthood authority is the means by which Godly revelation affecting all of humankind occurs. And revelation, wherein truth is revealed, is another evidence of God. "One of the grand fundamental principles of Mormonism," said Joseph Smith "is to accept truth, let it come from whence it may."[25] Brigham Young claimed that "God has revealed all the truth that is now in the possession of the world, whether it be scientific or religious. The whole world [is] under obligation to him for what they know and enjoy; they are indebted to him for it all."[26]

But all truths are not equal, according to Apostle Dallin H. Oaks. "Seeking learning by study, we use the method of reason. Seeking learning by faith, we must rely on revelation .... Reason is a thinking process using facts and logic that can be communicated to another person and tested by objective, that is, measurable criteria. Revelation is communication from God to man. It cannot be defined and tested like reason. Reason involves thinking and demonstrating. Revelation involves hearing or seeing or understanding or feeling."[27]

Ursula Goodenough, biology professor at Washington University in St. Louis, suggested that science is forever having revelations of its own through reason and study. Libraries full of journals reporting all kinds of spectacular breakthroughs came only after countless frustrating experiments and dashed ideas. Like clockwork, she said, once a discovery is reviewed and published, the errata sheets [compiled errors found in a written text] start to pile up. As the next question in science is asked and the answer pursued, a mutant strain will show up or growing cells at a different temperature will skew the earlier observations. The next journal article will reflect these new findings and a new scientific revelation will be shared.[28] She wrote:

> "So I would say that scientific understandings represent revelations of a second kind. The acceptance that truth is provisional, the acceptance that each revelation represents but the next step in acquiring the next revelation, is the surest path towards anything, that, in my book, might be called an unveiling, not to mention wisdom and—dare I say it—salvation. There are elegant truths in religious texts, in philosophy, in the arts, in histories. But none, I would say, merits the insult of being considered a 'truth.' Each merits the promise of being taken back to the lab, back to the inquiring mind and heart, for yet another round of probing, evaluation, integration, and yes, often amendment or flat-out rejection."[29]

So while all truth comes from God, we have to be sure that what we may think is truth, actually is. This is especially true in areas of science, which often go back to the drawing board over and over as new information comes forth. On the other hand, with direct revelation from God to his anointed prophet, all ambiguity ceases. Once the prophet reveals to us what God revealed to him, the only testing required is for each of us to pray about it and put it into practice to receive our own personal witness.

Personal revelation is guaranteed to every devoted, obedient, and righteous person through the Holy Ghost, who is a revelator. Of course, since the Holy Ghost does not always strive with man because of issues of personal worthiness, having the priesthood available can help us with answers and blessings when we are weak. Apart from worthiness, because the sometimes enticing doctrines of man and temptations of the world can lead to confusion, having a true prophet of God on the earth provides an unambiguous pathway to understanding the truth of all things.

Distinguishing Revelation from Reason

Many of us find it somewhat difficult to distinguish through the myriad thoughts and feelings we have each day, which is how revelation comes, when an impression is actually coming from God. This lack of clarity is another stumbling block for those who doubt. They wonder why God couldn't make his message a little more loud and clear, which of course, he does from time to time, but generally speaking, he communicates through "the still, small voice, which whispereth through and pierceth all things" (D&C 85:6). When a voice is still and small and whispers, it may seem like an obstacle for the listener. But therein, lays another opportunity for us to become more like God. If God handed everything to us on a silver platter, we would never do the work required for spiritual growth. It's the yearning, the anguish, the prayerful supplication, the internal commitment to righteousness, and the being "doers of the word" (James 1:22), that bring the reward of revelation.

A soft voice also requires us to tune out worldly distractions in order to hear it. Apostle David A. Bednar said, "Because the spirit whispers to us gently and delicately, it is easy to understand why we should shun inappropriate media, pornography, and harmful, addictive substances and behaviors. These tools of the adversary can impair and eventually destroy our capacity to recognize and respond to the subtle messages from God delivered by the power of His Spirit."[30]

But God has not left us without guidance in determining the source—God, Satan, or ourselves—from which revelation/inspiration/prompting comes. General Authority and author Gerald Lund outlined five such guidelines or principles:

> *Principle 1:* It is God who determines all aspects of revelation.
> *Principle 2:* The content given in a revelation is more important than the form in which it comes.

Principle 3: True revelation does not contradict gospel principles or go contrary to established Church policy and procedure.

Principle 4: The Lord wants us to use our agency and develop spiritual self-reliance.

Principle 5: A person is not given revelation to direct another person unless they have priesthood or family responsibility for that person.[31]

There are many stories of personal revelation shared among family and friends and in religious meetings and publications around the world. Anyone can be touched by the Holy Ghost, whether in or out of the Church, if they live as righteously as they know how. These insights and promptings are given from a loving Heavenly Father to help us find our way in a difficult world.

In one such story, a young wife casually encouraged her husband to apply for a job in another state that a friend told her about. The husband initially rejected the idea because for one, the job was in a profession which didn't interest him, and two, he enjoyed his current job and knew it provided stability and a chance for advancement. But despite his initial assessment of the idea, he kept thinking about the job opportunity, so much so, that it began keeping him up at night and monopolizing his thoughts during the day. Still, he could see no valid reason to change jobs. Finally, he decided to interview for the job and ultimately was hired at a wonderful salary. The very next day he was unexpectedly laid off from the current job because the failing economy necessitated a downsizing at the company. There was no doubt in his mind that God had intervened through personal revelation to prepare him for what was to come.

In another example, Apostle Dallin H. Oaks once told a story about a personal revelation that came to his grandmother.

> "As a young girl, my grandmother Chasty Olsen Harris, was tending some children who were playing in a dry riverbed near their home in Castle Dale, Utah. Suddenly she heard a voice that called her by name and directed her to get the children out of the riverbed and up on the bank. It was a clear day, and there was no sign of rain. She saw no reason to

heed the voice and continued to play. The voice spoke to her again, urgently. This time she heeded the warning. Quickly gathering the children, she made a run for the bank. Just as they reached the bank, an enormous wall of water, originating with a cloudburst in the mountains many miles away, swept down the canyon and roared across where the children had played."[32]

A story from President Thomas S. Monson illustrates how we can receive revelation related to our stewardships. When he was a mission president over the Canadian Mission, President Monson met with a missionary whose father was not a member of the Church. Strongly prompted by what he called a "source not my own," he without hesitation, told this missionary if he would honestly and diligently serve God on his mission, his father would join the Church before the mission ended. With tears in his eyes, the young elder promised he would do all in his power to serve an honorable mission to see the promise fulfilled of his father's conversion. Day in and day out the elder worked hard to spread the gospel with no news about the father's possible testimony. But he continued to pray as though everything depended upon God and work as though everything depended upon him. Then finally, two weeks before Elder Monson and his wife were scheduled to leave their mission, Elder Monson received a letter from the missionary's father expressing his joy at his recent baptism.[33]

Now when it comes to revelation for the Church, only prophets of God are ordained to receive it. It is not only a distinguishing feature of the restored Church, but also the foundation for all of God's workings with man since the very beginning. It also makes sense. Would a loving Heavenly Father leave his children without a rudder for this ark of life we're on where humans are swayed with every wind of doctrine and temptations of the natural man? Mormons are nearly alone in the religious world in our belief in continuous revelation, which has been shunned and discredited as heretical and blasphemous by other Christian churches. But let me repeat—it makes sense.

Joseph Smith said he once told a group of non-Mormons "that the most prominent difference in sentiment between the Latter-day Saints and sectarians was, that the latter were all circumscribed by some peculiar creed, which deprived its members the privilege of believing anything not contained therein, whereas the Latter-day Saints have no creed, but are ready to believe all true principles that exist, as they are made manifest from time to time."[34]

An interesting dichotomy is that the prophet's teachings on the topic strongly resemble one of the most, shall we say, sacred aspects of the scientific method—that truth is unrestricted. Science is built upon the newest theory, the next discovery, and the latest breakthrough. And unlike mainstream Christianity which must adhere to a systemic theology that never grows or progresses, Latter-day Saint Christianity exemplifies the same unrestricted, open-ended quest for truth found in science. The fundamental Mormon tenet that "God will yet reveal many great and important things pertaining to the kingdom of God" (Article of Faith 9), is radical in most of Christendom but right in line with the basic framework of science. Both understand and accept the need for continuous revelation.

Miraculous Intervention

Author and former *Time* magazine correspondent Robert Blair Kaiser once described a miracle in his life. He wrote:

> "In 1994, behind the wheel of my Mercedes, I lurched out of my driveway and was awakened from my dreamy preoccupation by the sight of a speeding car bearing down on me, not five feet away on my left. I knew I was a dead man. All of a sudden, that car was on my right. The driver weaved a bit, braked for a moment and then drove off, shaking his head in disbelief, as I was. For it was clear to me, there was no way he could have missed crashing into me, no way he could have steered aside. His car had flashed through

my car, his steel and glass and rubber passing through my steel and glass and rubber like a ray of light through a pane of alabaster. This miracle moment was a turning point in my life, for I took it as a sign that God wasn't finished with me yet and that I had some new business to attend to."[35]

Miracles of all kinds are recorded throughout our existence and are a mainstay of Christian theology. Indeed, the atonement and resurrection of Jesus Christ is the greatest miracle of all. But the well-meaning doubter can't help but read and listen to these miraculous accounts with a raised eyebrow, not because he needs one of his own before he'll believe, but because it's all just so incredulous to his finite mind that is helplessly earthbound. Because we are told that miracles come by faith, and because the faith some of us have is so weak, it's easy to feel abandoned to a state of never knowing the wonders and miracles that others speak of with such passion.

Some people have a hard time digesting the concept that miracles are supernatural events in the physical world that deviate from the laws of nature because after all, the laws of nature are immutable aren't they? Shouldn't there be some kind of explanation based on science for events that seem to defy our known laws of nature? If God created those laws in the first place, then shouldn't it follow that he would not depart from his own laws?

Perhaps the answer is that we simply don't know all the laws of nature. Perhaps there are yet more laws out there that humans, whose current knowledge of such things is embryonic, can't possibly know compared to that of an omnipotent God. Consider our own history. Early inventions using electricity probably seemed miraculous to the average person who didn't fully understand the properties of electricity. None of us think of today's technology—smart phones, computers, medical devices, space travel, satellites, military drones, inter-continental ballistic missiles—as miracles anymore because we know the technology that makes them possible. If we look to the future, the truly miraculous might come in the form of human teleportation, time travel, personal force fields, faster-than-light acceleration, and telepathic communication. Yet even then it wouldn't mean an abandonment of natural laws, but rather a better understanding of them. These scientific discoveries are bits and pieces of what God, as the master scientist, has put into motion for the benefit of his children.

The Bible Dictionary explains that miracles should not be regarded as deviations from the ordinary course of nature, so much as manifestations of divine or spiritual power. Some lower law was in each case superseded by the action of a higher law. Apostle James E. Talmage said, "Miracles cannot be in contravention of natural law, but are wrought through the operation of laws not universally or commonly recognized .... We arbitrarily classify as miracles only such phenomena as are unusual, special, transitory, and wrought by an agency beyond the power of man's control."[36]

For example, one natural law says that when one billiard ball smacks into another, the amount of momentum lost by the first ball must exactly equal the amount gained by the second. A billiard ball will go a certain way if nothing interferes, but if one ball encounters roughness on the cloth, we will no longer have the expected unimpeded result. Or if someone slightly taps the ball with a cue stick to move it along, we end up with yet a third result. Nature in this case has been doctored from what would have happened if the ball had not been interfered with, but regardless, all interferences still leave the law intact. A physicist knows the behavior of the billiard balls will differ from what he expected, not because the law is false, but because it is true. It is, therefore, inaccurate to define a miracle as something that breaks the laws of nature. Nature digests and assimilates the unexpected with perfect ease and harmony.[37]

Miracles should reasonably be seen in two ways: Deviations within the expected laws of nature, or the results of higher laws of nature not yet understood. Either explanation provides a home for the miraculous in our lives. And like near-death-experiences and visions, the sheer quantity of miracles throughout history provides stark evidence of God. A look at some of the wondrous, yet enigmatic events in people's lives can help us understand the true nature of God's power, as well as his tenderness. Within the content of these stories are principles of faith, hope, love, and the assurance that each of us matters and are never alone.

Stories of Miracles

Traveling through the back roads of Wyoming on a two-lane highway in the old family van, David and Mary Durtschi and their seven children were heading home to Tennessee after a fun vacation in the Yellowstone and Grand Teton national parks. Driving late at night under a dark, moonless sky while his family slept, David was traveling, as he usually did, a few miles over the speed limit. He had 1,000 miles to go and needed to be back to work on time. Suddenly, his quiet, uneventful drive was interrupted by a man's voice telling him to "slow down!" David responded audibly with "Who said that?" When he realized it wasn't anyone in the van, he decided to heed the voice and let up on the accelerator. When nothing alarming happened, he began to pick up speed again.

Soon the voice came again, but this time with a forceful urgency: "Slow down now!" Heart pounding, David immediately slowed from 65 mph to 40 when his headlights picked up a herd of deer crossing the road some 50 yards ahead. But as soon as he spotted the deer, the headlights on the battered old van went out and he was engulfed in thick, black darkness. Unable to see anything at all, he screeched to a halt, praying he wouldn't leave the road or hit the deer. It was truly a miracle that neither happened, which may not have been the case had he not heeded the voice to slow down.

"If I had not listened to that voice," David recalled, "the lives of those seven precious little ones, my beautiful wife, and 21 unborn grandchildren could have been lost. I know the Lord is mindful of our family and I can only hope we all live up to our potential. I am eternally grateful for the whisperings, and sometimes yelling, of the Spirit."[38]

The next account is a story in the January, 2000, *Dallas Morning News*, that described the contents of a letter received by a columnist detailing a remarkable miracle. The writer's five-year-old granddaughter, Heather, suddenly became feverish and lethargic. Her breathing was difficult and her lips had turned blue. By the time she arrived at the hospital, her kidneys and lungs had shut down, her fever was 107 degrees, and her body was bright red and covered with purple lesions. Toxic shock syndrome was the diagnosis, and doctors said she was dying. As word spread, family and friends from across the country began praying for the little girl. At the grandfather's request, a special prayer service was held in their Church of Christ congregation in Waco, Texas. Miraculously, Heather survived and was released from the hospital in a little over a week. The columnist concluded that Heather "is living proof that God does answer prayers and works miracles."[39]

There is a well-known story about Apostle Matthew Cowley being asked by a young father to give his new baby a name and a blessing. Elder Cowley responded,

> "All right, what's the name? So he told me the name, and I was just going to start when he said, 'By the way, give him his vision when you give him a name. He was born blind.' It shocked me, but then I said to myself, why not? Christ said to his disciples when he left them, 'Greater things than I have done shall you do' (see John 14:12). I had faith in that father's faith. After I gave that child its name, I finally got around to giving it its vision. That boy is about twelve years old now. The last time I was back there I was afraid to inquire about him. I was sure he had gone blind again. That's the way my faith works sometimes. So I asked the branch president about him. And he said, 'Brother Cowley, the worst thing you ever did was to bless that child to receive his vision. He's the meanest kid in the neighborhood; always getting into mischief.' Boy, I was thrilled about that kid getting into mischief!"[40]

A final story in this chapter speaks to the heart of a parent's worst fear. On January 30, 2010, the Staker family's nightmare began when their 16-month old son, Bronson, was pronounced dead on arrival at a Utah hospital. Bronson's mother Sara had become distracted during bath time, and briefly left him unattended in the tub. She returned to find her precious little boy floating lifeless in the bath water. Despite frantic attempts by Sara and the emergency response team, Bronson could not be revived. But Bronson's story did not end there. Connected to life support, the toddler remained in a medically-induced coma for 56 hours while undergoing an experimental procedure called "therapeutic hypothermia," in hopes of reducing brain damage. Doctors were unsure about the possibility of Bronson's survival and even more skeptical about his recovery. As the news of Bronson's story spread, people began to pray for a miracle. And once again the heavens opened and a loving Heavenly Father provided one. Bronson overcame the odds and made a full recovery.[41]

The stories are endless and come in all shapes and sizes. Many in the Church tell of getting spiritual help in genealogy research, warnings of danger, avoiding or surviving accidents, healings, missionary work, and testimony growth. Miracles can come to any of God's children, whether in or out of the Church, because he loves them and wants to turn their hearts to him. Sometimes they come without any preconditions, but often they come after a show of faith, which is the foundation for miracles. "For if there be no faith among the children of men, God can do no miracle among them" (Ether 12:12). Modern revelation teaches that miracles and signs do not create faith. Rather, miraculous events follow those who possess faith. So in a way, miracles among us serve as a barometer by which we can gauge the level of our faith and our relationship with God.

Understanding the Miracles of Jesus

Recorded in the New Testament are 39 miracles performed by Jesus Christ during his mortal ministry. They were intended as proof to the Jews that Jesus was the Christ (Matthew 11:4-5; John 2:11; 10:25; 20:30-31). His miracles were almost always beneficial and were always done to further God's plan and purposes. Here are a few that can be found in just the four gospels:

> *Matthew*: The curing of two blind men (9:27-31); the casting out of a devil from the dumb man (9:32-34); the stater in the fish's mouth (17:24-27).

Mark: The healing of a deaf and dumb man (7:31-37); the restoration of the sight of the blind man at Bethsaida (8:22-26).

Luke: The draught of fishes (5:4-11); the raising of the widow's son (7:11-16); the healing of the woman with a spirit of infirmity (13:11-17); the healing of the man afflicted with dropsy (14:1-6); the cleansing of the ten lepers (17:12-19); the healing of Malchus (22:50-51).

John: Water made into wine (2:1-11); the healing of the nobleman's son (4:46-54); the healing of the impotent man at Bethesda (5:1-16); the restoration of sight to the man blind from birth (chapter 9); the raising of Lazarus (11:1-45); the net full of fishes (21:1-24).

Miracles are a major part of the gospel of Jesus Christ. We are told by prophets that if miracles cease, it is because faith has ceased (see Mark 6:5-6; Mormon 9:10-20; Ether 12:12; *Bible Dictionary*, p. 732).

Some scholars have attempted to find temporal explanations for some of Jesus' miracles without palpable success. Jesus simply controlled nature for the benefit of man, and we just don't know how he did it. Talmage tells us that Jesus brought elements together to effect a chemical transmutation that changed water into wine at the Cana wedding. He enlarged the amount of bread and fish to feed the crowds who listened to him by increasing their growth more rapidly than would occur naturally. In the healing of so many physical maladies, he removed the impurities in their bodies more quickly than doctors would have been able.[42]

But skeptics are always looking for ways to explain away such miracles. For example, some have said that the miracle of Jesus walking on the water during a horrible storm on the Sea of Galilee was merely a desert mirage, which often gives the appearance of a sea of shimmering water. The truth is we simply don't know what natural law or principle took the place of the law of gravity in this instance. We don't even know whether the story itself is an allegory. But the meaning behind this single act, together with Peter's failed attempt to also walk on water, is a great affirmation about the principle of faith. It is the foundational power requisite in becoming like God, who is able to subdue the forces of nature.

Conclusion

It is well to discuss faith, prayer, and revelation as avenues to miracles, but they won't avail us much if they don't lead to personal conversion. A loving Heavenly Father did not provide them simply to astound and impress us with his power, but to arouse the light within and motivate us to move in the direction of his glory. It is truly miraculous when a person embraces the beauty and solemnity of the restored gospel and is transformed by it. Their very nature changes as they begin to live by inspired precepts and find solace in celestial answers to life's greatest questions. Apostle David A. Bednar taught,

> "The essence of the gospel of Jesus Christ entails a fundamental and permanent change in our very nature made possible through the Savior's atonement. True conversion brings a change in one's beliefs, heart, and life to accept and conform to the will of God (see Acts 3:19; 3 Nephi 9:20) and includes a conscious commitment to become a disciple of Christ. Conversion is an enlarging, a deepening, and a broadening of the undergirding base of testimony. It is the result of revelation from God, accompanied by individual repentance, obedience, and diligence. Any honest seeker of truth can become converted by experiencing the mighty change of heart and being spiritually born of God (see Alma 5:12-14)."[43]

Life's ultimate goal is gospel conversion, whether in this life or the next, so that we can reap the benefits of eternal life. If you are in doubt about the validity of God, use the inspiring stories you hear about or experience, as stepping stones to your own miracle of conversion. Be open to the possibility of God, so that as you learn from others' experiences, you can let the converting power of the Holy Ghost witness the truth of it to your soul. An open heart and a contrite spirit will go a long way toward building faith sufficient for conversion, which is after all, the thing for which you long.

CHAPTER SIX

Origins of Religion

An enormous number of religions have come and gone throughout history or still remain on the world stage. Those who doubt sometimes see the colossal number of religions as evidence that God does not exist, or at least, that he somehow made a mistake. They wonder how God could have let this happen if there is indeed, one true religion. The concern is valid, but when we look at the origins, differences, and similarities of world religions we find some interesting answers.

It's important to understand just how many religions we're talking about. Researchers agree there are 22 "major religions" in the world today, 10,500 "distinct religions," and an estimated total of 15,000 distinct religions expected in another quarter-century. Religion is defined as any specific system of belief about deity, often involving rituals, a code of ethics, and a philosophy of life. With this definition in mind, Christian denominations alone have risen to a current total of about 35,500.[1]

The *CIA's World Fact Book* puts the world population at 7,021,836,029 as of July 2012. It listed major religions as Christian: 33.39% [of which Roman Catholics are 16.85%, Protestants are 6.15%, Orthodox are 3.96%, Anglicans are 1.26%], Muslim: 22.74%, Hindu: 13.8%, Buddhist: 6.77%, Sikh: 0.35%,

Jewish: 0.22%, Baha'i: 0.11%, other religions: 10.95%, non-religious: 9.66%, and atheists: 2.01%.[2]

A study by the Pew Forum on Religion and Public Life in 2010 indicated 84 percent of the world's inhabitants identify with a specific religion. The "religiously unaffiliated," numbering 1.1 billion or about 16% of people worldwide, covers all those who profess no religion, from atheists and agnostics to people with spiritual beliefs but no link to any established faith.[3]

"Many of the religiously unaffiliated do hold religious or spiritual beliefs," the study indicated. "Belief in God or a higher power is shared by 7% of unaffiliated Chinese adults, 30% of unaffiliated French adults, and 68% of unaffiliated U.S. adults."[4]

So where does the Church of Jesus Christ of Latter-day Saints fit in to all of this? Although studies show the Church is the fastest growing faith in America, its worldwide membership is just 15 million, a meager 0.21% of the world's population. This is not a particularly high number when you consider its claim to be God's true Church that will one day fill the earth.

While finite numbers alone don't really matter in the eternal scheme of things, it's interesting to see what the future may hold with regard to Church population numbers. We are at the threshold of a major worldwide Mormon expansion, according to Mark Koltko-Rivera, Ph.D., an award-winning LDS social scientist, in his book, *The Rise of the Mormons: Latter-day Saint Growth in the 21st Century*. Koltko-Rivera, who holds a doctoral degree from the Department of Applied Psychology at New York University, said the expansion of Mormonism is due to an increase in missionaries, improvements in their preparation, and the recent establishment of stakes in places like India and Russia. His analysis was derived from Mormon membership figures, global population, and social trends.[5]

With more than 90 percent of LDS Church growth resulting from convert baptisms, Koltko-Rivera estimated that the Church will grow to more than 2.6 billion members worldwide by 2120. That would make it the largest Church on Earth, and the second-largest religious body in the world, following Islam, provided growth of other religions continues at their current pace.

He predicted it will be the largest in the U.S. by 2106. That's only about 100 years from now— just one generation.[6]

A population of Latter-day Saints in numbers like that would provide incredibly fertile ground for all the work of salvation required during and just prior to the Millennium. Of course, no one knows when the Savior's reign will begin and I'm certainly not making a prediction. But if there's a need to increase our Church population so the gospel can be "preached unto every nation, and kindred, and tongue, and people" (D&C 133:37), such numbers and time frames seem within our grasp. With 80,000 missionaries currently serving in 405 missions worldwide, as of 2013, many feel this prophesy has already been fulfilled. Maybe, maybe not. What we do know is that if the Church grows in 100 years as projected above, it will provide enough laborers in the vineyard to sew the gospel seeds in the hearts of people everywhere in preparation for the Savior's reign. The LDS Church will no longer be seen as obscure compared to other religions and will be positioned to impact the world as never before through missionary and temple work during the Millennium.

Differences and Similarities of World Religions

We are often more aware of the ways in which religions differ than we are of the surprising correlations among them. While they each offer distinctive techniques for accomplishing their religious goals, when examined carefully, we find embedded within those differences, nuggets of the restored gospel. True, such bits and pieces have been changed and modified, but many still resemble the word of God in its original form. Many world theologies converge and overlap in ways that greatly benefit the entire human race and point to a common origin.

In 1978, the First Presidency stated: "The great religious leaders of the world such as Mohammed, Confucius, and the Reformers, as well as philosophers including Socrates, Plato, and others, received a portion of God's light.

Moral truths were given to them by God to enlighten whole nations and to bring a higher level of understanding to individuals."[7]

Confucians believe our humanness is more fully developed by entwining ourselves in complex systems of social relations. Daoists believe we accomplish the same thing by disentangling ourselves from social relations. For Muslims, Muhammad had three core human qualities of piety, combativeness, and magnanimity. The Buddha was also magnanimous but didn't even believe in God so was far from pious. Jesus was also magnanimous, but when the need for combat arose, he turned the other cheek. It's easy to see the shared belief structures rooted within their theological differences. Unfortunately, societies in general, too often use these differences as political tools or to justify going to war for theological reasons.[8]

Getting along with our religious rivals may indeed be a fundamental part of why we're here. Because inherent in the purpose of life is learning to love and accept all people, the existence of varying theologies provides an opportunity to do just that. And history shows we haven't always done a very good job. Too often some in various religions have used their deistic differences to justify going to war against their theological enemies. The Muslim conquests [beginning in 634], the Christian Crusades [1095-1291], the Christian taking of the Iberian Peninsula called the Reconquista [722-1492], and the French Wars of Religion [1562-98] are frequently cited historical examples.[9] Now we can add the horrific attacks in the name of God on New York's World Trade Center and the U.S. Pentagon on September 11, 2001. Trying to get along in our religious differences is really no different from husbands and wives who are polar opposites learning to peacefully coexist, or fans of the Los Angeles Clippers and Lakers living and working genially together.

But because history is jam packed with holy wars and individuals continue to act out their religious beliefs in a variety of ways, it appears interreligious civility is not only an uphill battle, but also highly unlikely on a global scale, at least until the Millennium. Stephen Prothero, professor of religion at Boston University observed, "Allah tells them to blow themselves up or give to the poor, so they do. Jesus tells them to bomb an abortion clinic or to build a Habitat for Humanity house, so they do. Because God said so, Jews,

Christians, and Muslims believe that this (holy) land is their land, so they fight for it in the name of God or Jesus or Allah."[10]

In the U.S. alone, bookstores and airwaves are buzzing with sometimes hostile debate between secular progressives and the traditional religious right. Theological bickering does not appear to be ending any time soon. But a look at the similarities of world religions can help us understand their common biblical root. It also can show that God still has a hand in teaching all of his children without taking away their agency.

For instance, as Christians, we believe true religion—the gospel of Jesus Christ—started with Adam and Eve in the Garden of Eden. Several other religions also have an interpretation of that event. Muslims see Adam and Eve's roles as that of the father and mother of mankind. According to the Quran, both Adam and Eve ate the forbidden fruit in a *Heavenly* Eden. As a result, they were both sent down to Earth as God's representatives. Jews adhere to information in the second century BC *Book of Jubilees*, which states that the serpent convinced Eve to eat the fruit on the 17th day of the second month of the eighth year after Adam's creation. In the Baha'i Faith, Adam is seen as a manifestation of God, and the Adam and Eve narratives are seen as having divine mysteries and containing universal meanings, but are also seen as having mythical features.[11]

All three of the Abrahamic religions, Judaism, Christianity, and Islam, believe one powerful God created the world, made humans in his image, gave them agency, and will redeem the world. They all have a holy book of scripture, receive revelation through prophets [and a Messiah in the case of Christianity], and believe that God is active in the lives of people and events occurring in the world. They all believe in a final judgment before God for a chance to live with him in a heavenly realm based upon their obedience, faith, and righteousness.[12]

Similarities between Eastern religions and Christianity also exist. Hindus in India and Buddhists in central and eastern Asia believe in reincarnation, where the soul passes into another body at death. They also believe in karma, where a person's actions in one life directly affect who and where they are in the next. There is some similarity in Christian doctrine that teaches being a good person on Earth helps one advance into Heaven. Mormons believe it also helps us advance *within* Heaven. Hindus become saved when the cycle of death and rebirth through reincarnation ends, and Buddhists will no longer be reincarnated once they learn to become unattached to the things of ordinary existence. Again we see similarities with the Christian ideal of setting our "affection on things above, not on things of the earth" (Colossians 3:2).[13]

These Eastern religions, along with Taoism, Confucianism, and Shinto, do not worship a God, per se, but teach that power in the universe, which can enlighten human kind, comes from some kind of divine essence [think of the power of the Holy Ghost or the priesthood] or is derived through the power humans can acquire developing control over their own minds.[14] In the latter, what they're saying is that God is within us. What an interesting concept when compared with the Mormon tenet that within us is the capacity to become like God.

Religions, in general, express belief in a higher power as well as the need for self-mastery through righteous living in order to progress to a higher level of existence. That concept seems to cover the main ideologies of life for most people. Researchers have found that the ethics of the world's religions are almost identical, even when a religion has had very little contact with the rest of the world. For example, the Talmud, a post-biblical commentary on Jewish law and legend, has a saying on the value of community: "Sticks in a bundle are unbreakable, but sticks alone can be broken by a child." This same ethical lesson using nearly identical wording is found in the Masai tribe of sub-Saharan Africa.[15]

The golden rule, "Do unto others what you would have them do unto you" (Luke 6:31), appears almost verbatim in many different faiths. Islam teaches, "No one of you is a believer until he desires for his brother that which he desires for himself." In Hinduism, a passage in Mahabharata 5, 1517 reads, "Do naught onto others what you would not have them do unto you." Buddhism's Udana-Varga 5, 18 states: "Hurt not others in ways that you yourself would find hurtful."[16] These examples are among thousands found in all faiths that share a vision of human virtue. This means despite religious differences, the very core of each is built upon the same foundation of ethics and morality, not to mention nearly identical language.

Reasons for so Many Theologies

In studying these theological similarities, we learn that there is a common thread linking all religions to a central source: Adam and Eve. Because they and their posterity had the fulness of the gospel, they were literally the first Christians on Earth. But the fulness they enjoyed in the beginning was gradually replaced by periodic "famine[s]" of "hearing the words of the Lord" (Amos 8:11). Records indicate that as ancient Israel fell away from teachings that originated with our first parents, they changed ordinances, broke covenants, and rebelled against God (see Isaiah 24:5; Ezekiel 2:3).

Similarities among religions indicate they each have remnants of the true gospel in ancient times. Differences, according to Elder Neal A. Maxwell, indicate there was a "fragmentation, diffusion, and distortion... to a wide variety of world religions—Christian and non-Christian."[17] Each of these religions kept various tenets of truth they had acquired from God's revealed gospel anciently, but they allowed the teachings of man to take them in a variety of erroneous directions.

Deviation from True Doctrine

Just like world religions, this deviation from true doctrine is also seen in Christianity through the apostasy that occurred after the death of Christ and the apostles. Historical documents clearly show how and why this apostasy took place. Researchers believe the simple truths taught by Jesus and his apostles initially became perverted because of the Hellenistic influence of ancient Greece. Even before the apostles were all killed, Paul recorded how early followers of Christ were beginning to be deceived by false teachers (see Galatians 1:6-9).

According to American writer, historian, and philosopher Will Durant, "The Greek language, having reigned for centuries over philosophy, became the vehicle of Christian literature and ritual .... Christianity did not destroy paganism; it adopted it."[18] Eventually, the dominating, philosophical traditions of the Greeks replaced Christianity's trust and confidence in revelation.

Joseph Fielding McConkie, BYU professor of ancient scripture, described well what early Christians were up against.

> "The Christian convert stood alone, overshadowed by the influence of the Jewish temple on the one hand and the Greek academy on the other. From the temple came the Judaizers, who wouldn't let go of their traditions; while from the academy came those indoctrinated in the monotheism of Plato. As if that were not enough, there were also the Gnostics … straining everything through the veil of mysticism. And so the newly converted, wanting neither to give offense nor to appear as fools, sought common ground and a spirit of conciliation. In so doing, they modified the Christian message until it passed as it were into a new dialect, one that would have been very strange to the ear of those initially commissioned by Christ."[19]

One by one, the apostles were killed, and leadership in the Church completely deteriorated, opening the door ever wider for outside influences to take over. This loss of the true gospel plunged the world into the Dark Ages, which lasted about 1,000 years from the fall of the Roman Empire to the Renaissance, where all nations fell into illiteracy and ignorance. James E. Talmage recorded, "There were numerous sects and parties, cults and schools, each advocating rival theories as to the constitution of the soul, the essence of sin, the nature of Deity, and a multitude of other mysteries. The Christians were soon embroiled in endless controversies among themselves."[20] During this time, Constantine, who became the emperor of Rome in AD 306, converted to Christianity and furthered the falling away by setting up man-made creeds which established false tenets. Unnecessary pomp and ritual were added to Christian worship until any resemblance to the original Church was completely gone.

But reformers, beginning in 1517 with Martin Luther, a Catholic monk, revolted against the papal Church and fought to bring Christianity back to its roots. He was joined in this Reformation movement over the next 300 years by others including Phillip Melanchthon, Ulrich Zwingli, John Calvin, and John Wesley. Many played a major role in reforming doctrines of the Catholic Church, which dominated Christian theology. This reformation opened the way for the restoration of God's true gospel through the boy prophet, Joseph Smith. It was truly miraculous that his simple prayer concerning the correct church to join would lead to the re-establishment of sacred truths that had been lost for centuries.

Because of this restoration of all things, we know that God has not yet, and never will abandon us. He knew the nature of his children, along with the power of evil to confuse and deceive, would require divine intervention along the way. And so he continues to work with us through prophets and personal revelation to teach truth. We are human, which means being fallible and easily deceived, quick to jump to conclusions, and prone to mistakes. It was inevitable that religions in the numbers we have would germinate from some small deviation from the truth, and grow into entire theological movements.

Look at any mass movement in history, for good or ill, and you'll find it began with someone, usually dissatisfied in some way with a social or theological norm. This person then brought ideological changes into the milieu of thought and perpetuated them until they caught on. Luther, Calvin, Lincoln, Gandhi, Trotski, Lenon, Hitler, Churchill, and Nehru are a few that come to mind. Obviously, not all of them were being inspired by God and the movements of those who weren't eventually faded away, while the movements of those who were had long lasting influence for the good of society.

This, however, leaves us to wonder whether God also speaks to other people claiming to be prophets in other religions. Are their visions and revelations to be totally discounted or do they contain truth as well? A good way to answer this question is through an examination of Mohammed, the proclaimed prophet of Islam. Joseph Smith and Mohammed, who both brought forth mass movements in theology, have been compared to each other because they both saw flaws in Christianity. An examination of both will help us understand how this led to each of them reporting revelations and seeing angels designed to bring Christianity back to its original form.

Both Islam and Mormonism believe Christianity was a true religion established by Jesus Christ, but went astray over time and eventually moved beyond any possibility for reform. So, each sees its founder as a prophet who was chosen by God to once again bring forth the true faith. But their views of Jesus Christ differ in that Mormons say he is the promised Messiah while Muslims agree that Jesus was a prophet, but not the Son of God or divine in any way. They believe he was just a mortal man.

It is reasonable to accept the various truths inherent in Islam, and that on some level, Mohammad's revelations actually occurred. Church General Authority B. H. Roberts said, "While the Church of Jesus Christ of Latter-day Saints is established for the instruction of men; and is one of God's instrumentalities for making known the truth yet he is not limited to that institution for such purposes, neither in time nor place. God raises up wise men and prophets here and there among all the children of men, of their own tongue and nationality, speaking to them through means that they can comprehend; *not always giving a fullness ... of the gospel of Jesus Christ; but always giving that measure of truth that the people are prepared to receive*".[21]

While truth is truth no matter where it comes from, sometimes it gets diluted or changed when mingled with the ideas of man. There are many similar teachings within Islam and Mormonism and by extension, Christianity, indicating that some revealed truths were correctly received and retained in the Muslim world. But as with the founding fathers, who were inspired by God when they drafted the U.S. Constitution, inspiration is not always part of every thought or action by those same people all the time. Even modern-day prophets in the Church recognize the difference between when they speak by revelation from God and when they speak as men. Mohammad, and other visionaries who started religions throughout history, certainly had some of the truth. But over all, they were probably proceeding on imprecise vision interpretations, cultural influences and traditions, and lack of true continuous revelation that left them to their own devices.

This must be exactly how God wanted it to be or he would reveal more of the answers in greater detail to his chosen prophets. It would be so easy for God to just tell his prophets how the creation of the universe and of man, for instance, was actually accomplished and avoid all the angst and confusion about it. But he hasn't seen fit to do that, and so we are left to seek our own way through prayer, study, and faith, based on what he has revealed.

Bible Stories Appear in Other Cultures

Hugh Nibley, BYU professor of biblical and Mormon scripture, found that preliminary studies of each of the world's great empires show "that they had more or less intimate ties with the great Classical and Middle Eastern civilizations. Even the findings of archaeology in the great civilization of China, which is thousands of years older than any Western culture, had its origins among the people of Genesis."[22] Every ancient culture is rooted in the Bible, he said, and the same can be said of any ancient text, suggesting that all fields of study converge on the oneness of the ancient world. The interrelationships between ancient writings are so close, scientists proclaim that all ancient literature, "sacred and profane, Jew and Gentile, may be regarded and must be read as a single great book."[23]

President Joseph F. Smith said certain laws and rites were "carried by the posterity of Adam into all lands, and continued with them, more or less pure, to the flood, and through Noah .... to those who succeeded him, spreading out into all nations and countries. ... What wonder, then, that we should find relics of Christianity, so to speak, among ... nations who know not Christ, and whose histories date back ... beyond the flood, independent of and apart from the records of the Bible."[24]

As we understand our shared beginnings, we are compelled to unravel fact from fiction among all our stories, histories, and theologies. Nibley said the common ground on which all cultures and religions meet and fuse is *ritual*.

"This should have been clear from the outset, since myths and legends are innumerable while the rites and ordinances found throughout the world are surprisingly few and uniform, making it quite apparent that it is the stories that are invented—the rites are always there."[25] He went on to say, "So when the ancient myths from all over the world show us the same situations and same adventures and monsters recurring again and again, we may look upon this endless repetition not as discrediting the historicity of those events and situations but as confirming it. These myths tell about such things happening because that was the type of thing that did happen, the ritual nature of the event guaranteed that it should happen not once but over and over again."[26]

Language is no different. Scholars now believe all the languages of the world have retained recognizable ties to a parent language from which they separated long ago. In the mid-nineteenth century, the folklorists were beginning to notice that the same myths and legends turned up everywhere in the old and new worlds, and philologists were discovering the same thing about languages. Linguists Charles Hockett and Robert Asher declared that "phonological systems [of all the languages of the world] show much less variety than could easily be invented by any linguist working with pencil and paper."[27]

Detractors of Christianity and religion, in general, sometimes argue that many Bible stories were copied from earlier myths and legends in religious and pagan history. A look at a few of these stories will help to see if this charge rings true. Keep in mind that even though the examples given here are presented to rebuff the charges of skeptics who cry plagiarism, there are indeed, many variations on Bible stories seen throughout world cultures and religions which support the concept that we all came from the same biblical roots.

Noah's ark. The story of Noah's ark and the great flood has been said by some to be an adaptation of *The Epic of Gilgamesh*, a poem from Mesopotamia. It describes a man who dreamed that because God was going to send a flood to destroy the wicked, he was to build a large boat, put animals on it, and survive the flood. The poem was discovered on clay tablets in Iraq in 1853, from the Nineveh library of the last great Assyrian king, Ashurbanipal, who reigned in the 7th century BC. Historians date these tablet fragments from about 2,600 years before Christ, which roughly corresponds with when the first pyramids in Egypt were built. Aside from that, none of these tablets actually pre-dates the events in the writings of Moses, who authored the Bible's first five books. Because Noah's story predates all others by at least a millennium, the details in Gilgamesh are borrowed from the biblical record, not the other way around.

Furthermore, translations of Gilgamesh mention a flood in just a handful of places where occurrences of the English word are found in the documents. When taken in what little context there is in these tablets, most of these details bear no resemblance to anything in the Genesis account of Noah.[28] And because the Jews were meticulous in passing down information generationally, Genesis is seen by many as far more historical than *The Epic of Gilgamesh*, which is viewed mainly by scholars as a work of mythology.[29]

Moses in a basket. Detractors have said the story of Moses as a baby was lifted from a pagan myth about Sargon, a Semitic Akkadian emperor, who was placed in a reed basket and sent down the river by his mother. Sargon was rescued by Aqqi, who then adopted him as his own son. That sounds a lot like the story of Moses in Exodus 2, and since Sargon lived about 800 years before Moses was born, it looks like a good case of plagiarism in the Bible. But it's not. What we know about Sargon comes from legends written many hundreds of years after his death. Sargon's story of being placed in a basket and sent down a river comes from two 7th century BC cuneiform tablets from the library of the same Assyrian king that contained the story of Gilgamesh. It was written hundreds of years after the book of Exodus indicating the borrowing of the story to be the other way around.[30]

Jesus Christ. There is also a multitude of erroneous information claiming the story of Jesus was stolen from first century pagan myths or other religions that were present long before the life of Jesus. Right away we need to remember that the Bible is loaded with instances where prophets foretold the coming of the Messiah as well as a mountain of rich symbolism that accomplishes the same thing. The crucifixion of Jesus was even foretold in Psalm 22:16-18 about 1,000 years before his birth and long before this type of execution was even used. Symbols include such events as Abraham's sacrifice of Isaac, the Passover meal of Exodus 12, and the mission of Joseph who was sold into Egypt. Jesus' coming was long predicted and so available for the plucking of any other group who wished to borrow it.

Take Hinduism's Krishna, for instance. Almost every written parallel between Krishna and Jesus comes from Kersey Graves, a 19th century author who thought Christianity came from pagan myths. Scholars have shown his works to be false for years, but people are still swayed by his arguments. What they don't understand is the assertions of Graves and other critics can be easily disproved through a simple comparison of the Bible with Hindu texts. The facts tell us that Krishna's life does not compare to the life of Jesus at all.[31] Here are the facts:

- Critics claim Krishna was born to the virgin Maia, but Krishna's parents already had seven children before him.
- Critics claim a tyrannical ruler issued a decree to kill all infant males prior to Krishna's birth, but the Hindu legend states only Krishna's brothers were targeted, not every male child in the land under two as with Jesus.
- Critics say Krishna was born in a stable, but Hindu texts say he was born in a prison.
- Though critics claim Krishna was crucified, this is mentioned nowhere within the Hindu texts which say he was accidentally shot in the foot by a hunter's arrow. Skeptics really try to stretch this one by claiming the arrow that shot Krishna impaled him to a tree, thus crucifying him.
- There is no evidence to back up claims that Krishna descended into the grave for three days and afterward appeared before many witnesses. Instead, the actual account says Krishna immediately returns to life and afterwards speaks only to a single hunter.[32]

Likewise, according to Egyptian mythology, the life of Horus, the sky, sun, and moon god represented by a man with the head of a falcon, is said to be the source of the story of Jesus. The recorded facts do not affirm this.

- In the two different accounts of Horus' birth, neither depicts a virgin birth.
- Like Jesus, Horus had twelve disciples, but the similarity comes to an abrupt halt when we learn that Horus' disciples were actually the twelve signs of the zodiac. Jesus' disciples were actual men whose lives are recorded by historians.
- Horus is never said to have been crucified, and there is nothing remotely in Egyptian texts that speaks of a resurrection. There is, however, an account of Horus' mother piecing back together the dead body of Horus' father and resurrecting him so she can conceive an heir to avenge his death.[33]

For doubters who have heard about these false claims of literary bootlegging, be aware that most people can make a case for anything by taking bits and pieces of some truth in history and stretching it to appear to fit into anything they want. It's done all the time in courtrooms, advertising, storytelling, excuse making, and in the formation of scientific theories, to name a few. On the other hand, if all similar religious stories sprang from the ancient progeny of Adam as depicted in the Bible, and were carried off with migrating groups throughout history, changed and culturally assimilated along the way, then their very existence is evidence of one true God. When we see similarities in religious stories and doctrines, it's a time to rejoice not reject, because they serve as a connection to the God and Father of us all.

Scripture Stories: Fact or Fiction

When discerning scripture, there is a basic question that must be answered before true understanding can begin: Is the scripture or passage of scripture figurative or literal? This same question was asked by the brothers of Nephi after he read to them what we know as chapters 48 and 49 of Isaiah. Joseph McConkie and Robert Millet, LDS authors and BYU professors of ancient scripture wrote:

> "Short of the actual destruction of scriptural records, Satan has no more effective way of opposing scriptural truths than confusing the figurative and the literal. Like potter's clay, some simply mold the scriptures into the likeness of the theories of men. Conversely, by making scriptural metaphors literal, the most marvelous truths are distorted beyond recognition. The bread and wine of the sacrament are an obvious illustration. By eating the sacramental bread, do we literally eat the body of Christ? And in drinking the wine or water in a sacramental ritual are we figuratively drinking Christ's blood, or doing so literally, as some suppose? Such is the issue, ever present in scriptural interpretation: Is the passage, the story, or the book to be interpreted figuratively or literally?"[34]

The Church's official website states:

> "There is a broad range of approaches within the vast mosaic of biblical interpretation. For example, biblical inerrancy maintains that the Bible is without error and contradiction; biblical infallibility holds that the Bible is free from errors regarding faith and practice but not necessarily science or history; biblical literalism requires a literal interpretation of events and teachings in the Bible and generally discounts allegory and metaphor; and the 'Bible as literature' educational approach extols the literary qualities of the Bible but disregards its miraculous elements. The Church does not strictly subscribe to any of these interpretive approaches. Rather, in the words of Joseph Smith, it regards the Bible to be the word of God, 'as far as it is translated correctly'" (8th Article of Faith).[35]

As with other topics such as the earth's origin and the theory of evolution, the Church has not declared any particular doctrine on the matter of biblical allegory, although many Church leaders have made statements about it. We are left to find a balance in our own minds and hearts between some of the astounding and seemingly impossible stories found in holy writ and our faith and understanding that with God, all things are possible. But if we look at the overall purpose of the Bible permeating through every teaching and story, whether literal or allegorical, we conclude that its contents provide what God intended: A pathway to Jesus Christ.

Apostle M. Russell Ballard, called the Bible the bedrock of all Christianity and one of the pillars of the Church. Furthermore, he described the preservation of the Bible's 4,000 years of sacred and secular history as a miracle, in and of itself, one that has turned people to Christ for centuries. [36]

Taking these stories as literal or allegorical really doesn't matter if we, in fact, gain the insight from them that was intended. Some stories, like Jonah in the belly of the whale, Moses' story of the burning bush, Lot's wife turning into a pillar of salt, or the afflictions of Job, are not events that impacted the world or portions of it in any substantial way and so are of subjective interest. Other stories, such as Adam and Eve, Noah and the flood, the Tower of Babel, Abraham and his children and grandchildren, or even the life, death, and resurrection of Jesus, himself, do have ramifications for us on a global scale. A better understanding of the truthfulness of these accounts can be critical in our overall comprehension of the world.

Adam and Eve and the Garden of Eden

LDS Church leaders have said that while the events that took place in the Garden of Eden were real and did occur, many elements of the story are allegorical and not literal.

- Brigham Young said, "When you tell me that father Adam was made as we make adobes from the earth, you tell me what I deem an idle tale …. There is no such thing in all the eternities where the Gods dwell."[37]

- Parley P. Pratt said, "Man, molded from the earth, as a brick! A woman, manufactured from a rib .... O man! When wilt thou cease to be a child in knowledge?"[38]
- Spencer W. Kimball said, "The story of the rib, of course, is figurative."[39]
- Boyd K. Packer referred to the creation recorded in Genesis, the Book of Mormon, Moses, Abraham, and in the temple endowment this way: "We are told it is figurative insofar as the man and the woman are concerned."[40]
- Bruce R. McConkie also referred to Eve coming from the rib of Adam as being written "in figurative language."[41]
- McConkie also said, "Again the account is speaking figuratively in Moses 3:16-17. What is meant by partaking of the fruit of the tree of knowledge of good and evil is that our first parents complied with whatever laws were involved so that their bodies would change from their state of paradisiacal immortality to a state of natural mortality."[42]
- John A. Widstoe taught, "The statement that man was made from the dust of the earth is merely figurative. Likewise the statement that God breathed into man the breath of life is figurative and refers to the existence of the spirit within the body."[43]

The story of Adam and Eve was plainly meant to teach us about God's intentions for humanity, not about cosmology, anthropology, or biology. The language and imagery are highly symbolic to teach us who we are and how we need to evolve in our growth and knowledge to fulfill God's purposes. The biblical and Moses accounts of the temptation with the fruit is a symbolic picture of the first time a human, alive both spiritually and physically, responded to the moral principles within a divine law.

While the Garden of Eden to Mormons is a real place, in part because we believe that a resurrected Adam will return to the earth to fulfill a major role at Adam-ondi-ahman, it is also used as a parable or symbol. Examples elsewhere in the Bible clearly depict the Garden of Eden that way. In Ezekiel, we are told that Assyria is a tree in the Garden of Eden: Assyria "was a cedar in

Lebanon with fair branches and with a shadowing shroud, and of an high stature; and his top was among the thick boughs. The waters made him great ... and under his shadow dwelt all great nations .... Nor any tree in the Garden of God was like unto him in his beauty .... All the trees of Eden that were in the garden of God envied him" (Ezekiel 31:3-9). Because Assyria is not literally a tree, its reference to the Garden of Eden makes it a symbolic story, with the trees in the garden becoming symbols of the various nations God created.[44]

Also in Ezekiel, God tells the king of Tyrus, "Thou hast been in Eden, the garden of God" (Ezekiel 28:12-13). The king wasn't literally in Eden, indicating it is a symbol for wisdom and perfection. In addition, the Tree of Life is mentioned many times in the scriptures but is always spoken of as a symbol of wisdom and understanding (Proverbs 3: 8, 13). Gardens, trees, and fruit are common in the scriptures as symbols of knowledge sprouting up in the souls and minds of mankind. While Eden is a literal place, to Mormons it is also a garden of the soul, a spiritual state in which righteousness can grow in a person's mind. The Garden of Eden is rich in symbolism and like man, is both spiritual and physical.[45]

Noah and the Flood

Although the story of the flood should be viewed as real, we need to give space for the possibility that it didn't occur the way mainline Christianity says it did. Literalists believe the flood covered the entire planet but a look at a few word meanings provides a different viewpoint. In Hebrew, the word 'earth' means 'land,' and not 'planet' or 'world.' Even though in Genesis 4:14 we read that Cain complains of being driven "from the face of the earth," he didn't really go to a different planet but to a different land. In Hebrew, the word *erets* means land. Israel today is called *Erets Yisrael*, the Land of Israel.[46]

Taken literally, when the Bible says that Noah took two of every 'kind' of animal into the ark, it would have included dangerous carnivores, making such a journey virtually impossible. The Hebrew says two of every *behema*; which means a dumb or mute animal like an ox, a cow, etc., or in other words, a domesticated animal. It doesn't say that two or every *Beiyr* [wild beast] was taken aboard the ark. A better interpretation of the flood is that yes, it happened, but it was in a local area as the original Hebrew seems to indicate. The flood covered the entire land where Noah lived, not the entire earth. Two of every domesticated animal and fowl was aboard the ark because they had to take with them what they needed for food, clothing, and hunting.

This interpretation of the account easily solves some of the problems inherent in the literalist view such as how only 15 cubits of water, about 23 feet, could cover the whole earth as indicated in the Bible when the world's mountains are all unequal. Also, if all the animals after the flood came from the ark, why are there indigenous animals on all the continents?[47]

Another consideration is if the amount of fossil carbon in the earth's crust constitutes the remains of all the organisms that lived together when they were decimated by the flood, there would not be enough room on the earth to hold them. LDS Author Frank Salisbury calculated the living flesh would amount to over a thousand tons per square meter of the earth's surface. We know that calcium from organisms need to be deposited gradually over long periods of time leaving a universal flood next to impossible.[48]

A look at nature in the Mesopotamia area, now southern Iraq, where the Tigris and Euphrates rivers join, shows that this region is prone to severe flooding. There is geographical evidence that flooding actually caused some major disruptions to ancient communities of people, who from their limited perspective could have thought a local deluge, appeared to be global.[49]

Tower of Babel

In the story of the Tower of Babel, we learn in Genesis that all the people spoke with "one language" until God intervened to confuse the languages so they could "not understand one another's speech" (Genesis 11:6-7). We also learn in the Book of Ether that the Jaredite nation began when the tower was built and the language of the people was "confounded." After the brother of Jared prayed that God would "not confound us that we may not understand our words" (Ether 1:33), the Jaredites were spared this language punishment. Literalists would say there was an instantaneous change from one language to many among the people, and that the event happened exactly as recorded. But another approach is that the event did happen, but with the understanding that "confound" means to "mix together" or "pour together," according to Hugh Nibley. "The only way we can fail to understand our own words is to have words that are actually ours change their meaning among us," and that would have to happen over time.[50]

Another possibility is that the confounding of tongues is a myth used to explain the reasons why something exists—in this case, the divergence of languages. Such myths are actually legends that represent "types" or models. They may exaggerate a real event, squeeze several events into one story, or make false assumptions from a sketchy understanding of the facts. It's also true that ancient societies and their prophets wrote down their stories according to their own understanding of the world around them.[51]

Within Judaism, the words *Babylon* or *Mesopotamia* were used to represent the wicked, and the word *Zion* to represent the righteous. The mythological erecting of a tower or temple to imitate God-like power would represent a false priesthood and a false temple of wicked people who opposed the true priesthood of God.[52] The fact that Ether also spoke of such a tower in the Book of Mormon from which the Jaredite nation sprang, tells us there were multi-generations of people [25 by some counts] handing down this very ancient story. Moroni, who along with Mormon abridged the story, would have been familiar with the brass plates where the story of the great tower was also recorded. Church commentator Michael Ash explained, "Regardless of whether he [Moroni] abridged Mosiah the younger's translation of Ether or if he retranslated and redacted Ether's original record, it's possible that he edited the text to fit his view and understanding of Jaredite origins from an Old Testament perspective."[53]

The Message in the Story

When prophets of our day reference such stories as these, they only emphasize the messages they contain, not whether they are figurative or literal. If this account in Ether and other stories in both the Book of Mormon and the Bible are inspired but figurative, they don't invalidate the teachings of the Church in the least.

A mythological approach to the tower story, for example, doesn't mean that the Nephites were fictitious because ancient narratives and scriptures can contain myths as well as actual events. Remember Brigham Young called the creation of Adam from dust as a "baby stor(y)," and President Kimball said the creation of Eve from the rib of Adam was figurative. Because the Book of Mormon and the Bible were written by the ancients, both will include elements of ancient mythology.[54] But here again we can appreciate a Church built upon the agency of man to choose to believe the ideas that build his faith best in the absence of revealed doctrine.

Some non-LDS Bible scholars, such as Harvard and Bar Ilan University Israel Professor James Krugel, say many of the stories in the first part of Genesis had no religious significance originally. He called stories such as the Garden of Eden, Cain and Abel, and those associated with the wanderings of Abraham, "etiological legends," which means they were used as explanations of how "things" originated. Such things include why men must labor for their food, why childbearing brings women pain, why there are no legs on snakes, how the Kenites [a nomadic clan of coppersmiths and metalworkers] got their name and came to live among the Israelites, and how names were given to certain wells and rock formations. Stories in Genesis answer such questions through etiological legends, which are also found in all societies throughout the ages.[55] Basically, what he is saying is that stories in the Bible had nothing to do with any theological tenet or moral until later writers included them in scripture.

But there's a major problem with this thesis, according to BYU English Professor and folklorist Eric Eliason. He explained,

> "The problem with [Krugel's] contention is not that Bible stories do not have an etiological component or likely oral narrative antecedents; they do. The problem is that Krugel seems unaware of how the last few decades of scholarship have qualitatively changed how folklorists see the significance of etiological legends .... Etiological stories are *not* primarily about how something came to be. By looking closely at the various cultures that tell them, folklorists have discovered that the etiological nature of the story is usually

secondary to its main purpose—not only secondary but actually in service to the main purpose of the story, which is moral teaching after all. But the moral teaching, in the tradition of the best oral literature, is often subtle, oblique, nondidactic, and laid out by a trickster's negative example."[56]

Other scholars such as Keith Basso and Barre Toelken suggest that etiological legends, rich in symbolism, were passed on *primarily* for their moral content and to serve as reminders of that teaching to those who know the stories.[57] The Bible is rich in such narratives. Eliason suggested that "if we want to recover the original meaning and purpose of biblical stories with etiological motifs, it is probably best not to discount the story of the serpent in the Garden of Eden as a morally insignificant tale of origins. Rather, every time we see a snake in all its slithery legless glory we might be prompted to remember the importance of resisting temptation and not seeking to thwart the plans of God."[58]

Book of Mormon Authenticity and Symbolism

Mormons are drawn to physical evidences of the Book of Mormon's authenticity by LDS and non-LDS scholars, because they enjoy adding physical evidences to the testimonies they already acquired through the Holy Ghost. They also enjoy having answers and evidence for critics who have nipped at the Church's heels since its inception. Here is just a tiny sampling of the many physical evidences scholars have discovered to support the truthfulness of the Book of Mormon:

1. There are elaborate examples of ancient Hebrew poetic forms and writing styles found in the Book of Mormon, the Bible, and other ancient Middle Eastern works. These include:

    - Parallelism, the use of word pairs that are either synonymous or antithetical to each other, is a literary structure found in both the Book of Mormon and Hebrew poetry.

Book of Mormon example of parallelism:
A – like as one crying from the *dead*, yea,
    B – even as one speaking out of the *dust?*
(Moroni 10:27)

Bible example of parallelism:
A – Why do the heathen *rage*,
    B – and the people imagine a *vain thing?*
(Psalm 2:1)

- The presence of Chiasmus, a form of inverted parallelism, in the Book of Mormon is strong evidence that its writers knew of and used this ancient Semitic literary tradition, something Joseph Smith could not have known. Chiasmus has only come to light in the last 100 years and is still not very well known even among educated people today.[59]

Book of Mormon example of Chiasmus:
A – I will visit them
    B – in my *anger,*
    B – yea, in my *fierce anger*
A – will I visit them (Mosiah 12:1).

Bible example of Chiasmus:
A – He that *findeth* his life
    B – shall *lose* it
    B – and he that *loseth* his life for my sake
A – shall *find* it (Matthew 10:39).

2. Physical evidence that links the Old with the New World has been found through discoveries of other ancient texts.

- The Dead Sea Scrolls, dating from approximately 250 BC to AD 68 and written in Hebrew or Aramaic on parchment, chronicled an ancient sect called the Essenes. Discovered in 1947, at Qumran, the scrolls show similarities between these people and those in the Book of Mormon. Writings indicate the Essenes believed they were a covenant people, strictly observed the Law of Moses, believed in the coming of the Messiah, understood the importance of the temple, had priesthood leaders among them, trusted in prophesy and revelation, and believed there was a war between good and evil going on around them.[60]

- The Lachish letters, discovered in 1935 and written in Hebrew, parallel Lehi's story in form, style, subject matter, and in the mention of specific names and events. Other striking parallels also are found in the comparison of early Christian writings called "Forty-Day Literature," and Christ's post-resurrection mission to the New World in 3 Nephi.[61]

- The Pseudepigrapha records a tradition involving Jews leaving Jerusalem in Jeremiah's and Lehi's time, and traveling across the ocean to a land of promise.[62]

3. Writings on metal plates hidden in stone boxes or other containers have been found all throughout the Near and Middle East, supporting Joseph Smith's account of the gold plates.

- Many such records were engraved on gold, silver, bronze, copper, and tin plates, hidden away, and preserved for future generations. Some examples include the 1926 discovery of an inscription of Darius on gold and silver plates hidden in a foundation between square hewn stones; the 1933 discovery at Persepolis of stone boxes with square inscribed plates of gold and silver buried in the ground beneath a building corner; a copper scroll included in the Dead Sea Scrolls stored in clay pots.[63]

- Orphic bronze plates found in Greece describe the fate of the soul in the spirit world. Also, a gold plate was found on the Lower Rhine at the site of a Roman camp containing names and incantations identified as Egyptian, Jewish, Phoenician, and Babylonian.[64]

4. An ancient trade route across the Arabian Peninsula accurately, and in impressive detail, matches the Book of Mormon account of Lehi's flight into the wilderness.

- Researchers discovered Lehi's actual route in an ancient merchant trail known as the Frankincense Trail. It runs from Damascus to Salalah in Oman, and goes on to Aquaba on the Red Sea. This route would absolutely be able to provide the food, water, wood for shipbuilding, bow making materials, and iron ore in the mountains that Lehi's group is recorded to have used on their journey. Comparisons in topography, climate, and descriptions of specific places like Bountiful (1 Nephi 17:5) and Nahom (1 Nephi 16:34), where they all dwelt for a time, have been verified along this trail.[65]

- Experts have discovered that neither of the libraries available to Joseph Smith in 1830—the Manchester library and the Dartmouth College library—had works dealing in any detail with Arabia. In fact, there was simply not enough available in print anywhere in the 1820s, for Joseph to have produced such accurate and confirmed details of this Arabian journey.[66]

5. Statistical techniques that detect author identification called stylometry, confirms Joseph Smith's claim that the Book of Mormon was written by more than two dozen separate individuals and not any writer from the 19th century, as critics have claimed.[67]

- This conclusion is drawn from four major stylometric analyses of the Book of Mormon conducted since 1980. Each of these studies applied stylometry in different ways to test for Book of Mormon authorship, and each came away with the same conclusion. They determined that Joseph Smith, Sidney Rigdon, and Oliver Cowdrey did not write the Book of Mormon. They also confirmed the two dozen ancient individuals who did write it, by using "word prints" that show unique characteristics in each of their writing styles.[68]

The list of physical evidences goes on and on, and can be gleaned in many scholarly works available to the public. B.H. Roberts, who spent a lifetime studying the Book of Mormon and pursuing answers to the accusations of critics said, "We who accept it as a revelation from God have every reason to believe that it will endure every test; and the more thoroughly it is investigated, the greater shall be its ultimate triumph."[69]

Interestingly, the Book of Mormon is much easier to accept at a literal level than the Bible, because it was not subjected to the erroneous translations and compilations of those who put the Bible together. But the Book of Mormon, too, contains symbolism and allegory, which in fact, is a hallmark of ancient writings, and so helps support it as an authentic ancient text.

There are a number of figurative stories within the text, such as the narrative of the Tree of Life in Lehi's dream. It is rich in allegory and symbolism and actually finds root in the Egyptian redemption ritual for the dead. Elements in the dream are a symbolic portrayal of the Christian message of redemption for mankind.[70] From Nephi, who then has his own vision explaining his father's dream, we learn a number of interpretations such as the "fountain of filthy water" symbolizing "the depths of hell" (1 Nephi 12:16). Likewise, we learn the symbolic meanings of the rod of iron, the great building, and the dark mists.

But this account and others, like the allegory of the Olive Tree in Jacob 5, are written by their authors specifically as allegories, and so there's no guesswork on our part about whether they are literal or figurative. But other chronicles are left for us to determine. Some commentators have suggested that stories about "deliverance" permeate the Book of Mormon which they say is actually the theme of the entire book of scripture. Look at stories such as Nephi and his brothers' deliverance from Laban (1 Nephi 4:3); Alma's rebuke to the people of Ammonihah for failing to recognize how the Lord had delivered them (Alma 9:10); Helaman's 2,000 stripling warriors who were delivered from their enemies in battle. Such stories are symbolic of the greatest deliverance of all: The redemption of every living soul through our Savior, Jesus Christ.[71] That message can be found in nearly every story or event described in the Book of Mormon.

Other commentators point out that the many group journeys recorded among the Nephites are meant to represent our individual sojourns on Earth. These include Lehi and Nephi's exodus to the promise land, Alma the elder's journey from the land of Nephi to the land of Zarahemla, Ammon and King Limhi's trek to Zarahemla, and the Jaredite crossing to the New World. All of these stories, like the exodus stories in the Bible, were included because of the principles they teach through embedded symbolism. They teach us to have faith during trials, rely upon the Lord, understand the consequences of not listening, and appreciate the atonement of Christ in our lives.[72]

The Book of Mormon is filled to the brim with stories of death, destruction, wars, violence, and adversity which sounds a lot like today's world. Because Moroni told us his words were for the people of our day who were shown to him in vision (Mormon 8:34-35), it becomes clear the focus of the record is for us. Their stories of battle and triumph symbolize the destruction of our souls when we fail to overcome our weaknesses or obey God's commandments. Strategies for winning battles orchestrated by prophets and leaders, including their defenses and fortifications, represent principles that if followed, can strengthen individuals and families during adverse conditions.[73]

Does this mean these accounts did not happen? No. It means the way these historical events were presented was through the use of shadows, symbols, and types to instill in us messages of help and motivation to live as God would have us live. We must remember that the purpose of the Book of Mormon was not historical but rather for "the convincing of the Jew and Gentile that Jesus is the Christ, the Eternal God, manifesting himself unto all nations."[74]

There are volumes of books in our libraries and bookstores that delve deeply into every aspect of the Book of Mormon—from physical evidences of its authenticity to the sacred messages nestled within its narratives and symbols—providing a wealth of knowledge about this ancient text. I encourage people everywhere to do the research and study, and feel for themselves why Joseph Smith said, "the Book of Mormon was the most correct book of any on Earth, and the keystone of our religion, and a man would get nearer to God by abiding by its precepts, than by any other book."[75]

Gospel Globalization

When you study the history of religion with the understanding that all religions are joined at the hip through Adamic beginnings, you begin to see a pattern regarding the history of the earth and God's plan of salvation. The inhabitants of the earth began from a single source, grew in both their righteous and unrighteous choices, scattered to the four quarters, and engaged in their own often times borrowed and changed theologies, rituals, and customs. During this time, the true gospel of Jesus Christ, as revealed and taught by prophets, was upon the earth for people to embrace or adulterate as they saw fit. This occurred unless wickedness became so great the gospel was withdrawn altogether, such as during the Dark Ages.

God has always been in our corners trying to help his precious offspring choose the right through prophets, the Holy Ghost, and the light of Christ, so as to accomplish his purpose of bringing to pass "the immortality and eternal life of man" (Moses 1:39). He knew what he was up against because he knew the nature of his children to yield to temptation and "every wind of doctrine" (Ephesians 4:14). He knew their innate compulsions to search for supernatural answers to life would drive them to worship things and ideas contrary to his gospel. He knew it all, and yet he let it happen because we needed to gain physical bodies and experience the pain, sorrow, joy, learning, and growth of our second estate.

And now we've come full circle. With the restoration of the gospel of Jesus Christ in its fulness during this last dispensation, there's a ratcheting up of God's efforts to save his children. While wickedness is heavy around us, so are the power of the priesthood and the ubiquitous influence of the Holy Ghost. The kingdom of God in the form of the Church of Jesus Christ of Latter-day Saints, with its marching orders from God, himself, is rolling forth as never before to unite a historically divided world and bring them back to a true understanding of Deity.

Joseph Smith once wrote, "The Standard of Truth has been erected; no unhallowed hand can stop the work from progressing; persecutions may rage, mobs may combine, armies may assemble, calumny may defame, but the truth of God will go forth boldly, nobly, and independent, till it has penetrated every continent, visited every clime, swept every country, and sounded in every ear, till the purposes of God shall be accomplished, and the Great Jehovah shall say the work is done."[76]

When the Church was first organized in 1830, there were a mere six members within the ranks. Despite the communication inadequacies of Joseph's day, the Saints took seriously the words of their prophet, as well as other prophets like Daniel, that God would "set up a kingdom, which shall never be destroyed" (Daniel 2:44), but would roll forth and fill "the whole earth" (see Daniel 2:26-44). The Church's website records:

> "It took 117 years, until 1947, for the Church to grow from the initial six members to one million. Missionaries

were a feature of the Church from its earliest days, fanning out to Native American lands, to Canada and, in 1837, beyond the North American continent to England. Not long after, missionaries were working on the European continent and as far away as India and the Pacific Islands.

"The two-million-member mark was reached just 16 years later, in 1963, and the three-million mark in eight years more. This accelerating growth pattern has continued with about a million new members now being added every three years or less. Growth consists both of convert baptisms and natural growth through the birth of children. Church membership today is nearing 15 million."[77]

As never before in the history of the earth, man's ability to accomplish Joseph's and Daniel's prophetic words are within our grasp. Today's technology of instantaneous communication has made it possible to accelerate the preaching of the gospel and the gathering of Israel. We live in a world of cyberspace with the Internet, satellites, cell phones, video and music downloading, social networks, text messaging, podcasts, and blogs. New Media is facilitating immediate dialogue in every corner of the world on all subjects, including religion, among all people. And the Church is taking full advantage of it. This kind of gospel globalization was never possible before in human history. So how are we doing? What are we doing to fulfill Joseph's divine directive?

We're doing it through divinely called apostles and prophets, through 80,000 missionaries teaching in 405 missions all over the world, through the lifting of language barriers where Church materials are now printed in 177 languages; through respectful relations with world governments to permit our entrance and increase our stature; through the building of meetinghouses and temples [141 in operation, under construction, or announced]; through family history centers [4,689 in 128 countries]; through humanitarian aid in 179 countries; through 10,138 welfare service missionaries who help with food acquisition, employment, counseling, adoption services, addiction recovery support groups, and resources for social, emotional, and spiritual challenges. Communication and participation in the world is the key to the process and is better accomplished through the inspired technology developed in these latter days.

Conclusion

Just before the turn of the 21st Century, Gordon B. Hinckley spoke of the opportunities we have to accomplish God's work in this uniquely enlightened age.

> "This is the focal point of all that has gone before. This is the season of restitution. These are the days of restoration. This is the time when men from over the earth come to the mountain of the Lord's house to seek and learn of His ways and to walk in His paths. This is the summation of all of the centuries of time since the birth of Christ to this present and wonderful day ....
>
> "The centuries have passed. The latter-day work of the Almighty, that of which the ancients spoke, that of which the prophets and apostles prophesied, is come. It is here .... There has been a flowering of science. There has been a veritable explosion of learning. This is the greatest of all ages of human endeavor and human accomplishment. And more importantly, it is the season when God has spoken, when His Beloved Son has appeared, when the divine priesthood has been restored, when we hold in our hand another testament of the Son of God. What a glorious and wonderful day this is. We stand on the summit of the ages, awed by a great and solemn sense of history. This is the last and final dispensation toward which all in the past has pointed."[78]

Rest assured, the world's history moved and progressed as expected by God. He provided pathways leading to our very day and time when it was ripe and ready to finally receive his true message everywhere at the same time. No more would only pockets of the world be privy to direct revelation through prophets while the remainder is left with myths, legends, and folklore from a sifting process of the truth over time. No more would theological confusion prevail from historical narratives that were often derived from true events but had lost the details along the way. This is the dispensation of the fulness of times, and we are all needed to prepare the way for the Second Coming of Christ.

CHAPTER SEVEN

Salvation of the Dead

Where am I going after this life is over? This is the age old question pursued by people of all cultures and generations from the beginning of time. It's the perplexing query that spawned religions of all kinds, and is likely the impetus behind much of our thirst for scientific knowledge. But how can we know for sure the right answer to that question as well as the myriad other theological questions that are rolled up into it? The obvious answer, and certainly the right one, is we can listen to a prophet's voice. When a true prophet of God answers the questions as he receives them from on high, we can be assured the information we receive is genuine.

But in order to believe it and embrace it, we must first study and understand it. Included in that process, should be an examination of the evidence. So what should a true plan of salvation from God that answers our questions look like? Reason would suggest it would need to be fair, universal to everyone who ever lived, provide mercy as well as justice, be consistent throughout history, triumph over evil, and ultimately ring true in the depth of our souls. If it contains these elements, then we have our evidence that the plan of salvation presented is truly from God.

In the melting pot of answers among the religious and non-religious alike, are the profoundly simple doctrines of salvation brought back to mankind through the Prophet Joseph Smith. What he taught about man's mortal and immortal journey through eternity, though scorned and derided by the unenlightened, not only holds up in antiquity, but also brings assurance and peace about who we are and where we're going.

In order to possess this comfort and confidence, we need to be clear about what scripture and the prophets are saying in connection with the gospel plan. Confusion can arise when words like salvation, redemption, glory, eternal life, and exaltation appear to be used interchangeably in many instances. Perhaps a definition can help.

Salvation. The root of the word means to be saved, or placed beyond the power of one's enemies. It is deliverance from the bondage of sin and death, through the atonement and resurrection of Jesus Christ.[1] On one hand, salvation is being resurrected, and is synonymous with immortality. It is universal except for the sons of perdition, who, after their resurrection, will dwell in a place of endless torment.[2] On the other hand, salvation is eternal life in the celestial kingdom. To be saved is to be exalted, possess eternal life, and have a continuation of seeds forever (D&C 132:19-20, 24, 55).

It's important to note that when passages of scripture or Church leaders refer to salvation, "almost without exception they mean eternal life or exaltation," wrote Apostle Bruce R. McConkie. "They use the terms salvation, exaltation, and eternal life as synonyms, as words that mean exactly the same thing without any difference, distinction, or variance whatever."[3]

Spirit World Evangelization

Since all people in every generation would not have a chance to hear the gospel in their lifetime, it's reasonable to expect that God, because he loves us, would provide that opportunity after mortality. The LDS doctrine of gospel evangelization in the spirit world fills that criterion. Because all of Christianity has had to tackle questions about what happens to people who never even heard of Jesus Christ, we will examine five major positions among Christian theologians on the topic.

1. *Universalism* – All people will, in fact, be saved by Jesus. No one is damned forever.
2. *Inclusivism* – The unevangelized may be saved if they respond in faith to God based on the light they have.
3. *Postmortem Evangelism* – The unevangelized receive an opportunity to believe in Jesus after death.
4. *Universal Opportunity Before Death* – All people are given an opportunity to be saved when God sends the gospel through various means, such as angels and dreams, or at the moment of death, or by middle knowledge [God's foreknowledge of future events].
5. *Restrictivism* – God does not provide salvation to those who fail to hear of Jesus and have faith in him before they die.[4]

From an LDS perspective, we can immediately rule out Universalism and Restrictivism, both of which are unfair and at odds with any view of a magnanimous Deity. They appear to violate everything we know about the love of God and Christ and their desire to bring us back into their presence. The others have merit and are worth our examination.

Universal Opportunity Before Death {middle knowledge}. The basic premise is that God not only knows everything that possibly could happen and all the events that actually will happen, but he also knows what *would* have happened had something in the circumstances of an event been different. So this suggests that God already knows who will or won't accept the gospel if it were presented to them, and could save them or not, based upon his middle knowledge. Joseph Smith even suggested this idea when he spoke about an 1836 vision of his brother, Alvin, who had died as a young man. His concern was how Alvin could be in the celestial kingdom when he had not been baptized into the Church. Through revelation, Joseph was told that those who died without knowledge of the full truth would be saved if they would have accepted it, had they known of it. This particular explanation has merit for the mentally ill and for those born into such repugnant circumstances that having a fair chance to receive the gospel would be impossible. But for all of us, at some point in time, there are certain requirements attached to salvation, namely, that one, people must hear or be exposed to the gospel of Christ (Acts 4:12), and two, they must act in faith (James 3:14-20). It seems that some level of exposure and activity regarding the gospel of Christ is required of all people, and if it didn't happen in this life, it would need to happen in the next.[5]

Postmortem Evangelization. This suggests that these two requirements of exposure to the gospel and acting in faith could be met after death. Mormons believe that departed faithful friends and relatives of the deceased will serve as missionaries to share the gospel in the spirit world. The Bible shares insight on this position (see Mark 16:16; Matthew 10:32-33; John 5:25), with the classic text used to support it being 1 Peter 3:18–20, 4:6: "For Christ also hath once suffered for sins, the just for the unjust, that he might bring us to God, being put to death in the flesh, but quickened by the spirit: By which also he went and preached unto the spirits in prison; which sometime were disobedient, when once the longsuffering of God waited in the days of Noah, while the ark was a preparing, wherein few, that is, eight souls were saved by water .... For for this cause was the gospel preached also to them that are dead, that they might be judged according to men in the flesh, but live according to God in the spirit." Because circumstances may make it difficult for a person who hears the gospel in this life to accept it, condemnation by God would be unjust.[6]

Inclusivism. According to this position people can progress in the next life if they live according to the light that they have in this life. It gives space for people of all religions to at least live within the righteous teachings of their faiths, or even for non-religious people, to live by their conscious understanding of right and wrong. Evidence of this idea can be found in scriptures where God went beyond his dealings with his chosen people in Israel, and looked favorably upon other nations (Deuteronomy 2:5, 9, 19, 21-22; 2 Kings 5:1). It is also found in passages showing God dealing with non-Israelites like Melchizedek, Jethro, Job, the Queen of Sheba, the Canaanite woman (Matthew 15:21-8), and the Roman centurion (Matthew 8:10). The Gentiles, we're told by Paul, will benefit from the atonement of Christ, even though they don't have the gospel, if they will live by nature the principles within it (see Romans 2:6-16). Most Christian religions adhere to inclusivism as a tenet, making it a near consensus among them.[7]

All three of these positions have place within the parameters of the LDS Church and help to provide answers. We must remember that people don't receive harsh judgment from God because they haven't heard the gospel, but rather, because they have sinned beyond some point of no return. The atonement generally helps us not get to that point. Whether a person receives the gospel on Earth or in the spirit world, may be of less consequence than we think, because God views the progress of his children as one continuing course. And because the deceased will carry their same personality, prejudices, and urges with them, it should be a fairly level playing field for gospel acceptance or rejection.

"We shall enter into the other sphere of existence with the same spirit that we have here," said President George Q. Cannon. "If we were animated by the spirit of the telestial kingdom we shall have that, if by the spirit of the terrestrial kingdom we shall have that, if by the spirit of the celestial kingdom we shall have that. We shall go from this condition of existence into the other sphere with the same feelings, to some extent, at least, as we have here. If we have had knowledge, we shall have it there."[8]

A look at near-death-experiences can also shed some light. In his NDE, Dr. George Ritchie described how he saw people in various stages of progression depending on the kind and amount of love they possessed. Many he described as vile, self-absorbed and totally devoid of love. He saw honorable people who loved their fellowmen and chose to follow the Savior, but also saw beings who were still tied to the earth by their physical appetites and desires for worldly endeavors. The experience was a stark reminder to Ritchie that "we have to be careful of what we grow to love so much that we let it control us, for it can lead us into becoming bound on this earth to the things that we made into false gods."[9]

We also know that a "fair" chance must be given to everyone to accept or reject the gospel, or God would be neither just nor merciful. Joseph Fielding McConkie wrote, "In principle, it should be neither easier nor harder to exercise faith or to repent in the spirit world. Were that not the case those in that estate could not be judged according to men in the flesh. For some it will be natural and easy to accept and live gospel truths, for that will have been the practice of a lifetime. For others it will be very difficult to do so, for eschewing the things of the Spirit will have been the practice of a lifetime. The difference is not in the gospel but in the hearts and souls of those to whom the message is being presented."[10]

We have to remember that this life only represents a snap of the fingers in comparison to the timeless state of eternity. This concept of timelessness is difficult to get our heads around because our mortal minds are so time oriented, but God has an eternity to help us find all the answers and work our way back into his presence. One of the most important reasons for Earth life is to gain a physical body. We use it to learn and grow in our earthly school of life, where the requirements for graduation, although the same in both this life and the next, are attainable because of the atonement of Christ. We must not get hung up on "when" every human being will hear the gospel, but rather celebrate the fact that everyone "will."

And this truth is very much a part of the historical record. Ancient texts are full of references regarding the preaching of the gospel to, and vicarious baptism for, the dead. Hugh Nibley uncovered information about a Coptic papyrus found in Egypt in 1895 that elicited a confirming response from a highly respected early Christian historian, Adolf von Harnack. Nibley said Harnack concluded that it was an "authentic statement of certain important doctrines of salvation and resurrection common to the whole Christian church at a very early date."

Nibley went on to say, "Shortly after, Carl Schmidt, second only to Harnack in his knowledge of early Christian documents, produced a number of ancient fragments, matching the Coptic text word for word in a half dozen languages and showing it to be derived from the Greek original of an apostolic general epistle which had enjoyed widespread authority and popularity in the church at least as early as the second century. The subject of this epistle was salvation for the dead, a doctrine which, as Schmidt demonstrated, was believed in the early church to have been the main theme of Christ's teaching after the resurrection."[11]

According to Nibley, many other early texts of the oldest Christian writers showed that the main weight of early doctrine "was not on the cross but on the work of the Lord as a teacher, marking the way of eternal progress for the living and the dead according to a pattern first followed by Adam, to whom the texts attribute an importance out of all proportion to the teachings of the later church."[12]

For example, in the early third century, Origen, a scholar and early Christian theologian, is recorded as saying, "We assert that Jesus not only converted no small number of persons while he was in the body . . . but also, that when he became a spirit, without the covering of the body, he dwelt among those spirits which were without bodily covering, converting much of them as were willing to himself."[13] This statement is consistent with LDS doctrine that the early church taught the doctrine of the dead being free to accept or reject the gospel once it is preached to them, the same as the living.

Degrees of Glory

The next principle involved in the salvation of the dead would be God's judgment of his children and their assigned eternal rewards. Mormon doctrine on this is very different from mainstream Christianity. Here's what we know through scripture and modern-day revelation. There are three degrees of glory—celestial, terrestrial, and telestial—where all resurrected persons, except sons of perdition, will go (D&C 76; 1 Corinthians 15:39-42; Revelations 21). After their resurrection, the sons of perdition will be cast out with the devil and his angels. We know that only the faithful saints [whether in this life or the next] will receive a celestial reward and live with God, and that within that kingdom, are three heavens, the highest of which is reserved for only those who are married and sealed in the temple (D&C 131:1-4). The nature of the other two degrees within the celestial kingdom have not been described, except to say that the people who go there will become "ministering angels" (D&C 132:16-17).

In further support of this doctrine, the Lord said, "In my Father's house are many mansions" (John 14:2), and that rewards will vary between and within kingdoms (D&C 76:98, 1 Corinthians 15:41; D&C 76:71-79). Such revelation negates the general Christian dogma of people going to either a heaven or hell. When you add to that God's teachings that men will be judged according to their works, and because their works are varied, so too will be their rewards (Revelations 20:12-14; Luke 19:16-26), we get a clear picture of both his justice and mercy.

Joseph Smith explained, "I do not believe the Methodist doctrine of sending honest men and noble minded men to hell, along with the murderer and adulterer .... There are mansions for those who obey a celestial law, and there are other mansions for those who come short of the law, every man in his own order."[14]

This doctrine of the three degrees of glory was not just something made up by Joseph Smith. In fact, it was very much a part of early Christian teachings but, like so many other tenets, was lost through apostasy once Christ and the early apostles were taken from the earth. There is abundant evidence to show that this doctrine was a true teaching of Jesus Christ among early theologians. Let's look at some of that evidence.

Clement of Alexandria, born around AD 150, who was venerated as a saint in early Catholicism, also expressed belief in the three degrees. He said, "Conformably, therefore, there are various abodes, according to the worth of those who have believed .... These chosen abodes, which are three, are indicated by the numbers in the Gospel—the thirty, the sixty, the hundred. And the perfect inheritance belongs to those who attain to 'a perfect man,' according to the image of the Lord .... To the likeness of God, then, he that is introduced into adoption and the friendship of God, to the just inheritance of the lords and gods is brought; if he be perfected, according to the Gospel, as the Lord Himself taught."[15]

Clement also taught that people must act in certain ways to qualify for the three gradations of glory. The first way is " ... right or perfect action, which is characteristic of the perfect man and Gnostic alone, and raises him to the height of glory. The second is the class of ... medium, or intermediate actions, which are done by less perfect believers, and procure a lower grade of glory. In the third place he reckons sinful actions, which are done by those who fall away from salvation."[16]

Origen also compared, as did Paul, the kingdoms of glory to the sun, moon, and stars: "Our understanding of the passage indeed is, that the Apostle, wishing to describe the great difference among those who rise again in glory, i.e., of the saints, borrowed a comparison from the heavenly bodies, saying, 'One is the glory of the sun, another the glory of the moon, another the glory of the stars.'"[17]

St. John Chrysostom, one of the greatest early church fathers of the 5th century, was another witness that early Christians believed Paul's passage referred to degrees of reward. "And having said this, he ascends again to the heaven, saying, 'There is one glory of the sun, and another glory of the moon.' For as in the earthly bodies there is a difference, so also in the heavenly; and that difference no ordinary one, but reaching even to the uttermost: there being not only a difference between sun and moon, and stars, but also between stars and stars. For what though they be all in the heaven? yet some have a larger, others a less share of glory. What do we learn from hence? That although they be all in God's kingdom, all shall not enjoy the same reward; and though all sinners be in hell, all shall not endure the same punishment."[18]

Along with Chrysostom, there were other early church fathers who taught the doctrine of varying degrees of glory. They include Irenaeus, Cyprian, Ambrose, and some lesser-known fathers, Macarius, Quodvultdeus (died 453), who was bishop of Carthage and a friend of Augustine, Severus, bishop of Antioch (died 538), and Caesarius, bishop of Arles.[19]

There is even evidence of this doctrine in both Muslim and Jewish antiquity. In his article, "The Seventh Heaven," Jewish commentator Dr. Eliezer Lorne Segal, found that the term 'seventh heaven' comes from "the popular Muslim conception of paradise, which is divided into several celestial levels, awarded according to the degree of righteousness achieved during one's mortal lifetime." Interesting as that is, Segal said the doctrine actually predates the rise of Islam by "many centuries" and has "deep roots in Jewish tradition."[20] As doctrine of the three kingdoms became changed over time, new ones emerged such as the seven heavens, although they still included differing degrees of glory. Scholars don't know exactly how the doctrine was completely lost, but the Greeks seemed to be influential in changing it to a two place condition for the saved and the damned.[21]

Even Christian reformers after the Dark Ages like John Wesley spoke of degrees of reward in the hereafter. He said, "There is an inconceivable variety in the degrees of reward in the other world .... In worldly things men are ambitious to get as high as they can. Christians have a far more noble ambition. The difference between the very highest and the lowest state in the world is nothing to the smallest difference between the degrees of glory."[22]

Doctrine of the three degrees of glory was just one of many that needed to be restored to the earth after centuries of loss. It is a doctrine that gives promise and purpose to our lives and illustrates well God's desire to save all his children to an eternal dwelling place that befits who they are. The scriptures teach "that through him all might be saved whom the Father had put into his power and made by him; who glorifies the Father, and saves all the works of his hands, except those sons of perdition who deny the Son after the Father has revealed him" (D&C 76:40-43).

Justice and Mercy

As we come to understand who we are, why we do what we do, and the enormity of all the forces at work to influence the outcomes of our lives, it naturally leads us to wonder how it will all be reconciled. A truly loving God, as well as one who is just, would provide a plan of salvation that reflected both justice and mercy. This then, would be another evidence of God for the Doubting Thomas. A look at the plan, itself, as revealed in scripture, must be dominated by these two elements in order to reflect a true and living Deity.

This incredible plan of spirit world teaching and varying rewards, trumps any other Christian interpretation about life after death by providing specific details about our eternal destiny. There is comfort in knowing such details, and yet even with all that we know through revealed truth, finding and understanding the balance between justice and mercy can be difficult. Some tough questions about the judgment are often concerning for some in the Church.

1. What are the criteria God will use to judge a Church member who goes inactive and lives decently, but not in accordance with what they once believed?
2. Do they have a second chance in the spirit world like the rest of God's children who never heard the gospel, or are they automatically destined to lesser degrees of glory?
3. How will forever families be eternally happy, as they're often told they will, if one or more of its members are consigned to a lesser kingdom?
4. If a person has a chance to accept the gospel in the next life and receive the full glory of the celestial kingdom, why would they put themselves through living the strict standards of the Church in mortality?

These are very tender questions, ones that tear at the heart strings of many in the Church who have family members who have strayed. The answers must reflect both mercy and justice in order to stand as evidence of God. As I have researched the scriptures and the words of Church leaders, I have been struck by the seemingly perfect balance between both in his plan of salvation.

Boyd K. Packer gave one of the most moving illustrations of this principle that I have ever heard. He told us to imagine a man who went into great debt for something he wanted to own now instead of when he could afford to pay for it. He signed a contract in which he agreed to give up this possession and go to prison if he couldn't pay for it when the debt became due. Over time, the item brought the man much pleasure, but making payments on it only sporadically was not enough to expunge the debt. Eventually, the creditor demanded payment in full but the man was unable to pay. When the creditor declared his intensions to repossess the item and throw the man in prison as the contract stipulated, the man pleaded for mercy.

It seemed they were at an impasse with one seeking justice and the other mercy. Neither could have his way except at the sacrifice of the other. How could both eternal ideals be served? The story revealed that, indeed there was a way in the form of a mediator who was a friend of the debtor. The mediator loved the man and wanted to help, so told the creditor that he would pay the man's debt in exchange for the creditor returning the man's possession, releasing him from the contract, and keeping him out of prison. The creditor agreed to these terms, and the debtor was relieved and thankful for this intercession that saved him from his own foolishness.[23]

We too are in need of a mediator because we live on a kind of spiritual credit, said Elder Packer. That someone is our Savior, Jesus Christ. His mediation, through the atonement, satisfies the demands of justice, so that mercy is not capable of robbing it (Alma 42). Even if a person is riddled with faults and misdeeds throughout his or her life, and at some point becomes truly repentant, the Savior's atonement pays the price for that person, so that mercy can be extended. Too often, well-meaning Mormons put way too much weight on the justice part of the scales, and forget that the atonement has weight sufficient to save us all.

"Listen to him who is the advocate with the Father, who is pleading your cause before him—Saying: Father, behold the sufferings and death of him who did no sin, in whom thou wast well pleased; behold the blood of thy Son which was shed, the blood of him whom thou gavest that thyself might be glorified; Wherefore, Father, spare these my brethren that believe on my name, that they may come unto me and have everlasting life" (D&C 45:3-5).

The atonement is not just in effect for mortals. It extends to each of us throughout the eternities. On January 21, 1836, Joseph Smith learned this principle in a vision. The Lord told him, "All who have died without a knowledge of this gospel, who would have received it if they had been permitted to tarry, shall be heirs of the celestial kingdom of God; also all that shall die henceforth without a knowledge of it, who would have received it with all their hearts, shall be heirs of that kingdom" (D&C 137:7-8).

King Benjamin affirmed this when he taught the Nephites that, "his blood atoneth for the sins of those who have fallen by the transgression of Adam, who have died not knowing the will of God concerning them, or who have ignorantly sinned" (Mosiah 3:11).

So it's clear who will qualify for celestial glory upon acceptance of the gospel in the spirit world. But we're also told that not everyone will be eligible for the highest kingdom and will be assigned to lesser degrees of glory. "These are they who are honorable men of the earth, who were blinded by the craftiness of men. These are they who receive of his glory, but not of his fullness" (D&C 76:75-76).

This is just. But because God is also merciful, the atonement of Christ ensures even rejection of the gospel in this life does not necessarily disqualify a person from hearing it again in the spirit world. God takes into consideration the circumstances of our lives that may have unfairly clouded our choices, and only he can judge these things fairly. Joseph Fielding McConkie taught, "We must allow, however, for circumstances in which people were prisoners to experiences in this life that prevented them from having a fair chance to embrace gospel principles here. When they are freed from those bitter chains, many of them will seek the blessings of the gospel."[24] Joseph Smith declared,

> "While one portion of the human race is judging and condemning the other without mercy, the Great Parent of the universe looks upon the whole human family with a fatherly care

and paternal regard; He views them as His offspring .... He is a wise Lawgiver, and will judge all men, not according to the narrow, contracted notions of men, but 'according to the deeds done in the body whether they be good or evil,' or whether these deeds were done in England, America, Spain, Turkey, or India .... We need not doubt the wisdom and intelligence of the Great Jehovah; He will award judgment or mercy to all nations according to their several desserts, their means of obtaining intelligence, the laws by which they are governed, the facilities afforded them of obtaining correct information, and His inscrutable designs in relation to the human family; and when the designs of God shall be made manifest, and the curtain of futurity be withdrawn, we shall all of us eventually have to confess that the Judge of all the earth has done right."[25]

Of the judgment day, Elder M. Russell Ballard said that the Lord will, "Take all things into consideration: Our genetic and chemical makeup, our mental state, our intellectual capacity, the teachings we have received, the traditions of our fathers, our health, and so forth."[26]

How Many Will Be Exalted?

We may wonder in light of these assurances just how many of God's children will actually inherit the celestial kingdom. The words of prophets and apostles provide assurances on this question.

Wilford Woodruff: "There will be very few, **if any**, in the spirit world, who will not accept the gospel."[27]

President Joseph Fielding Smith: "All who hear and believe, repenting and receiving the gospel in its fulness, whether living or dead, are heirs of salvation in the celestial kingdom of God."[28]

President Lorenzo Snow: "When the gospel is preached to the spirits in prison, the success attending that preaching will be far greater than that attending the preaching of our elders in this life. I believe there will be a **very few** indeed of those spirits, who will not gladly receive the gospel when it is carried to them."[30]

Apostle Melvin J. Ballard: "When you die and go to the spirit world you will labor for years, trying to convert individuals who will be taking their own course. Some of them will repent; some of them will listen. Another group will be rebellious, following their own will and notion, and that group will get smaller and smaller until every knee shall humbly bow and every tongue confess."[31]

There is hope in the words of the prophets and apostles that when all things are considered, those who get a second chance in the spirit world to accept the gospel will still inherit the celestial kingdom. Ultimately, the kingdom of glory received by those who accept the gospel will be based on God's knowledge of whether they "would have received it with all their hearts," as manifested by their works and the "desire of their hearts (D&C 137:8-9). It is both just and merciful that conditions pertaining to the judgment are not always what mere mortals would consider black and white.

Many of his children have simply been unable to fight off the immensity of moral pollution surrounding them, and have stumbled and fallen in the war against evil. I love the words of BYU Professor Dr. Robert Millet, who said, "Surely in the postmortal spirit world, men and women will have burdens such as abuse, neglect, false teachings, and improper traditions—all of which can impose obstacles to embracing the truth—torn away like a film. Then perhaps they will, in that sphere free from Lucifer's taunts, seen as they are seen and know as they are known." He then quoted Wilford Woodruff who said, "I tell you when the prophets and apostles go to preach to those who are shut up in prison, thousands of them will there embrace the gospel."[32]

With innumerable hosts to be saved, doubters might wonder about the scriptures that speak of the "strait gate" and "narrow way" to eternal life and the "broad gate" and "wide way" to destruction (D&C 132:22, 25; Matthew 7:13-14). Some have said that given what we know about the multitudes who will accept the gospel in the spirit world, perhaps the scripture should include this caveat: "Strait is the gate, and narrow is the way, and few there be that find it IN THIS LIFE."[33] Clearly, Christ is speaking to a very small group of people who will come in contact with the gospel during mortality.

Brigham Young also explained, "If people are not saved, it is because they are not disposed to be saved."[34] Apostle George Teasdale concurred when he said, "Straight is the way and narrow is the path that leadeth to the exaltations, and few there be that find it. Why? Because they do not want it."[35]

Certainly, the numbers of those not interested in righteousness, even the wicked, at any point in time, always outnumber the small band of believing disciples by a large margin. But the right perspective on the matter makes clear that in the long run God, as our eternal parent, will save many more than he will lose.[36] Millet and McConkie offered a convincing list of the enormous numbers of those who will *automatically* be saved:

1. Billions who never heard the gospel in mortality but afterwards received it with glad tidings.
2. Those with limited accountability because of a mental disability in mortality.
3. Innumerable hosts who qualified for exaltation from Enoch's city, from Melchizedek's Salem, and from the golden era of the Nephites.
4. Billions of children who died before the age of accountability from Adam to the Millennium.
5. Countless billions who will be born during the Millennium where "children will grow up without sin unto salvation" (D&C 45:58). Because of the paradisiacal state [no disease or evil] of the earth during Christ's thousand year reign, it's likely more people will live on the earth then, than the combined total of all the previous six thousand years.[37]

We do not know why multitudes of God's children were not required to go through the trials and growth processes required of the rest of us, but he does, and so we can be assured that all is as it should be. But their automatic exaltation leaves plenty of room in the lesser kingdoms for individuals whose hearts were just not aligned enough with the Savior's. They will still partake in redemptive glory and enjoy the ministrations of Christ in the terrestrial, and angels in the telestial. Their lives will be far better, in all ways, than they have been in mortality. As for members of the Church, we don't have to be perfect in this life but we must align ourselves with the teachings of Christ as much as possible to continue the lengthy process of becoming the kind of beings who can abide in God's presence. If we do that, according to Elder Bruce R. McConkie, "then it is absolutely guaranteed—there is no question whatever about it—we shall gain eternal life."[38]

There also are supplementary evidences that, like bells in a tower sounding the ubiquitous gong of truth, proclaim the vast majority of us will be exalted. For one thing, the many titles for the plan of salvation found in scripture, indicate the plan was not intended to punish or damn us but rather, promote our happiness in this life, and save and redeem us in the next. Elder Packer compiled a list of these titles that make plain the happy ending God's plan was meant to have:

- The merciful plan of the great Creator (see 2 Nephi 9:6).
- The plan of mercy (see Alma 42:15).
- The great plan of mercy (see Alma 42:31).
- The great plan of redemption (see Jacob 6:8; Alma 12:25-26, 30, 32; 17:16; 18:39; 22:13-14; 29:2; 39:18; 42:11, 13).
- The eternal plan of redemption (see Alma 34:16).
- The great plan of redemption (see Alma 34:31).
- The plan of salvation (see Jarom 1:2; Alma 24:14; 42:5; Moses 6:62).
- The plan of our God (see 2 Nephi 9:13).
- The great plan of the Eternal God (see Alma 34:9).
- The eternal plan of deliverance (see 2 Nephi 11:5).
- The plan of happiness (see Alma 42:16).
- The great plan of happiness (see Alma 42:8).
- The plan of restoration (see Alma 41:2).
- The plan of the Gods (see Abraham 4:21).[39]

Do these descriptions sound like a plan intended to fail? No. The plan was designed by a perfect being, one who could create a perfect plan to accomplish a perfect outcome. It is not in the nature of God to design a plan that would ultimately damn, or stop the progression of most of his children. It's simply incomprehensible.[40]

When the plan was presented to us in the spirit world, the scriptures tell us we were so excited about it that we shouted for joy (Job 38:7). BYU Educator Alonzo L. Gaskill suggested, "Clearly, those of us who shouted for joy sensed that what God was telling us was good and desirable. Clearly, we felt that the odds were in our favor. There is no sense of foreboding or fear of fear! If the Father had informed us that 'there's good news and bad news'—and had He continued, 'the good news is there is a plan, but the bad news is most of you are not going to make it back ... —surely we would not have felt reason to rejoice."[41]

It would seem that God is planning to be victorious in numbers by saving and exalting the vastly greater portion of his children. While the damage being done by Satan for the souls of mankind may seem great, in the end, God will win the fight, and by extension, so will we.

Of course, repentance is still necessary, because that's a stipulation of the contract we agreed to in the spirit world with our mediator, Jesus Christ. Joseph Smith said, "The dead who repent will be redeemed, through obedience to the ordinances of the house of God, and after they have paid the penalty of their transgressions, and are washed clean, shall receive a reward according to their works, for they are heirs of salvation" (D&C 138:57-59).

But the soothing words of Apostle Dieter Uchtdorf of the First Presidency, reminds us that repentance is a healing balm that is built into the plan. He said, "Remember, the heavens will not be filled with those who never made mistakes, but with those who recognized that they were off course, and who corrected their ways to get back in the light of gospel truth."[42]

Wayward Children to Be Saved

What about wayward children born under the covenant? This is one area that has caused substantial angst and confusion among Church members.

Many have interpreted the scriptures in a way that dooms their children to the demands of justice, leaving no room for a second chance. But once again, mercy is included in the judgments of God to protect these children of the covenant. There is a distinct advantage for members of the Church, whether born into an eternal family or adopted through convert baptism. By virtue of the baptism and temple ordinances which come to them as members of the Church, they become part of the House of Israel and heirs to the promised blessings.

Joseph Fielding Smith said those born under the covenant "have claims upon the blessings of the gospel beyond what those not so born are entitled to receive. They may receive a greater guidance, a greater protection, a greater inspiration from the Spirit of the Lord" than those not so born.[43] They are rightful heirs of the promises made to Abraham and have claim upon all the ordinances of salvation (Abraham 2:9-11).

Just as physical or temporal inheritances can be handed down through the generations, so too, can spiritual birthrights. This gives parents of wayward children of all ages every reason to hope. Joseph Smith said, "When a seal is put upon the father and mother, it secures their posterity, so that they cannot be lost, but will be saved by virtue of the covenant of their father and mother."[44] According to Apostle Orson F. Whitney,

> "The Prophet Joseph Smith declared—and he never taught a more comforting doctrine—that the eternal sealings of faithful parents and the divine promises made to them for valiant service to the Cause of Truth, would save not only themselves, but likewise their posterity. Though some of the sheep may wander, the eye of the Shepherd is upon them, and sooner or later they will feel the tentacles of Divine Providence reaching out after them and drawing them back to the fold. Either in this life or the life to come, they will return. They will have to pay their debt to justice; they will suffer for their sins; and may tread a thorny path; but if it leads them at last, like the penitent Prodigal, to a loving and forgiving father's heart and home, the painful

experience will not have been in vain. Pray for your careless and disobedient children; hold on to them with your faith. Hope on, trust on, till you see the salvation of God."[45]

Now some might call this favoritism—certainly not a trait one would expect of a fair minded Deity. But when you think about who the covenant people really are, and for what divine purpose they were reserved for Earth life at this time, you begin to realize how important they are as soldiers in God's army. Heavenly Father's children, who were purposefully placed into the lineage of Israel, were faithful and strong before this life and because of this are a marked generation to help ensure that the forces of righteousness will finally win.[46] Mormons are taught that all of us, as latter-day children of Israel, are a royal generation preserved to come to the earth in this time for a special purpose.[47] We would be singled out and strategically placed upon the earth to perform the special work of redemption of souls, because in our premortal life we "conformed to the image of [God's] Son" (Romans 89:29).

Clearly, God needs our help to get the job done, both in this life and in the next, for all who have ever lived since the world began (D&C 128:22-24). In comparison to all the hosts of heaven who chose Earth life, our numbers in the Church are few. Using 2009 numbers, LDS Author Larry Barkdull calculated that with the world population then at about 6.6 billion and the Church membership at the time, at 13 million, our latter-day generations represent approximately one in 508. Then comparing Church membership against the estimated 100 billion people who have ever lived, we are only 1 in 7,692.[48]

Is it any wonder that God cannot afford to lose even a single child of the covenant? That is why he has promised through his prophets to bind them "to their parents by an everlasting tie, and no power of Earth or hell can separate them from their parents in eternity."[49] And that is why "their future glory and exaltation is secured unto them."[50] Of course, there are no guarantees in this matter. Like everyone else, God's covenant people must exercise their agency by actively choosing and living the gospel of Christ at some point before all promises are binding. But God will make every effort to save them and keep them, and he has an eternity to do it.

And he may well need to use that entire eternity for some of his children. Joseph Smith counseled us to never give up on our children because, "there is never a time when the spirit is too old to approach God. All are within the reach of pardoning mercy."[51] Lorenzo Snow added, "If you succeed in passing through these trials and afflictions ... you will, by the power of the priesthood, work and labor, as the Son of God has, until you get all your sons and daughters in the path of exaltation and glory. This is just as sure as that the sun rose this morning over yonder mountains. Therefore, mourn not because all your sons and daughters do not follow in the path that you have marked out to them, or give heed to your counsels. Inasmuch as we succeed in securing eternal glory, and stand as saviors, and as kings and priests to our God, we will save our posterity."[52]

There is another principle that helps us understand how God can save so many of his children: The law of justification. This law is a safeguard in his plan to ensure that no unworthy soul is rewarded with exaltation not earned.[53] But that same safeguard is also used to help those who are weak in the faith but still desire salvation. Here's how it works. Justification "is a scriptural metaphor drawn from the courts of law: A judge justifies an accused person by declaring or pronouncing that person innocent. Likewise, God may treat a person as being 'not guilty' of sin."[54] Justification is a tool that safeguards members who have received the ordinances and appear to be living worthily but, in fact, have difficulty with aspects of righteousness because of weak testimonies. They may eventually leave the Church, leaving their loved ones to wonder and worry about what will become of them in the eternities. Many people, sadly, write them off to a lesser kingdom.

But unless the Holy Spirit of Promise, which is the Holy Ghost, ratifies or approves of an ordinance or contract with God, it is not binding in this life or the next (D&C 132:7). It is as if it never happened. To get the ratifying seal, the person must be worthy through personal righteousness. If they never fully believed when an ordinance was performed, such as a spouse who joins the Church simply to please his or her partner, it would not have been sealed by the Holy Spirit of Promise in the first place. In the case of our covenant children, their baptisms and even temple ordinances may have been justified by the Holy Spirit of Promise at some point. But if they go astray, the ratifying of those contracts will be removed, which in effect, takes away some of their accountability and opens the door for another chance. Repentance on their part will reinstate the ratification.[55]

Advantages to Conversion Here Instead of There

Emily and David had been converts to the Church for about 10 years, but struggled during that time because of the lifestyle membership required. They missed the social life they once had with friends involving drinking, partying, and R-rated movies. They also found such things as the Word of Wisdom, Sabbath observance, wearing garments, and Church callings restrictive. They truly loved the message of the restoration and the plan of salvation, but ultimately, left the Church because they felt it was difficult to live. Here is what they reasoned: If people can hear and accept the gospel in the spirit world and still receive exaltation, why not wait to do it then so you don't have to live such a strict lifestyle here. So the question becomes, what are the advantages to Church membership and gospel testimony in this life as opposed to the next?

This is a good question. One obvious answer is it may be too late for the already baptized, if the Lord decides their rejection of the gospel is sufficient to receive a lesser kingdom.

God's plan is not risk free. If we were all given a free pass because of being born under the covenant or adopted into it, it would sound a lot like Lucifer's plan to force obedience and guarantee redemption for all. Since that is not the case, the choices we make while exercising our agency will weigh heavily in the judgment we receive. We take a risk if we wait until the gospel is offered in the spirit world without the foreknowledge of membership in the Kingdom of God on Earth. It's quite possible that leading a less righteous lifestyle in mortality could create in our minds a comfort level we feel is more suited to a lesser kingdom. Remember, we choose by our deeds in mortality as well as the desires of our hearts, where we will reside for eternity.

Purposeful rejection of the gospel in the flesh, if [and this is a big if] God determines that person was truly converted, may certainly result in a lesser kingdom despite God's mercies. In May 1898, Elder Whitney taught that "they who reject the gospel here, and put off the day of their salvation, and have to be preached to in the spirit world ... they who put off the day of their salvation, and think 'we will have a good time here and will obey the gospel hereafter,' they must answer for this neglect, and after they have answered for it and realized what they have lost, they will be saved—not in the celestial kingdom, but in a lesser kingdom called the terrestrial."[56] This is most likely because our natures will have changed over time away from spiritual inclinations toward Godly goals. Elder James E. Talmage said failure to respond to the gospel's call and to repent in this life would not be easily repaired in the next. He said, "As the time of repentance is procrastinated, the ability to repent grows weaker; neglect of opportunity in holy things develops inability."[57]

And for those hoping God's love is so great and so unconditional that it will mercifully excuse them from obeying his laws, are playing Russian roulette with their eternal lives. His laws are invariable, which is another great evidence of his love for his children. Remember that mercy cannot rob justice.[58]

Besides the pain involved in the repentance process in the spirit world, another disadvantage of choosing to wait for spirit world conversion is how long a person may have to wait in spirit prison. Their agency is hindered, because even if they accept the gospel in the spirit world, they may have to wait for ordinances to be done for them. Many probably wait a precious long time. Parley P. Pratt said,

> "The question naturally arises—Do all the people who die without the gospel hear it as soon as they arrive in the world of spirits? To illustrate this, let us look at the dealings of God with the people of this world. What can we

reason but from what we know? We know and understand the things of this world, in some degree, because they are visible, and we are daily conversant with them. Do all the people in this world hear the gospel as soon as they are capable of understanding? No, indeed, but very few in comparison have heard it at all .... I have not the least doubt but there are spirits there who have dwelt there a thousand years, who, if we could converse with them face to face, would be found ... ignorant of the truths, the ordinances, powers, keys, priesthood, resurrection, and eternal life of the body ...."[59]

Accepting the gospel in this life will bring immediate blessings beyond the veil. People who wait until the spirit world to accept the gospel also must wait for the blessings while they undergo gospel learning and repentance. Some of these blessings include:

- Dwelling in "a state of happiness, which is called paradise, a state of rest, a state of peace, where they shall rest from all their troubles and from all care and sorrow" (Alma 40:12).
- Being resurrected sooner than those who rejected the gospel in mortality, who will be "reserved in chains of darkness until the judgment of the great day" (Moses 7:56-57).
- Having the Father, Jesus, and angels speak to us, and live in the company of the just and the pure who are in the spirit world until the resurrection.[60]
- Having an absence of evil influences. Brigham Young taught that Lucifer and the third part of the heavenly hosts that followed him, as well as the spirits of wicked men who lived on earth, would no longer be allowed to influence us. All other spirits are more or less subject to them, the same as when they dwelt in the flesh.[61]
- Enjoying the same priesthood power. It will continue to operate as it did on Earth.[62] (see D&C 124:130).

- Having our lives organized within families. We will be organized according to priesthood order in family groups and organizations.[63]
- Helping mortal family members. When there is need, we are able to bring them messages of warning, reproof, or instruction.[64]
- Participating in missionary work in the spirit world and preaching the "gospel of repentance and redemption ... among those who are in darkness" (D&C 138:57).

What wonderful blessings beyond the grave are available to those who receive and live the gospel during mortality, and what sadness those who rejected it will feel when they witness what they could have had. Joseph Smith said, "The spirits of the just are exalted to a greater and more glorious work; hence they are blessed in their departure to the world of spirits. Enveloped in flaming fire, they are not far from us, and know and understand our thoughts, feelings, and motions, and are often pained therewith."[65] On the other hand, said Joseph, "The great misery of departed spirits in the world of spirits, where they go after death, is to know that they come short of the glory that others enjoy and that they might have enjoyed themselves, and they are their own accusers."[66]

Conclusion

The Doubting Thomas should begin to realize that there is nothing out there in the tenets of other theologies that even comes close to the plan of salvation revealed though the Prophet Joseph Smith. It is comprehensive, universal, merciful, and just. It is brilliantly glorious in every detail, offering evidence of a purpose to life and a reason to hope beyond all imagination. It is a simple plan that only requires a willing heart and a contrite spirit to enjoy its greatest rewards. But some reject it because they look for something more—something spectacular, something grander.

It brings to mind the Old Testament story of Naaman the leper, who was told by the prophet Elisha, to wash seven times in the Jordan River to be healed. Naaman chose not to do it, and was incredulous (see 2 Kings 5:10-12) at the idea that a miraculous healing could be accomplished through such a simplistic act. He was looking for something more impressive and grand and so nearly missed out on being healed, which only occurred after he had a change of heart and did as the prophet directed. Let us not, likewise, be in danger of walking away from the reprieve God extends to us through the simplicity of his gospel plan.

Too often we fool ourselves into thinking God's requirements are complicated and unattainable. We don't believe that he would so easily forgive and reward. We somehow think his offered grace, through the atonement of Christ, has strings attached beyond our efforts to live the best we can, and repent when we fall short. But if we fully understood how much he loves us, we'd cast aside all doubt, rejoice in his goodness, and never look back.

It was his love for us that made him devise a plan of salvation in the first place. Until people embrace that ideal, they may continue to doubt and continue to reject the plain and precious truths of the gospel. "He that loveth not knoweth not God; for God is love" (1 John 4:8); "... God is love; and he that dwelleth in love dwelleth in God, and God in him" (1 John 4:16). The love of God is everywhere if we would but see it. It is in the earth, itself, that sustains our physical needs. It is in our relationships with family and friends. It is in the miracles and Godly interventions that, from time to time, save us from our self. It is echoed in poetic utterances by prophets through the ages, and captured fluidly in scripture and sacred literature that speaks to our souls.

This then, is the key to accepting the simplicity of his gospel. Because we are his literal offspring, made in his image and with his attributes, we like him, possess the innateness of love. If we can use the love we feel for family and friends as a springboard to loving God, we can begin to know why he answers prayers, reveals truth, and accepts our efforts to live according to the light that we have. He loves us so much he gave us an eternity to embrace his gospel.

It is my hope, that if you desire to have a personal relationship with Heavenly Father and his Son, Jesus Christ, you will come in or come back to the fold as soon as possible. You are loved and you are needed. Your intrinsic value to God is unquestionable because he truly sees you as a pearl of great price.

CHAPTER EIGHT

Symbolism and Ritual

*I*t is not unusual for some Church members to feel frustrated in the temple or when reading the scriptures because the rich symbolism they encounter is hard to understand. They wonder why God couldn't just deliver his message outright, in plain language with clear definitions, to avoid potential misunderstanding. Appropriate here is the analogy of a gold mine that only provides its sought-after treasure after the miner puts in an incredible amount of work to extract it. Likewise, the wealth of extractable meaning embedded within ritual and scripture will enlighten our beings when we diligently work to dig them out of the content and patterns of the restored gospel. "It is the glory of God to conceal a thing; but the honor of kings is to search out a matter" (Proverbs 25:2).

The *Dictionary of Word Origins* will help us better understand exactly what symbols are. "Etymologically, a *symbol* is something 'thrown together.' The word's source is Greek *sumballein* .... The notion of 'throwing or putting things together' led on to the notion of 'contrast,' and so *sumballein* came to be used for 'compare.' From it was derived *sumbolon*, which denoted an 'identifying token—because such tokens were compared with a counterpart to make sure they were genuine—and hence an 'outward sign' of something."[1]

Simply put, symbolism is the practice of comparing unlike things to express deeper meaning. An example of a metaphor [figure of speech using symbolism] would be, "her smile is a sunset." The sun is not literally bursting inside her mouth but the comparison of the two unlike things suggests that her smile provides the warmth, peace, and beauty usually associated with a sunset.

Church leaders have provided ample counsel regarding symbolism surrounding sacred ordinances. Apostle John A. Widtsoe taught,

> "We live in a world of symbols. We know nothing, except by symbols. We make a few marks on a sheet of paper, and we say that they form a word, which stands for love, or hate, or charity, or God or eternity. The marks may not be very beautiful to the eye. No one finds fault with the symbols on the pages of a book because they are not as mighty in their own beauty as the things which they represent. We do not quarrel with the symbol G-O-D because it is not very beautiful, yet represents the majesty of God .... There are men who object to Santa Claus, because he does not exist! Such men need spectacles to see that Santa Claus is a symbol; a symbol of the love and joy of Christmas and the Christmas spirit. In the land of my birth there was no Santa Claus, but a little goat was shoved into the room, carrying with it a basket of Christmas toys and gifts. The goat of itself counted for nothing; but the Christmas spirit, which it symbolized, counted for a tremendous lot. We live in a world of symbols."[2]

Societal Symbolism

An examination of religious symbols and rituals is the main purpose of this chapter, but a look at a few of the symbols, images, types, metaphors, euphemisms, and allegories found within the social fabric of our world, can give us a foundation from which to start. It is amazing how steeped we are as a people in the language of symbolism in nearly every facet of our lives. Symbolism is not a casual notion or a curious happenstance. It is a natural part of being alive to surround ourselves with images that reinforce, augment, and increase our understanding of the human experience.

Symbols appear in widely scattered parts of the world, suggesting a transfusion of ideas among civilizations. Traders and artists in the ancient world traveled far and wide exchanging merchandise and ideas, which explains how symbols popped up far away from where they originated. This is how Islam reached Southeast Asia, Buddhism extended to Japan, and Portuguese is spoken in the heart of South America. One example is the dragon. In China, it is a symbol of the glory of the emperor and the sun, while in European Christian art the dragon represents the baser part of humans.[3]

The examples of symbolism in our language are nearly endless. Here are a few: Time is money, life is a roller coaster, I am a rock, falling in love, racking our brains, hitting a sales target, climbing the ladder of success, all the world's a stage, and light as a feather.

Symbolism is found in colors:

- Black - death or evil.
- White - life and purity.
- Red - blood, passion, danger, or immoral character.
- Purple - royalty.
- Yellow - violence or decay.
- Blue - peacefulness and calm.

Objects are often used as symbols:

- Chains - coming together of two things.
- Ladders - relationship between heaven and earth or ascension.
- Mirrors – sun, but when it is broken, it means an unhappy union or a separation.

- Five interlocked rings - Olympics.
- Flags, badges, coats of arms - country, honors, and family.
- Barber shop poles – bloodletting.
- Scales - legal profession.
- Red cross - humanitarian work.

Even flowers can be symbolic:

- Roses - romance.
- Violets - shyness.
- Lilies - beauty and temptation.
- Chrysanthemums - perfection.

As a people, we also design our own symbols through graphic design. Noted graphic designer Patrick Cramsie observed, "We live in a world of signs and symbols. Street signs, logos, labels, pictures and words in books, newspapers, magazines and now on our mobiles and computer screens; all these graphic shapes have been designed. They are so commonplace we seldom think of them as a single entity, 'graphic design.' Yet taken as a whole they are central to our modern way of life."[4] We have icons for gender affixed to the doors of public toilets; hazard symbols such as the skull and cross bones for poison; the lion as a symbol of courage; an eagle for the United States, and a pine tree for Christmas.

Political movements also are rife with symbolic icons. In U.S. politics, icons of the donkey represent the Democratic Party and the elephant the Republican Party. A dove is the symbol of the United Kingdom Liberal Democrats Party. The swastika of the Nazi Party during and just prior to World War II, was once isolated as a symbol of anti-Semitism, but has since morphed into something even more heinously universal.

Good, old-fashioned American movies also contain symbolism, both in the script lines of the characters and in objects of importance to the story. Batman and the Lone Ranger are excellent examples:

Batman

Bruce Wayne: "People need dramatic examples to shake them out of apathy, and I can't do that as Bruce Wayne. As a man, I'm flesh and blood. I can be ignored, I can be destroyed, but as a symbol, I can be incorruptible, I can be everlasting."[5]

The Lone Ranger

John Reid: "Silver bullets will serve as sort of a symbol.... I want to become known to all who see the silver bullets that I live and fight to see the eventual defeat and proper punishment by law of every criminal in the West."[6]

Like symbols, rituals too are integral parts of human existence with common elements found in all cultures. While some may consider rituals archaic and no longer meaningful today, the opposite is actually true, with rituals of old finding place in our lives right alongside new ones.

Look at all the rituals of everyday life: We brush our teeth and other morning routines, wave to people, embrace, shake hands, offer a toast, give and receive gifts, conduct meetings, and use accepted social etiquette. We commemorate birthdays, holidays, anniversaries, retirement, marriage, deaths, and school graduations. We wear lucky hats, carry lucky objects, or repeat special words [like break a leg] to emphasize our hope for success in a situation. We celebrate Valentine's Day, Easter, Kwanzaa, Fourth of July, Memorial Day, Halloween, New Year's Eve, Hanukkah, and Christmas with zeal and commitment, because of what they represent to us. All of these are rituals that started somewhere in time and continued because of how they connected us to each other.

Religious Symbols and Rituals

Human nature to adopt symbols and rituals is also replete in religion. Here are a few examples of word symbols:

- Damnation - fire, flames, hot temperatures and heat.
- Death or endings - gravestones, cemeteries, grim reaper, day of the dead, skulls, candles, coffins, bell ringing, cross bones.
- Reincarnation - phoenix rising from flames, crosses, rainbows, passing storms, dawn, sunrise, broken chains.
- Love - apple, cupid, harp, heart, shell, triangle, maple leaf.
- Salvation - crosses, angels, haloes, clouds, churches.
- Knowledge - book, candle, lamp.

The Christian cross, symbolizes Christ's crucifixion and sacrifice. The olive is a symbol of peace dating back to at least the 5th century BC. Symbols of Noah and the flood, the dove, and olive branch also were used on currency on early Roman coins, and later on American and British coins.

Christian religious rituals:

- Genuflecting in front of a cross.
- Saying grace or blessing the food.
- Candle lighting at an altar.
- Worship services that usually include singing, prayer, and a sermon.
- Scripture reading.
- Baptism.
- Communion.
- Pilgrimages.
- Last Rites.
- Exorcism.
- Funeral or graveside services.

While Mormons use some of the symbols commonly employed by other Christian religions, we also have symbols unique to our faith and culture. Some of the less ritualistic symbols include the iron rod, handcarts and covered wagons, seagulls, the tree of life, CTR rings, religious paintings and pictures, the Liahona, statues of Moroni on some temples, and the beehive.

Of deeper significance are the sacrament of bread and water, baptism by immersion, priesthood blessings and ordinations, and temple ordinances.

There also are architectural symbols on temples, such as the carvings of suns, moons, and stars on the exterior of the Salt Lake Temple representing the degrees of glory. The Salt Lake Temple also has three towers on the west side, representing the Church's Presiding Bishopric, and three slightly taller towers on the east, representing the Church's governing First Presidency. In the basement of each temple is a font for baptisms that is built upon the backs of twelve stone or bronze oxen, representing the twelve tribes of ancient Israel. In the sealing, or marriage rooms of the temples, large mirrors are mounted on opposite walls, creating a reflective symbol of an eternal union between married couples.

Sometimes writers will reach for metaphors and similes when trying to describe something they have never seen before, as did Joseph Smith and Sidney Rigdon when they tried to describe the Savior. "His eyes were *as* a flame of fire; the hair of his head was white *like* the pure snow ... his voice was *as* the sound of the rushing of great waters" (D&C 110:3.)

Anthropologists say ritual is a universal feature of human social existence. In the field of Interaction Ritual Analysis, pioneered by Erving Goffman and Emile Durkheim, we learn that everyday secular life is organized by a set of rituals among people who live in a society. The idea is that people are constant in who they are and how they react—as seen in sayings such as, everyone is unique, be yourself, don't give in to social pressure, to your own self be true—but they have a need to be part of a group or social order. Rituals provide a powerful social mechanism that reinforces group coherence and produces social solidarity. This can be seen in the collective singing of the national anthem or the recitation of the Pledge of Allegiance in the U.S. We see it in the group watching of sporting events when fans collectively wear team insignias and engage in such show-of-spirit activities as "doing the wave" or storming the basketball court after a win. These rituals provide a focal point for emotional processes and generate symbols of group membership. They help people to experience a shared sense of exaltation and group transcendence.[7]

This same principle holds true with religious groups. Durkheim's theory implies that (a) any object could become socially defined as sacred; and (b) repeated veneration of sacred objects creates stable social relations. Rituals are foundational to voluntary collective action and "fulfill the need which the believer feels of strengthening and affirming, at regular intervals of time, the bond which unites him to the sacred beings upon which he depends." Church attendance, prayer, and scripture reading are the most common measurements of religious behavior, both inside and out of formal worship.[8]

Religious rituals also link the community backwards to primordial time. They link people to a religious history that provides reminders that their religious rituals go back in unbroken succession throughout time and into the future. This is most obvious in Judaism, Christianity, and Islam, where adherents are ever reminded of the vast generational span of their religion through scripture and historical and symbolic events.[9]

It is evident how symbols and rituals have found their way into every aspect of our lives, not just in modern times, but also throughout recorded history. Why is this important? It's important because humans have an innate attraction to symbolism, which makes it the perfect avenue for God and Christ to teach the gospel. Symbolism is truly an art, a transcendent way to give meaning to the every day and obscure conventions and ideologies of life. Its meanings go beyond the obvious, to adorn and beautify the world around us as well as help us energize our minds and spirits to search for deeper insights about God.

Jesus taught through the symbolism of parables because it was a way of veiling or revealing truth based on the mind-set of the listener. The disciples, after hearing all the parables now recorded in Matthew 13, realized that Jesus was making them dig deeper for meaning beyond the literal, beyond face value. There was method to his ministrations and the disciples were beginning to grasp it.

Gaskill offered six possible reasons the Savior would choose to use symbols when teaching or establishing modes of worship and ritual. He said symbols require people to ponder and dig for insights; they protect sacred ideals from those not prepared to receive them; they translate well into all cultures; they bring to our memories over time the associated meanings we originally gave them; they're multilayered nature can give different degrees of insight; and they clarify abstract concepts.[10]

God knew that gospel teachings would have a greater and more lasting effect on us if taught through symbolism rather than a simple recitation of a principle. He knew we'd have to search and struggle to gain the insight inherent within the symbolism, which would by extension, cause us to grow and progress in a deeper way.

For example, imagine if Alma never offered his beautiful allegory of planting the seed of faith in our hearts, nourishing it, and having it grow into a tree that produces fruit unto everlasting life (see Alma 32). If he had, instead, taught blandly that the people should listen to his counsel and do what he instructed to find truth, there would be far less spiritual impact, producing far fewer conversions. It's the melody and imagery of Alma's symbolic language that beckons the listener [reader] to accept his invitation and begin the process of increasing their faith.

Unfortunately, some in the Church get discouraged because of their inability to understand the symbolism, and so withdraw from participation in the gospel. My hope is that they will not give up, but will seek harder to receive the truths contained within. For those who hunger for truth and clarity, the intensive process of digging and struggling to learn the language of revelation will not dissuade them from the enlightenment they seek. Church leaders and scholars tell us that fluency in the language of the spirit means fluency in the language of symbolism.[11]

Symbolism in the Scriptures

The scriptures are literally bursting with symbolism that involve body parts, clothing, colors, numbers, directions, people, names, animals, and Christ, himself. For instance, the *arm* suggests power and strength in some circumstances and shows submission and humility when folded in prayer. The use of the word *bowels* can connote compassion, or if linked with the loins, represent fertility.

The symbol of the olive is found throughout the Apocrypha, the Pseudepigrapha, the Mishna, and Talmud, with the olive wreath representing kingship, authority, and the tree of life. Because the olive was of economic and religious importance in the ancient world and was very much at the heart of Judaic customs, its allegorical rendition in Jacob 5 is very intriguing. The allegory of the olive tree is a beautiful expression of the desires of God concerning the house of Israel." Let's look at a few of the items in scripture that contain symbolic meaning.

Numbers. In addition to usage among Christians, numbers were used symbolically among the Hebrews, Greeks, Romans, Babylonians, Egyptians, Aramaeans, and Gnostics, many of these long before Moses authored the oldest biblical books.[12] Seven is the most common number used symbolically in scripture, followed by three. Examples of seven include, God rested on the seventh day, Israel was exiled to Babylon for 70 years, seven devils left Mary of Magdala, forgive until seventy times seven, and seven angels having the seven last plagues.

The number three is seen in the Godhead, the length of Jesus' mortal ministry, the number of times Satan tempted him, and the three days his body laid in the tomb. The references go on and on: Jonah spent three days in the belly of the great fish; God spoke to the Nephites three times before they knew it was him; Christ was crucified at the third hour. It also emphasizes the distinct and separate nature of the Godhead. The use of numbers as symbols is all throughout the standard works.

Geographical directions. East, the direction used the most in LDS scripture, represents God. If something came from the east it was representative of something being sent by God—both blessings and punishments. The other directions also are symbolic. South means literally right or right hand, and west traditionally connotes negativity—something to be discarded or lacking in priority.[13] North is used as a direction of orientation, but also as a symbol for darkness, obscurity, and apostasy. References to the lost tribes returning from the north, implies they will come back out of darkness and apostasy, not an actual northern location.[14]

Symbols for Christ. These are seen throughout scripture in the form of people, animals, objects, food, events, and places, to show that all things truly testify of Christ. Most LDS and non-LDS commentators suggest that every prophet recorded in scripture was actually a type for Jesus Christ.[15] Abraham's offering of his son, Isaac, as a sacrifice, parallels God's offering of his Beloved Son, Jesus. Despite Job's suffering, he was described as being "perfect and upright," (Job 1:1), emulating Jesus' lack of sin. Jonah's experience in the belly of the whale for three days and three nights symbolizes Christ's death, burial, and resurrection (Matthew 12:38-40).

When you look at the story of Cain and Abel, you see a distinct typology for the conflict between Jesus and Lucifer in the preexistence. This is evident in a number of story elements between the brothers. Abel was a shepherd while Cain was a "tiller of the ground" (Moses 5:17). Cain's offering was rejected by the Lord and Abel's was accepted. Cain killed his brother and convinced many of his siblings to leave their parents and the gospel to dwell in another land.[16]

The *sacrificing of animals*, often the first born, found throughout scripture, are types of Christ. *Food* is also commonly used in scripture for Christ, the best known being manna as the "Bread of Life" (John 6:35). *Objects* can symbolize Christ, as in the seventeenth chapter of the book of Numbers, where twelve dead branches were brought to the tabernacle, and on the next day, only the one belonging to the Tribe of Levi blossomed. Not only did this indicate which tribe would be given authority to officiate in the priesthood, but also attested to the resurrection of Christ from the dead.

Events also attest to the mission of Christ. In the story of Noah's ark, the Hebrew word *kpr*, translated as *pitch* or a waterproofing substance used on the wood denotes a protective covering. In every other instance where this Hebrew word is found, we know it is referring to the atonement, another kind of protective covering. Furthermore, Noah knew that as the waters covered the land on which he dwelt because of sin, the result of the Fall, the ark [Jesus Christ] would be the only means of survival from death and sin.[17]

Of special interest to Mormons is the idea that *places* also are used as types for Christ as is seen in Abraham's account of Kolob, the planet or star nearest to the throne of God (Abraham 3:3, 9). It is not solely an account about astronomy, but is a symbol for Christ and contains a greater message about God's plan for our exaltation.[18] Gaskill described several passages that show this:

- The name of "the great one" is Kolob because it is near unto God (Abraham 3:3, 16) – Jesus is the Great One because of his nearness to God.
- Kolob is the star or planet nearest to the throne of God (Abraham 3:2) – Jesus is nearest to God in attributes and relation.
- Kolob is "after the manner" of, or in the likeness of, the Lord (Abraham 3:4, 24) – Jesus is in the likeness of the Father (Hebrews 1:3).
- Kolob is the "first creation" (Abraham 3:2) – Jesus is the Firstborn of the Father (D&C 93:21).[19]

The parables and allegories Jesus used ranged from simple stories about life during his time to those meant to aid us in our relationships. The story of "The Good Shepherd" (John 10:1-18) and "The Vine" (John 15:1-8) are good examples of biblical allegories. In religious history, most teachers have used some form of parable in their instruction, but none so exclusively as Jesus at one period of his ministry.[20] In modern times, some have questioned this method of teaching as did his disciples of old (Matthew 13:10). But just as so many Old Testament and ancient Hebrew stories pointed to Jesus Christ and his mission, many of Jesus' own parables bore specific testimony of his mission and coming atonement. These include the parables of the lost sheep, lost coin, prodigal son, laborers in the vineyard, unmerciful servant, Good Samaritan, wicked husbandmen, ten virgins, and wedding supper.

This is just a small taste of what the scriptures hold in the way of symbols and types. They provide us with a stunning realization that to fully comprehend God we must find a way to comprehend his language of symbolism. It requires thinking and searching along with prayer and faith, all of which are at the very core of why we are here.

The Temple

Other than when the priesthood was removed from the earth during the Dark Ages, God's people have always been commanded to build temples for ordinance work and as a place of worship. In cases of extreme poverty or emergency, these ordinances have sometimes been done on a mountaintop (see D&C 124:37-55). We see this in Mount Sinai, the Mount of Transfiguration, and in the portable tabernacle of Moses during the Israelites' wilderness wanderings. In the Book of Mormon, we see it when the brother of Jared spoke to and saw the Lord, and when Nephi climbed a mountain to gain knowledge on building a boat. The most familiar temple from biblical times was Solomon's temple built in Jerusalem, destroyed in 587 BC, and rebuilt by Zerubbabel about 70 years later. It was then somewhat burned in 37 BC and partially rebuilt by Herod the Great until it was finally destroyed by the Romans in AD 70.[21]

Unfortunately, many truths of the gospel were lost through the apostasy, including baptism by immersion, apostles and prophets, a lay ministry, and the Godhead as separate personages. Also lost were temple rites and practices, though many vestiges remain in the form of ceremonies, architecture, and priestly clothing in various religions. The temple is not merely a fabrication of Joseph Smith as some doubters might think. It has roots in ancient Christian and Jewish practices that became borrowed and corrupted over time. It is perhaps the greatest loss, because the temple is the spiritual base of LDS theology, and acts as a compass to give our lives direction and meaning. Hugh Nibley once called the temple "a scale model of the universe."[22]

Such a description holds true historically. According to the Talmud, the temple at Jerusalem existed before the foundations of the world (*Pesahim* 54a-b). It was considered a cosmic center, or navel, of the earth. The Muslims established the Kaaba [a sacred cuboid building] in Mecca by imitating both Jewish and Christian ideas about the temple as the center of the earth. Traditions originating from the temple at Jerusalem went forth all over the Jewish, Christian, and Muslim worlds.[23]

It is a given that temples were an important part of the Abrahamic religions, so it makes sense that some of our everyday symbolic behaviors would actually have a tie to temple rituals. The simple extended hand when greeting someone in our Western culture goes back to the ancient ritual of requesting a "token of recognition" from someone encountered. The act of bowing or kneeling in prayer connotes submission. Bathing, over and above hygiene, is a metaphor for washing or scrubbing one's body to remove impurity.[24]

The Endowment in Antiquity

For those who struggle to understand aspects of temple ordinances, it might help to learn that those ordinances have been around for a long time. They did not originate with the restored gospel, but were ancient rituals brought back, along with other lost truths, during this dispensation of the fulness of times. A look at the historical record will bear this out and provide us with a deeper connection to these sacred practices.

Some of this historical record comes from the Apocrypha and the Pseudepigrapha, which are a collection of Jewish writings dating from approximately the 13th - 3rd centuries BC. They are not included in the Christian Bible. However, the Apocrypha are still included in the canon of the Roman Catholic and Orthodox churches, while the Pseudepigrapha are not, nor are they included in the Apocrypha or Jewish literature. Both records are of interest to scholars, because they help explain how Judaism and Christianity came to be.[25]

There are a number of documents from the second century BC through the fifth century AD that describe parts of the temple endowment, demonstrating its ancient beginnings. Of these elements Brigham Young said, "Your endowment is, to receive all those ordinances in the House of the Lord, which are necessary for you, after you have departed this life, to enable you to walk back to the presence of the Father, *passing the angels who stand as sentinels, being enabled to give them the key words, the signs and tokens, pertaining to the Holy Priesthood,* and gain your eternal exaltation in spite of earth and hell" (italics added).[26]

Elements of the endowment are found in a number of early Jewish and Christian texts. Epiphanius, an early church father (*Heresies* 36.13), cites the Gospel of Philip as saying, "The Lord revealed unto me what the soul must say as it goeth up into heaven, and how it must answer each of the powers above." In the *Testament of Isaac* 6:4, we read, "Then they [the angels] took me by the hand and led me to the curtain before the throne of the father." Note also the following from *Apocalypse of Elijah* 1:7-11:

> "Therefore become sons to him since he is a father to you. Remember that he has prepared thrones and crowns for you in heaven, saying, 'Everyone who will obey me will receive thrones and crowns among those who are mine.' The Lord said, 'I will write my name upon their forehead and I will seal their right hand, and they will not hunger or thirst. Neither will the son of lawlessness prevail over them, nor will the thrones hinder them, but they will walk with the angels up to my city.' Now, as for the sinners, they will be shamed and they will not pass by the thrones, but the thrones of death will seize them and rule over them because the angels will not agree with them."[27]

Also, recorded in the Pseudepigrapha, Isaiah had a vision that Jesus gave passwords to the angels he passed while going through the seven heavens to be born on Earth: "And those who kept the gate of the (third) heaven demanded the password, and the LORD gave (it) to them in order that he should not be recognized …. And again I saw when he descended into the second heaven, that there again he gave the password, for those who kept the gates demanded (it), and the LORD gave (it) …. And again I saw when he descended into the first heaven, that there he gave the password to those who kept the gates …. And again he descended into the firmament where the prince of this world dwells, and he gave the password to those who (were) on the left …. And he did not give the password."[28]

The Handclasp

Handclasps in the temple, which detractors say were borrowed from Masonry, were very much a part of early Christianity, as supported by this excerpt from Todd Compton, Ph.D., an American historian in the field of Mormon history:

> "The handclasp continued in early Christian ritual, both gnostic and orthodox. According to Galatians 2:9, 'the right hand of fellowship' is given 'as a sign of friendship and trust,' though this does not necessarily suggest ritual practice …. The handclasp as marriage rite, however, continued in Christian surroundings. The salvific handclasp is nearly the trademark of the iconography of Christ's postcrucifixion descent into Hades. One of the most frequent scenes in this tradition is that of Christ grasping the hands of Adam and Eve to lift them up out of hell and to resurrect them. While sometimes he grasps their wrists … in other depictions he lifts them. .
>
> "The fifth-century *Gospel of Nicodemus* describes a true handclasp: 'And the Lord … took the right hand of Adam and went up out of hell, and all the saints followed him …. He went therefore into paradise holding our forefather by the hand, and delivered him, and all the righteous, unto Michael the archangel.' Here the [handclasp] starts the ascent, continues it, and ends it on the threshold of paradise. A similar handclasp is used in the apocalyptic 1 Enoch: 'And the angel Michael … seizing me by my right hand and lifting me up, led me out into all the secrets of mercy; and he showed me all the secrets of righteousness.'"[29]

Here we see how this important ritual within the temple endowment is found in the practices of early Christians. It also suggests the use of handclasps in ceremonies even earlier because of the existence of temples where sacred rituals were performed. Any other place where we find the use of handclasps must be viewed as having been borrowed from the temple endowment after exposure to it somewhere in history.

Names

Within the Bible and throughout history, the names people were given were significant and sacred. Names meant something to the parent giving the name such as Rachel naming her son Benoni [son of my sorrow] because of an intense labor (Genesis 35:18), or Hannah naming her son Samuel [heard of God] because she felt her son was an answer to prayer (1 Samuel 1:20). In Hebrew culture, sometimes names were changed to show a new phase in the person's life, such as with Abram, Sarai, and Jacob [changed to Abraham, Sarah, and Israel]. We also see it in the New Testament when Simon becomes Peter and Saul becomes Paul.

Emphasis on names can be seen throughout other ancient civilizations as well. Reflected in the ordinances of ancient societies was a belief that if one became privy to a secret name he must guard it carefully. It was believed that the discoverer of a person's secret name would give them power over that person.[30] Those who advance to the celestial kingdom will have a "white stone" on which is written "a new name ... which no man knoweth save he that receiveth it. The new name is the key word" (D&C 130:11).

Drama

The temple endowment occurs within a drama in which participants re-enact the plan of salvation from the creation of the world to their acceptance into the celestial kingdom. Some doubters may well ask why something as important as a temple ordinance is conducted via play acting. Interestingly, this method of teaching through dramatization is very much a part of what non-LDS anthropologist Erving Goffman says about life being a theater. He says sociologically, people live their lives as if using a front stage and a backstage to interact with others. The front stage of publicity is where the self uses lots of props, and works hard to present itself in a certain way, whereas in the backstage, the private self exists. The self, from Goffman's perspective, is more public than private because it is built on interaction with others. The interactions we have each day are akin to dramatization rituals that create our realities.[31]

From early on in religion, the theater was a tool to help man find explanations about himself that he couldn't find in nature. Over time, drama was used to attract the attention of and influence an audience on political issues, injustice, or controversial topics as well as religion, without getting into arguments. Anthropologists suggest theatrical rituals in religion can be powerful communication tools that make human foibles acceptable. They can also be understood by both educated and uneducated people because of the inner emotions drama can invoke. Goffman said that religion in one form or another has always used theatrical technique to communicate its messages.

An example is when the Egyptian Pharaoh around 2000 BC encouraged the worship of the God Osiris through a play called "Passion."[32] Dramatic religious rituals are all throughout religions of the world, many of which are still performed today, such as the Persians/Iranians reenactment annually of the martyrdom of Imam Hussein or the theatrical Christian Holy processions, or the Whirling Dervish dance in Islam. All use theater dramatization techniques in a ritualistic pattern.[33]

Creation Drama

Daniel Ludlow, BYU professor of religion and chief editor of *the Encyclopedia of Mormonism*, said over time the creation drama in the temple was diffused into many civilizations and was eventually corrupted and lost. It is seen in the Memphite theology of Egypt, in the Babylonian New Year's rites, in the great secular celebration of the Romans, in the *panagyris* and beginnings of Greek drama, in the temple texts of Ras Shamra, and in the Celtic mythological cycles. Persecutions arose because Jews and Christians tried to keep the ceremonies secret and claimed that they alone possessed the mysteries of God. Temple rites became subject to a variety of interpretations and were copied and modified in these various other cultures.[34] Through the restoration of the gospel of Christ, Joseph Smith was given the creation ceremony in its original form once again.

Patterned after God's temples of old, our temples today include ordinances of baptism for the dead, initiatory, the endowment, and sealings. All involve symbolic clothing and some involve various rituals such as handclasps. But the endowment alone uses both these elements along with a reenactment dramatization of man's journey of life. For the Doubting Thomas, please note that this use of theatrics in religious teaching is right in line with historical accounts in religions throughout the world. It also is right in line with modern fields of anthropology that have found the nature of humans is to actually interact with each other as if on a stage. Again, God knows our nature and has designed teaching methods that go to the core of our humanness to achieve the best possible outcomes for growth.

Because we can place key concepts of the temple endowment squarely in the ancient world, suggestions that it was made up by Joseph Smith are simply false. This and other ordinances performed there clearly originate anciently, and should provide some assurance that if they were from God then, they're still from God now.

Ancient Origin of Sacred Clothing

The word endowment originates from a Latin word that means the conferral or bestowal of a gift.[35] Our endowment in the temple should be seen as a gift from God to help us become exalted. A further look at ancient words and definitions brings us to the word *endue*, which Jesus used to refer to his disciples as being "endued with power from on high" (Luke 24:49). It is a Greek form and root of the word *endow*, which means "to clothe."[36] Joseph Smith sometimes used the word "endument" for endowment, which gives a clear signal about the importance of the act of being clothed in the temple. This gift of clothing was the first act provided by God to our first parents in the Garden of Eden after their Fall to help protect and uplift them in their journey through life.

Sacred clothing also is seen in antiquity as having special meaning in temple and other important rituals. Many believe the conventional robes of the Christian clergy were adopted late in the fourth century at best and are of pagan origin. But scholars of the Jewish and Christian apocalyptic tell a different story. Hugh Nibley said, "What they say is in closest agreement with the oldest writings of the Egyptians and Babylonians, for that matter, taking us into a world which has been completely forgotten until our own day and introducing us to concepts in modern times first made known to the world by Joseph Smith."[37]

Nibley's detailed research on sacred temple clothing is excellent and well worth the read, so I will not attempt to repeat it here. He also provides discussion about baptism for the dead, the early Christian prayer circle, sacred vestments, apocryphal writings, geometrical symbols, and much more. They can be found in *Mormonism and Early Christianity,* vol. 4, of *The Collected Works of Hugh Nibley* (Salt Lake: Deseret Book, 1987), and *Temple and Cosmos,* vol. 12, of *The Collected Works of Hugh Nibley* (Salt Lake City: Deseret Book, 1992). But a brief insertion from him here will provide a taste of some of what's out there and give the reader some evidence that the clothing in our temples is completely in line with the ancients, clear back to Adam and Eve. It only seems odd to some of us now because of their ancient origin.

Nibley pointed to a publication by Moshe Levine that describes in detail, through translated Hebrew, the priestly vestments worn in the temple by early Christians.

> "Thou shalt make holy garments for Aaron thy brother," the Lord tells Moses (see Exodus 28:2), *lekabod ultip'eret,* "both for glory and for magnificence"—to give an impression, to fill one with awe. And the Lord instructed Moses to say to all the people of "thoughtful-mindedness" and

intelligence "that they shall do so, and make such garments for Aaron, for holiness, and for his priesthood, to represent his priesthood to me" (see Exodus 28:3). "And these are the garments which they shall make; a breastplate, and an *'epod* ... and the *meʿîl*," "a cloak, a covering, a long garment;" "a *ketonet*," the "shirt;" "a *tashbets*," a thing elaborately woven in a checkerboard pattern, or something similar; "a mitre" *miznepet*, "a turban," "a round cap;" "and a girdle" or "sash;" "and these garments they shall make holy for Aaron, thy brother, and for his sons, to serve me in the priesthood" (Exodus 28:4).[38]

Additionally, the Testament of Levi (8:2-10) in the Pseudepigrapha, a document to which Joseph Smith did not have access, also mentions sacred temple clothing:

"And I saw seven men in white clothing, who were saying to me, 'Arise, put on the vestments of the priesthood, the crown of righteousness, the oracle of understanding, the robe of truth, the breastplate of faith, the miter for the head, and the apron for prophetic power.' Each carried one of these and put them on me and said, 'From now on be a priest, you and all your posterity.' They first anointed me with holy oil and gave me a staff. The second washed me with pure water, fed me by hand with bread and holy wine, and put on me a holy and glorious vestment. The third put on me something made of linen, like an ephod. The fourth placed ... around me a girdle which was like purple. The fifth gave me a branch of rich olive wood. The sixth placed a wreath on my head. The seventh placed the priestly diadem on me and filled my hands with incense, in order that I might serve as priest for the Lord God."[39]

When Hugo Odeberg, an influential Swedish theologian and professor at Lund University, translated the Hebrew book of Enoch, he found the ceremonial veil mentioned was marked with "the secrets of the world's creation and sustenance ... in short, the innermost Divine secrets." He found that as the person progressed through the ceremony, a change of some kind occurred with regard to the garment or robes implying an increase in glory.[40]

Garments as Coverings

Unfortunately, people sometimes scoff at the wearing of garments. Perhaps if they understood their history and significance, they would feel it more of an honor to wear them than a burden. When Mormons finish their work at the temple, they depart wearing a white undergarment, which serves as a tactile reminder of the temple experience and as a boundary between the believer and the profane world. Once again, history shows that sacred garments are not new to the modern world.

Ezekiel said special undergarments, "linen garments," the "linen bonnets upon their heads," and the "linen breeches upon their loins," were to be worn as part of temple work and worship, both anciently and in modern times (Ezekiel 44:17-18). Jewish tradition says the earliest raiment worn by Jewish priests was believed to be the garments of skin provided to our first parents after the Fall.[41] Mormons are told their garments will bring blessings and spiritual protection from the buffetings and temptations of the world. Interestingly, Louis Ginzberg, a non-Mormon scholar in Jewish studies said, "God killed certain animals in order to furnish Adam and Eve with clothes." They "received their garments [of skin] from God after the Fall ... and [Adam's] descendants wore them as priestly garments at the time of the offering of the sacrifices. Furthermore they ... [are said to have had] supernatural qualities."[42]

The scriptures are filled with references relating to garments and clothing. Enoch declared, "I beheld the heavens open, and I was clothed with glory" (Moses 7:3). Jacob suggested on the day of judgment, "we shall have a perfect knowledge of all our guilt, and our uncleanness, and our nakedness;

and the righteous shall have a perfect knowledge of their enjoyment, and their righteousness, being clothed with purity, yea, even with the robe of righteousness" (2 Nephi 9:14). Isaiah said, "God ... hath clothed me with the garments of salvation, he hath covered me with the robe of righteousness" (Isaiah 61:10). Alma mentioned "all the holy prophets, whose garments are cleansed and are spotless, pure, and white" (Alma 5:24).

These references suggest a two-fold purpose for sacred garments: Cleanliness and purity within our hearts and souls, and a spotless covering over that soul denoting a life of righteousness and consecration to God. The wearing of garments is very much in keeping with the symbolism behind Paul's admonition to "take upon you the whole armor of God" (Ephesians 6:13; see D&C 27:15).

Aprons

Clothing has always been important in ancient societies and was a way for prophets to make ethical exhortations, send theological messages, and indicate the status of people.[43] The most familiar article of clothing mentioned in scripture and the temple is the apron of fig leaves, which anciently, symbolized fertility and reproduction. When Adam and Eve opted to follow God's command to "be fruitful and multiply" they donned aprons of fig leaves, the very symbol of fertility and reproduction. An ancient Semitic custom has children wearing a loose cloak for raiment until they reach sexual maturity when they begin to wear an apron or loincloth, which represented adulthood.[44] So, it was appropriate for Adam and Eve to wear aprons once they had decided to reproduce, reaching maturity, as it were, both physically and spiritually. As with many symbols, the fig leaf has multiple meanings. "Covered their nakedness" also means to make excuses for one's actions, something the temple apron appropriately addresses.

LDS scholars believe that the two items of clothing possessed by Adam and Eve in the Garden—the apron (Genesis 3:7) and the garment of skins (Genesis 3:21)—had ritual meaning, and likely became archetypes for later sacred apparel used in the Israelite temple system.[45] Anciently, priests wore clothing to represent the clothing of God and angels, and were held to be so sacred that when they wore out they had to be burned in the temple. Dressing in sacred clothing in the temple, then and now, represents a role change from ordinary human to priest or priestess, king or queen, and shows a preparation for higher work.[46]

Robes

The scriptures provide many instances where people wore special robes as a depiction of priesthood power promised to all who entered the temple and kept the covenants made within (Isaiah 61:10, Revelation 6:11; 7:9; 19:8). It's easy to see how the robe as a symbol for power could have found its way through the centuries into all kinds of societal conventions in modern times. Think of the judge's robe and those worn by high school and college graduates. Both are symbolic of power or newly achieved power in our current world. We see them throughout other religions as well, such as minister robes, pulpit gowns, church vestments, rabbinical gowns, baptismal robes, choir robes, or doctoral robes.

Caps

The scriptures describe the wearing of hats or "miters," by men in the temple (see Exodus 28:4, 37, 39; 29:6; 39:28, 31; Leviticus 8:9; 16:4; Zechariah 3:3-5) symbolizing nobility and freedom.[47] The caps worn by the priests in the tabernacle (Exodus 39:28) were of white linen and flat on top.[48] Nibley said the flat, tasseled, mortarboard caps in graduation exercises came from temple clothing caps. He said the tassel is "the emergent flame of the fully enlightened."[49]

 LDS Author Matthew Brown's study of the temple indicated that the high priest of the temple wore a crown of pure gold. A single cord, string, or line [*pathil*] was used to secure the golden crown of the high priest onto the front of his white linen headdress (see Exodus 28:36–38; Leviticus 8:9).[50] Furthermore, in a ceremony called rajasuya, the king of India is clothed in sacred garments which are said to be marked in special ways, representative of the ceremony undertaken by the king. The garment includes a cap and the ends of it are tied into the upper garment. Throughout the ritual, the king is called by the name of the various gods whom he is impersonating. He is taken back into primordial time and performs the same functions symbolically which the gods and the first king did at that time, thus obtaining heaven ....[51]

Volumes more have been written showing evidence of sacred clothing and under garments associated with ancient temples. Suffice it to say, the evidence is great. But for the purpose of this book, my hope is the fact that such vestments were an integral part of ancient temple worship for those allowed to go within, will be sufficient reason for why they are still in use today. What was true then must still be true now if God is the same yesterday, today, and forever.

Embracing the Symbolism

J. Golden Kimball, First Council of the Seventy from 1892 to 1938, once said, "Every window, every steeple, everything about the temple speaks of the things of God, and gives evidence of the faith of the people who built it." I've heard this idea many times since going through the temple, and have tried very hard to look for the symbols and search out their meanings. The more I have pursued this topic, the closer I have come to answers that have increased my faith beyond measure. Each of us must likewise, search out our own meanings. The following is some of what I have learned and interpreted to give me a fuller, richer, more meaningful experience in the temple.

One of the functions of the endowment is to teach us the plan of salvation, beginning with the creation of Adam and Eve, who represent us all. Through the use of overflowing symbolism, we follow their journey through mortality, their redemption through the atonement of Christ, and their return to the presence of God. Even the Garden of Eden, itself, symbolizes the first temple on Earth.⁵² Scriptural accounts and the temple endowment place the garden at the east end of Eden, the holy direction, indicating it is a holy sanctuary within the area known as Eden, just like a temple.

Looking at the allegorical components of the story of Adam and Eve, we learn that Adam was created first, just like our spirits were created first. Eve was created figuratively from man, so represents the physical self, which was created second, after our spirits. I always thought that because Adam was created first, he is supposed to be over the woman in authority, but what the order may actually represent is that the spirit was first created, followed by the body. This interpretation suggests that the account of Adam and Eve may not be about male and female roles at all. It may be more about the importance of embracing our spiritual selves first, in order to help our physical selves grow in harmony with our spirits. In the temple we should remember that each individual going through the endowment, regardless of gender, is represented by both Adam and Eve, and not just men for men and women for women. Adam symbolizes the spirit, Eve symbolizes the body, but both pertain to each individual.

As for God's words to Eve that "thy desire shall be to thy husband, and he shall rule over thee" (Moses 4:22), it's perfectly reasonable to accept the above symbolic understanding and still accept that our first parents actually existed and were sealed by God as husband and wife in the garden (Genesis 2:22-24). Once the priesthood is introduced into the first family unit as it was in the garden, each took on different responsibilities. President Spencer W. Kimball explained that the Hebrew word translated as "rule" would better be understood as "preside" and even then, it's only in righteousness.⁵³ Correlatively, God introduced Eve to Adam in terms that are rendered into English by the phrase "an help meet for him." These words mean "to be strong, to help, rescue, or save" and "to meet, to correspond to, to be equal," thus indicating that Eve was to be a strong, saving partner in righteousness (Genesis 2:18).⁵⁴

When Mormons view the garden story as completely literal, they miss much of the light and knowledge that is embedded in the symbols of the temple. For instance, the tokens received in the temple are symbols, just like coin and paper money are tokens of our monetary system. The real value of the money lies in the worth of the tokens when they are redeemed for something else. Likewise, the real value of the tokens in the temple lies in the concept and redemptive power they represent. The endowment is to help Adam, or each of us, learn to understand and embrace what the tokens represent to prepare us in our journey to become like God. In fact, because man is so physically oriented, he may not even realize that he, himself, is the true temple and the endowment is the token. "Know ye not that ye are the temple of God, and that the spirit of God dwelleth in you" (1 Corinthians 3:16; also D&C 93:35).

We are taught that just about everything in the temple is a token or symbol of some sort, including the garment we wear, which represents the coat of skins given to Adam after being cast out of the garden. The garment, itself, also represents our bodies as the physical covering for our true temples. The garment and the apron of leaves used to cover our first parents' nakedness are alike in intent because they are used to cover Adam's nakedness or more symbolically, "lack of understanding." The apron was used in Eden whereas the garment was used in the lone and dreary world.

As we open our minds to the realm of the spiritual, we will more fully understand the tokens we are given in the temple and how they are to be used when we "pass by the angels who stand as sentinels." Tokens are simply proof of a covenant made and signs are closely linked to them. These remind us that covenants are a requirement to live with God. It is not the mysterious words or gestures of the tokens, symbols, or signs required at the veil that will bring us entrance into the presence of God, but evidence of what they represent, i.e., how well we have kept our sacred covenants. It is the level of our knowledge, wisdom, and righteousness that is required at the actual veil of exaltation.

Elder John A. Widtsoe taught: "Some have gone through the temple looking at the outward form and not the inner meaning of things. The form of the endowment is of an earthly nature, but it symbolizes great spiritual truths.... The endowment itself is symbolic; it is a series of symbols of vast realities, too vast for full understanding. Those who go through the temple and come out feeling that the service is unbeautiful have been so occupied with the outward form as to fail to understand the inner meaning. It is the meaning of things that counts in life .... No man or woman can come out of the temple endowed as he should be, unless he has seen beyond the symbol, the mighty realities for which the symbols stand."[55]

Conclusion

To learn the lessons in the symbols of the temple requires guidance from the Holy Ghost. Those lessons won't come by any other means, and there's a reason for that. Symbolism is God's way of both teaching his children as well as protecting them. It conceals sacred truths from those who are not prepared to receive them, while at the same time, offers deeper insight to those who are spiritually prepared. God does not want to reveal higher truths to his children who are not ready for them because he doesn't want to hold them accountable for knowledge they simply couldn't handle. If they obtain the deeper meanings of the temple too easily and then turn away because they weren't prepared to embrace them throughout life, they may have sealed their fate in the eternities.

So if you become frustrated by the symbolism and are tempted to turn away because of it, remember that God is doing it, in part, to protect you. But consider this: As long as you allow yourself to stay behind that protective wall of the unaware, you will remain forever unimpressed and stuck in your lack of temple understanding. Too often we sit in the temple as casual observers looking to have its sacred lessons spoon fed to us. By so doing, we miss the deeper meanings and the hidden treasures because we are not willing to put in the effort to dig them out.

It's much like the analogy of the gold mine provided at the start of this chapter. Just as the miner only obtains the treasure after working arduously to extract it, so also will only those who hunger and thirst after the spiritual lessons hidden in symbolism ultimately extract them. If they do the work to dig out the meanings through prayer, pondering, and personal revelation, their reward will be great in this life and the one to come.

It's time to dig deeper. To fully understand the symbolism of temple ordinances, we must look beyond the physical, beyond what we see and hear, and open our hearts and minds to the truly profound lessons contained within.

Let us not dismay because our finite understanding of things cannot be completely reconciled with the symbols, rituals, and rites displayed in the temple. Let us accept that they live and breathe in antiquity and that as we continue to serve within those hallowed halls, our faith will increase and the mysteries of God will be revealed to us. Reflect on the symbolism, search out the meanings embedded so richly within, then look unto the Lord and he will enlighten you.

CHAPTER NINE

A World of Evil, Tragedy, and Challenge

One of the most difficult challenges people face when struggling to cultivate a belief in God is how a perfect God of love who is capable of accomplishing all things merely by the word of his power, would create a world fraught with so much evil and suffering. It seems to be in opposition to everything for which God stands, and yet it is woven tightly into the very fabric of human existence. The reality of it is so distressing even scientists who were surveyed on their beliefs indicated evil in the world was their main rationale for not believing in God.[1]

Individuals and families face tragedy every day that seem arbitrary and unfair, sometimes straining their faith to the brink. Add to that mankind's record of mayhem and carnage, and suffering takes on a whole new meaning. The historical record is full of global atrocities of unimaginable proportions that seem to be repeating themselves at alarmingly accelerated rates.

How can we even fathom the cold-blooded murder of five to six million Jews in Nazi Germany, the heinous slaughter of Cambodians during the Vietnam War, or the genocide of 800,000 Rwandans? And what about the horrifying events on American soil such as the Sandy Hook Elementary, Virginia Tech, and Columbine High School shootings, or even the mowing down of 12 innocents at a Colorado movie theater? Add to that the Jonestown and Waco, Texas massacres, serial killings, and disgruntled employees who stalk their bosses and gun them and others down without remorse. And of course, we must include the Jihadist war on Americans and the West as exemplified in the killing of nearly 3,000 people at New York's World Trade Center on September 11, 2001, and the Boston Marathon bombings that terrorized the nation on April 15, 2013. Every day the news is filled with killings, sexual abuse of children, rape, incest, swindling of peoples' life savings, assaults and robberies, human trafficking, and any other human-on-human atrocities.

Surely, humans in the express image of God, who have inherited his qualities for goodness, could not commit such cruel and heinous acts simply because it's part of human nature. Surely, there has to be an outside influence with a persuasive power so compelling, so subjugating that the light of Christ gets smothered and all but extinguished for such atrocities to occur. This chapter will explore the effects of evil in the world and the causes and circumstances surrounding a person's choice to do evil. We will get to know Satan and how he operates, and ultimately conclude that he was "a liar from the beginning" (D&C 93:25) and was unleashed upon the world, to tempt and try us. It is he and he alone, who is the very nucleus of all evil.

Satan is Alive and Well

The Doubting Thomas who questions the existence of God usually also questions the existence of Satan. Those who doubt see it as a package deal, but the very reality of evil is also a testament to the existence of God. We know there must be "opposition in all things" (2 Nephi 2:11), and that all things have their opposite—night and day, right and wrong, health and sickness, happiness and sadness. The more we know about evil—where it comes from, how it works, why it's so effective—the better equipped we'll be to combat it. But first we must accept the fact that the power of evil thrives among us, and that Satan is real and is waging war on all the inhabitants of the earth. And he's doing it one individual at a time. Once one person is in his power, others seem to collapse like dominoes into a world of darkness that leaves them spiritually prostrate and broken.

When people don't believe in the existence of Satan, they unwittingly fall into his biggest trap. Nephi taught, "He saith unto them: I am no devil, for there is none" (2 Nephi 28:22). He even tries to portray himself as a ridiculous creature with horns and a forked tail so that none of us will take him seriously. He whispers to us all that the idea of the devil is just myth and that it is antiquated in this modern age. If he can get us to buy into this nonsense, we are giving him a free pass to plant any lie he wants in our vulnerable minds. Apostle David B. Haight said, "To deny the existence of Satan and the reality of his evil power and influence is as foolish as ignoring the existence of electricity."[2]

So what do the scriptures teach us about Satan? When you look at biblical references of Satan, you find there aren't as many as you'd think. Nephi explained that many things have been removed from the Bible (see 1 Nephi 13:28-35) and no doubt Satan made sure that one of those lost items was himself. In his book *Putting on the Armor of God*, LDS writer Steven A. Cramer actually counted references of Satan in all the standard works.

"The word 'devil' appears in scripture 205 times and yet there is not a single reference to this word in the entire Old Testament. There is a total of 2,476 pages in all four current books of LDS scripture. The Bible comprises 1,590 pages, or 64 percent of the text and yet it only contains 29 percent of the references to Satan or the devil. The other three books of scripture contain 886 pages, or 36 percent of scripture, and yet they contain 71 percent of all references to Satan and the devil. Clearly, Satan has not been successful in hiding himself in the modern revelation as he was in the biblical records."[3]

Modern day revelation also warns us that Satan will be working frantically in these latter days to win us over and spoil God's plan to redeem his children. He's running out of time before he will be bound during the Millennium, so he's pushing his agenda with a vengeance. An eye-opening description of how powerful and far reaching his influence truly is can be found in the experiences of Spencer as described by author John Pontius in *Visions of Glory*. During a vision, Spencer saw a young man in his underwear sitting at a computer in a small home office late at night viewing pornography. The man was a returned missionary with a wife and three children whom Spencer perceived to be a good man making a bad choice. Immediately, eight evil spirits—four who were once mortal and four who were unborn minions of Satan—appeared and began to shout in a frenzied fashion at the young man to urge him on. He completely caved to their influence of achieving sexual ecstasy when they kept him focused on his own body rather than on Christ or his cherished family.[4]

Spencer also was taken in vision to a nightclub where the number of evil spirits hanging around outnumbered mortals. The spirits were urging people to revel in worldly sensations brought on by the seductive and bawdy atmosphere. Spencer also witnessed the same thing at a race track, party, movie theater, and casino, where comparable quantities of evil spirits interacted with mortals.[5]

From these examples, we are faced with the blatant reality that the strength and numbers of evil forces per individual mortal, are overwhelming. It's downright frightening to contemplate. Apostle Neal A. Maxwell noted that estimates of the disembodied population of the spirit world—those who have already passed through mortality—is approximately 70 billion spirits.[6] Add to that another five billion mortals alive today and you have 75 billion people who represent the two thirds of God's children who voted to come to Earth and receive physical bodies, not counting the as yet unborn spirits. Do the math and over 37 billion represents the one third of God's spirit children who chose to follow Satan and are now at war with us. This tells us that Satan has at least seven evil spirits working on each mortal on Earth today, not counting children because he is not allowed to tempt them (see D&C 29:47). But because Satan's more interested in the righteous he assigns more of his manpower to work on them.[7] This doesn't even count the evil disembodied spirits who were once mortal and now in the spirit world that Spencer witnessed.

It seems clear that if an idea, action, or impulse is not directly generated from the influence of God—"all things which are good cometh of God" (Moroni 7:12)—it is generated from Satan. It's an either/or situation with nothing in between. Even in circumstances where a person has good intentions—maybe espouses a religious tenet that is just off the mark enough to direct people away from the whole truth—it is nonetheless from the devil, who uses it as a stepping stone to lead people astray.

Global Evil

Just as God delights in the saving of a single soul, Satan also delights at the ruination of a soul to wickedness and evil. But oh how much greater is his joy when he can turn the hearts of whole families, whole communities, whole nations, making them turn on one another in the most vile of ways. I can just picture him belting out a fiendish laugh watching us cringe in horror at news headlines like these: "Terrorists Attack New York, Pentagon" (Los Angeles Times, Sept. 12, 2001); "A Ghastly Act Leaves Hundreds of Children Dead" (Akron Beacon Journal, Sept. 8, 2004), "An Act of Terror in Boston" (Washington Post, April 16, 2013).

Satan loves it when he can get us to hate each other. It may start out as an annoyance toward someone or something, which can build in intensity if it is nurtured into a full-blown explosive rage. When you transfer this power of hate to a global setting, like a spark to tinder, it takes very little to see it ignite in the direction of those it targets. Sometimes it is fueled in individuals who have experienced a constant barrage of abuse. This makes them think hate is central to all relationships and is simply how the world works. Or even more insidiously, it makes them want to lash out at others in retaliation. It's a kind of perverse inversion of the Golden Rule—do unto others what was done unto you.

You see it in the cruelty of nations through authoritarian regimes that murder their own, subject women to near-slave status, flog, stone, and amputate for the slightest infractions. You see it among gangs within major cities who engage in violence and murder against rival gangs, making war zones of our inner cities. You see it within different ideologies or among the poor who begrudge the rich, those of little stature who hate those in power, and nations who feel threatened by other nations. History has shown that differences of any kind among humans have the potential to germinate into hatred and explode into violence.

What's at the heart of all this hate? Often it's what psychologists call projection—the tendency to blame others for our problems. This is one of Satan's favorite tools. He whispers it to violent husbands, feeling stressed and powerless in their jobs, who turn their frustration on their wives to feel power over something, anything. He screams it to whole nations looking for a scapegoat for their ills as with the Irish who blame the English for violence that happened clear back in the 12th century. He pushes it onto the Tutus and the Hutsis in Rwanda's longtime feud, or the Serbs and the Croatians, or the Hatfields and McCoys.

Look at our own history in the United States. The perceived existence of witches in Salem led to the torture and murder of innocent citizens. The perceived threat of the Japanese among us during World War II led to the internment of thousands of innocent Japanese Americans. Today we blame illegal immigrants for some of our country's ills, including how they steal our jobs, burden our welfare system, and increase our crime rates. Whether true or perceived, this view on immigration is merely an example of the foot in the door Satan looks for to fuel animosity.

This is certainly the mentality behind how the German people could inflict harm to the Jews while under the influence of the Nazi Party, which blamed all the country's ills on these people. Humans all too easily find themselves engaged in collective reasoning and get on the bandwagon of hurting people as a group dynamic. Under normal circumstances, the German people would never come close to doing such things.

This reality was verified by psychologist Solomon Asch who set up experiments in 1951 that tested the extent to which people would go along with the majority—even if they knew the majority was wrong. In the test, a person was asked to view two cards and determine which line on one card matched one of three lines on another card. A group of actors who were aware of the set up also chose a line, but in their case, the choices they made were incorrect. The lengths of the lines were purposefully drawn to be obviously different but despite that, one-third of subjects lied about which lines matched just to go along with the group. This harmless transgression serves as a small indicator of how conformity to the majority can lead to mass participation in human atrocities by evil regimes.[8]

But how did we get there? What is it about the human race that moves us to violence of global proportions? The answer appears to be that people are easily manipulated, and Satan knows it. When people are surrounded by conditions of evil they become weakened into submission. The same can be true about entire societies. According to Harvard psychiatrist and historian Dr. Kenneth Levin, "Segments of populations under chronic siege commonly embrace the indictments of the besiegers, however bigoted and outrageous. They hope that by doing so and reforming accordingly they can assuage the hostility of their tormenters and win relief."[9]

A big chunk of the world is currently under attack because of terrorism. It works globally because of the fear of future attacks it generates in its victims. But its ultimate goal is to capture our hearts and minds and convert us to the tenets it advocates. Countries victimized by terrorism sometimes walk on eggshells because of intimidation that, with enough time, could turn into sympathy and then conversion. That's what evil wants. That's how millions of people in Mao Zedong's China or Pol Pot's Cambodia went from relative freedom to collectively embracing the venomous principles of Marxism.[10] It appears Satan is doing a bang-up job.

Tools of the Devil

We were told to expect this kind of evil today because in the last days "iniquity shall abound," and "the love of men shall wax cold" (Joseph Smith Translation 1:30). It doesn't take much to see that this has come to pass completely. Sadly though, we know it will only get worse. He has a bag full of tools—precision instruments really—from which to draw, that are designed to inflict the greatest damage to our souls.

Throughout time, Satan has managed to influence us through the use of imitations and counterfeits. While we see similarities among religions that indicate shared origins as described in chapter six, we also see how false religions arose because of the establishment of counterfeits to God's true religion. The children of Israel were often attracted to the religions of other nations because Satan had helped these nations establish imitations of holy things such as temples, priests, sacred clothing, and sacrificial offerings. He also set up within these false religions false prophets, scripture-like texts, and tenets that appeared to be sacred. In these imitations of the true religion were carnal appeals such as unclothed idols, temple prostitutes, and other things that stimulated sex, greed, and power.[11] No wonder the Israelites, and by extension us, had trouble staying on the straight and narrow path. Satan takes his job of destroying lives seriously and has the backup to make it happen.

Other satanic counterfeits include the fortune teller's crystal ball imitating the Urim and Thummin, false prophets mimicking the Lord's prophets, false temples designed to look like God's temples, clairvoyants masquerading as God's seers, and lust and immorality as forgeries for true and eternal love. If there is anything true, righteous, or from God, Satan makes a copy of it to lead us away from the true gospel of Jesus Christ.[12]

One of the devil's most effective tools for leading us astray is the folly of pride. Apostle and counselor in the First Presidency, Dieter F. Uchtdorf, taught: "To some, he appeals to their prideful tendencies, puffing them up and encouraging them to believe in the fantasy of their own self-importance and invincibility. He tells them they have transcended the ordinary and that because of ability, birthright, or social status, they are set apart from the common measure of all that surrounds them. He leads them to conclude that they are therefore not subject to anyone else's rules and not to be bothered by anyone else's problems."[13]

On the flip side, he is a master at persuading us to believe we are insignificant and have no worth. If he can beset us with discouragement and convince us we are nothing in the eyes of God, he can slowly destroy lives and thwart the work of salvation. But he is a liar because, as Elder Uchtdorf explained, "the Lord doesn't care at all if we spend our days working in marble halls or stable stalls. He knows where we are, no matter how humble our circumstances. He will use—in His own way and for His holy purposes—those who incline their hearts to Him. God knows that some of the greatest souls who have ever lived are those who will never appear in the chronicles of history. They are the blessed, humble souls who emulate the Savior's example and spend the days of their lives doing good."[14]

Satan also loves to introduce divisive topics into our lives that cause us to question and doubt. These might include homosexuality, polygamy, politics, global warming, and women's issues. He wants to get us arguing among ourselves, so that what starts out as civil dialogue escalates to anger, hostility, and violence. It's a scary thought when you see how much of that very scenario is already happening around us. Certainly, within the Church we see it as individual members grapple with the love they feel for their homosexual family members and the Church's stance on the matter. We see it in the rumblings among women who struggle over perceived inequality that motivates them to petition the prophet to let women hold the priesthood. These real concerns are perfect opportunities for Satan to divide and conquer if we succumb to his enticing.

Also in the devil's arsenal is his use of addiction to rob us of our agency. When we are addicted to any one thing, we surrender ourselves to that thing until it takes control over our ability to make choices. Our brain has a "pleasure center" that is activated by certain drugs or behaviors and has the ability to completely overpower us when it kicks in. It destroys our self-control, judgment, common sense, and moral compass leading us to discard everything we know and believe about right and wrong.

Here's how it works. All pleasurable experiences from drugs, monetary rewards, sex, or even a great meal, are registered in the brain through the release of the neurotransmitter dopamine. This release is consistently tied with pleasure, and when illicit feel-good drugs are added, there is a particularly powerful surge of dopamine in the brain. What leads to addiction is the speed with which a drug or pleasurable activity promotes dopamine release, the intensity of that release, and the reliability of that release. Further activity in other parts of the brain produces memory and motivation to seek out the source of pleasure again and again. Thus, an addiction is born.[15]

Drug abuse. In 2007, the National Institutes of Health reported that nearly one in 10 Americans over the age of 12 is classified with substance abuse dependence. The emotional, psychological, and social toll that addiction takes on the country is immense. The economic costs alone are estimated to exceed a half trillion dollars annually due to health care expenditures, lost productivity, and crime. Only about 10 percent of the 23 million addicts in the U.S. are even receiving the treatment they need.[16] Add to that the sad statistic that one in four children grows up in a home where someone abuses alcohol, and you have a win/win for Satan.[17]

And it's not just younger people engaging in substance abuse. National surveys show an alarming movement among those in their fifties. The use of illicit drugs, including prescription drugs for nonmedical purposes, more than doubled in this age group from 2002 to 2010, going from 907,000 to 2,375,000, or from 2.7 to 5.8 percent in this population. Among those 65 and older, 414,000 used illicit drugs in 2010.[18] These statistics are all sad and scary at the same time because they indicate that Satan is rapidly advancing in his own war on drugs.

Gambling. This haunting addiction is so powerful it has single handedly destroyed individuals and families the world over. Its vise-like grip sends incessant impulses that push and prod and morph a person into only caring about their next bet. Sometimes gamblers must lose everything—family, job, material possessions—before they even begin to realize they have a problem. According to the National Council on Problem Gambling, an estimated two million adults in the United States meet the criteria for "pathological gambling," and four to six million are considered "problem gamblers." This addiction has no barriers in that it affects all economic classes.[19] As much as $5 billion is spent on gambling in the United States every year, with gambling addicts accruing tens to hundreds of thousands of dollars in debt.[20]

Pornography. According to a recent study, about 10 percent of Americans admit to having a pornography addiction, and the experts at OvercomePornography.com say that number is increasing annually. There is big money in the pornography industry. Research indicates that $97 billion is spent annually on porn, which is higher than the revenues of Microsoft, Google, Amazon, and eBay combined.[21] Las Vegas-based therapist, Ryan Wydner said, "Brain studies have shown that … it's harder to quit porn than crystal meth or crack."[22]

Idol Worship. Another trick Satan uses in his voluminous armory of deception is to get us to worship idols that have us spending all our time and money in their pursuit. Sometimes we idolize celebrities as our exemplars and spend too much time watching them and wanting to be like them. The examples they set are not always imitation-worthy with many engaged in lives of self-absorption and debauchery. Sometimes we idolize money, prestige, or power and spend our time literally worshipping them. Anything can be an idol—social media, technology, work, exercise, sleep, eating, and sports—if they cause us to spend more time in the pursuit of them than in the pursuit of righteousness.

The trick in all these cases is never to start, and if you have, get help immediately. That's why the Church, in all its repetitive glory, keeps hammering home warnings against gambling, sexual movies, risqué reading material, questionable Internet sites, sensual music and dance, video-gaming, and various kinds of texting. We may rationalize seeing an R-rated movie because of its historical backdrop, or tell ourselves that setting a monetary limit at a casino is no worse than spending the same amount to go out on a dinner date. But that's akin to saying "I'll just drink a little poison instead of the whole bottle." Between our own rationalizations, born of the natural man, and trying to swat away the hordes of evil spirits always on the attack, it's just a matter of time before some of us have emptied the whole bottle of poison and completely deadened our spirits to the messages of God.

Moral Agency and the Fight against Evil

Two things seem to be at the heart of why people do bad things in this world: Agency and Satan. It's hard to even include the two in the same sentence because agency is an incredible gift from a loving Heavenly Father and Satan stands as the antithesis to that gift. Nevertheless, both are the means by which various degrees of calamity happen to, by, and among all people. If we choose to disavow God because of such inhumanity, we are turning our backs on the very reason for our existence and ultimately surrendering to the evil influences that want us to do just that.

In the preexistence, God rejected Lucifer's plan to send him to Earth to "redeem all mankind that one soul shall not be lost, and surely I will do it; wherefore give me thine honor" (Moses 4:1). Then when he accepted the Savior's plan instead, God explained, "Wherefore, because that Satan rebelled against me, and sought to destroy the agency of man, which I, the Lord God, had given him, and also, that I should give unto him mine own power; by the power of mine Only Begotten, I caused that he should be cast down" (Moses 4:3).

Notice that Lucifer's rebellion involved the dissolution of agency, making that principle alone *the* reason for God's rejection of the plan. Of course, Satan took a moment to childishly display his narcissistic nature by demanding recognition and glory for the plan, but it was incidental to his demands about agency. This principle was so important during this pre-earth strategy session that it caused a third of the host of heaven to follow Lucifer, which incidentally, would not have been possible without agency in the preexistence. The very thing the devil was against turns out to be the thing that benefitted him the most.

But Heavenly Father knew that a perfect world where no one needed redemption would make Earth life pointless. An omnipotent God can do anything he wants but one who has a perfect knowledge will only seek to do what is doable. Apparently, it was not doable for God's spirit children to be saved and exalted without moral agency. Moreover, God gave us commandments to keep during our sojourn on Earth, which means we needed agency in order to accept or reject his commandments. Without being tested and given the opportunity to make mistakes and learn by them, humans could never become as God. Our first parents were given the first opportunity for mortals to exercise this magnificent principle and live with the consequences, good or bad. They paved the road for the rest of us to implement this natural law that has always existed, under which worlds without number have always operated.

But in total disregard of this reasonable and beautiful principle in theology, some in science insist it is not the human spirit at all that exercises moral agency, but rather, biology that produces and controls the moral choices we make or don't make. Neuroscientists say that guilt, compassion, or embarrassment, come about because certain areas are activated in the brain. Other areas of the brain set in motion reactions of indignation and disgust. Some in neuroscience say this is proof that moral decision making is solely a product of the brain.[23]

These same neuroscientists say our brains decide our choices in advance, making our freedom to choose our behavior an illusion. This, of course, is completely in opposition to the doctrine of agency in the restored gospel. What these scientists don't understand is because we are dual beings, created with both spirit and physical bodies, it's perfectly expected that our physical brains must be involved in the processing of our moral choices. If we combine brain functions with the ability of our conscious selves to imagine future scenarios and potential consequences of our actions, we are indeed better able to make educated choices. The fact that our brain functions are predictable actually helps us act more reliably in the choices we make.

William P. Cheshire, Jr., professor of neurology at the Mayo Clinic in Florida, said, "If free will is ultimately a delusion and human decisions are reducible to the blind product of material efficient causes, then there could be no reason to argue that one ought to choose to act in a certain way instead of another .... It would make no sense to appeal to reason as a guide to decisions if all thought ultimately reduces to the irresistible consequence of material causes prodding us as inexorably as lines of computer code."[24]

People are Inherently Good

Now that we understand humans can and do make moral choices, we can't help but wonder why so many of those choices are aligned with evil. It's beyond the comprehension of most of us how people can "choose" to engage in the awful things they do to one another, but the fact is, they do. The fact is we all do. Some people make evil choices involving atrocities that put them in a class of evil all by themselves, but we all are guilty of following Satan through lesser infractions that are nevertheless wrong. With all these bad choices going on, it begs the question: Are people inherently evil or inherently good?

In the Church, we know the "natural man is an enemy to God" (Mosiah 3:19), and Alma said that men had "become carnal, sensual, and devilish, by nature" (Alma 42:10). At first glance, this sounds like man is naturally evil. But a look at D&C 20:20, clearly shows that the word natural, or nature, does not mean something innate or inborn, but refers to the fallen state we're in because of disobedience. Interestingly, *Guide to the Scriptures* on the Church website defines the natural man as "a person who *chooses* to be influenced by the passions, desires, appetites, and senses of the flesh rather than by the promptings of the Holy Spirit." The key word here is "chooses." It's the choice we make to succumb to things of the flesh that is the natural man, not the things themselves. Again, everything in God's plan is centered on agency.

Social scientists also have studied the question and provide convincing evidence that evil acts are a product of choice rather than something innate. In studies years ago, when such experiments using human subjects were allowed, we learned just how much capacity to choose evil humans really have.

After World War II, psychologist Stanley Milgram set up an experiment involving a teacher and a learner to ostensibly test the effects of punishment on learning. But its real objective was to test the level of depravity to which people can go. A teacher [the experimental subject] was told to use electric shock on a learner [an actor and confederate of the experimenter] whenever they answered a question incorrectly, and to increase the voltage with each wrong answer. Both could hear each other but had no visual contact. The simulated shock generator consisted of 30 switches in 15 volt increments, up to 450 volts, along with a rating, ranging from "slight shock" to "danger: severe shock." The final two switches were labeled "XXX." Some teachers began to question the purpose of the experiment at 135 volts, paused, but continued after being told they would not be held responsible. A few showed extreme stress after hearing screams of pain from the learner, but they all continued up to 300 volts. In the end, 26 of the 40 subjects, or 65%, went all the way to the maximum 450 volts and continued to shock the learner even though they believed that the shocks were extremely painful.[25]

Another experiment was conducted after a number of prison riots in the early 1970s. Psychologist Philip Zimbardo set up a simulated prison at Stanford University and recruited students to play either guards or prisoners in the simulation. They tried to make the conditions as real as possible, even having the Stanford Police Department cuff, book, and jail those who would be prisoners. During the very first day, conflicts arose between the prisoners and guards resulting in harsh treatment of the prisoners. Some were put into solitary confinement or stripped of clothing and made to sleep on the floor. The prisoners eventually became submissive, even though they knew they could go home at any time, but because the guards continued to dole out harsher and harsher treatments, the experiment had to be ended on the sixth day.[26]

Many have pointed out that these studies don't automatically prove how evil people can be, but instead, show how environmental and social factors can be the catalyst for our choices. In both studies the students found it difficult to stop participating, and most saw it through to the end. The reason: Once they agreed to participate in their assigned roles, they felt obligated to finish so they wouldn't appear inconsistent, or be the one to ruin the study. Also, the violence occurred gradually providing no obvious time to declare "that is enough."[27]

So here again we see human tendencies in group situations that Satan knows about and exploits in a manner that moves us to abusive conduct. Some might attribute human behavior in these and other situations to personality characteristics, but Zimbardo dismissed that idea completely. He said we shouldn't underestimate the power of situational controls over behavior because (a) they are often subtle, (b) people can choose to not get into situations that might lead to such controls, and (c) we see people who don't behave as we think we would, as weak or deviant.[28]

These studies align well with Mormon doctrine in showing that the evil people do, is a product of Satan's ability to manipulate their human weaknesses in certain situations. And he is cunningly aware of just what those situations are. Any human weakness—not an innate propensity for evil—can be exploited to entice people to engage in evil. This is why we must be ever vigilant to ensure we rise above those enticements toward even the smallest inclinations of evil and maintain a crystal clear vision of right and wrong.

Interestingly, that moral compass inherent in all human beings has even been identified in infants. In 2007, the Yale Infant Cognition Center showed that babies are actually capable of making ethical judgments by showing that in a series of simple morality plays, 6- and 10-month olds overwhelmingly preferred "good guys" to "bad guys." They found that infants are born with pro-social tendencies and appear to be predisposed to care about other people and act in an altruistic manner. In another study, 19- and 21-month olds were found to have a keen understanding of fairness. They are naturally willing to help others at a cost to themselves, are concerned when someone messes up someone else's artwork, and love to divvy up earnings after a shared task.[29]

The Biology of Goodness

Goodness also appears to have a biological component. Medical research has discovered an explanation for a whole list of philosophical and religious questions by referencing a single chemical in the bloodstream: oxytocin. Being treated decently, it turns out, causes people's oxytocin levels to go up, which in turn, prompts those people to behave more decently. This was discovered when experimental subjects given an artificial oxytocin boost behaved more generously and trustingly, prompting its nickname, "the cuddle hormone."[30]

This phenomenon has been demonstrated in the "trust game" which pairs people up via computers, while keeping their identities anonymous. Person A is given some money, then invited to send a portion of it, electronically, to person B. Person A has a motive for doing so: According to the rules, which both players know about, any money that A sends to B will triple in value, whereupon B will have the option of sending some of it back as a thank you.

Conventional wisdom suggests that Person B, acting selfishly, has no reason to give any money back. Knowing this, person A simply wouldn't send any thus stopping the game before it even starts. Yet, in trials of the game, 90% of A-people send money, while 95% of B-people send some back. When analyzed, the oxytocin in their bloodstreams revealed that by sending money to person B, person A is giving a sign of trust. When B receives the money and recognizes it as a sign of trust, it causes oxytocin to increase in him too, motivating a generous move in return.[31]

These findings provide evidence of God-like selfless qualities in humans, and suggest further that our bodies also function to help us exhibit tendencies towards goodness. We often blame the weaknesses of the flesh, or the natural man, for the bad choices we make. But because we are dual beings, we are aided by both our bodies and our spirit selves through the light of Christ, making us fully equipped to choose the right. Unless someone is a sociopath or has some other severe mental illness that blocks their ability to make correct moral choices, we all have a conscience teaching us good from evil.

Even the devil knew this in the Garden of Eden: "And the serpent said unto the woman, ye shall not surely die: For God doth know that in the day ye eat thereof, then your eyes shall be opened, and ye shall *be as gods, knowing good and evil*" (Genesis 3:4-5). God, himself, underscored this point by saying, "And I, the Lord God, said unto mine Only Begotten: Behold, *the man is become as one of us to know good and evil*" (Moses 4:28). Even Lehi repeats it to his son, Jacob: "Men are instructed sufficiently that *they know good from evil*" (2 Nephi 2:5).

President Harold B. Lee made it very clear that "we get our answers from the source of the power we list to obey. If we're following the ways of the devil, we'll get answers from the devil. If we're keeping the commandments of God, we'll get our answers from God."[32]

This principle is taught well in a story I remember about an Old Cherokee chief talking to his grandson. The chief explained to the boy, "A fight is going on inside me. It is a terrible battle—between two wolves. One wolf represents fear, anger, pride, envy, lust, greed, arrogance, self-pity, resentment, lies, and cruelty. The other wolf stands for honesty, kindness, hope, sharing, serenity, humility, friendship, generosity, truth, compassion, and faith. The same fight is going on inside you, and inside every other person, too." The grandson reflected on these words for a minute and then asked his grandfather, "Which wolf will win?" The old chief simply replied, "The one you feed."

God Provides a Balance

Even when we consistently choose to feed the good wolf in our day-to-day lives, we will still be burdened with the effects of evil all around us. That is an inescapable part of mortality. We know that correct choices will generate more peace, because righteous living brings the calming presence of the Holy Ghost. This, of course, was designed by God who promised he would not leave us alone to fight our internal and external battles over good and evil. He has his own army to influence, comfort, and guide us as a counterbalance to the buffetings of Satan. In addition to the influence of the Holy Ghost, we are surrounded by numerous spirit beings, some, deceased family members or assigned caring souls, who are ever ready to help us choose the right. They are always present to whisper the encouragement we need to keep Satan at bay. The following three stories attest to the help we can receive against the forces of the adversary.

Vickie Soule nearly lost her son through suffocation until the Holy Ghost intervened. Five-year-old Kristopher suddenly passed out from swallowing a bunch of pennies that had lodged in his throat. She helplessly watched her little boy go limp and turn completely blue, and remembered being engulfed by an evil, dark feeling as a voice whispered, "Give up, Vickie, he's dead." Immediately a peaceful, loving whisper entered her mind: "Be calm, and do the Heimlich maneuver." When Kristopher didn't respond to that, the Spirit told her to check his throat, which she did. She was able to push the coins down which opened his throat again to air. "I know if I had not heard the Holy Ghost, My Kristopher would not be here," she said later. What a wonderful example of God rushing to the rescue to thwart Satan's attempt to confuse a frightened mother.[33]

Another example comes from Art Berg, a young man who had a car accident a few weeks before his scheduled temple marriage. His neck had broken and he became paralyzed from the chest down. Art described how he felt the tug-of-war between two opposing forces for his very soul.

"On one side were all the good, right, and encouraging things in my life, led by the Lord himself. On the opposing side were Satan and his hosts, complete with all of the negative and degrading things the evil one would have me feel. In those first few days I came to understand and appreciate the vast difference in roles between these two opposing forces and the length and depth to which they would go to hurt me or to rescue me."[34]

Satan took this young man's pain and fear and whispered, "I've got you now. I have destroyed your life. Without your body you are nothing. You'll live a despicable life, and when it is over, I will have won."[35] But God countered those lies with whisperings of his own:

"Into my mind and heart came some reassuring and powerful words I will never forget. A voice said, 'Remember, Art, back a long, long time ago, when you and I sat in a great council in heaven. Remember, I said you could become like me. You thrilled at the idea. But, then I told you it would be hard, sometimes very hard. I promised you, however, with an oath and a covenant, that I would never leave you to suffer alone. Art, when you suffer, I suffer. When you hurt, I hurt. And, when you cry, I cry. I promised you then, and I will not leave you now.'" [36]

The last example is told by LDS member Nancy Richardson, who joined the Church as an adult. She had an especially moving experience involving God's love when she was a child that has comforted her throughout the subsequent trials of her life.

> "When I was eleven years old, my sister, who is my only sibling, got married. She was twenty and I was distraught that she was leaving me. You see, my parents were physical fighters and they would wait until the middle of

the night to fight. They told me years later that they chose to battle it out at night because they thought we were asleep. But who could sleep? I was so afraid and tormented because of their fights that I slept with my older sister every night.

"Soon after her wedding when I was sleeping alone in my room, I was awakened in the middle of the night by the all familiar sounds of my parents fighting. This time I was alone, terrified, and trembling as I pulled the covers over my head and prayed for protection. In time I pulled the covers away from my face to discover an image in the corner of my room. It was not clear to me if it was male or female. What I saw was a glowing white image of a being that was elevated from the floor. I kept thinking I should have been afraid, but I was enveloped in a feeling of peace. After this comforting feeling calmed me down, I dozed off, but I remember waking up several times during the night to find this being still there. It did not talk to me, but I will never forget that feeling of peace, comfort, and assurance that I would never be alone. This experience is at the heart of my testimony that God lives and loves us. I know that I have a loving Heavenly Father who knows me and knows my needs. Since that one incredible night, I have never doubted that."[37]

Not everyone will have such dramatic interventions, but everyone is promised some kind of spiritual help in the battle against evil. As we've already learned, personal revelation does not always come when we'd like it to, but eventually, it does come, and when it does, it will clear our vision and lighten our load. God will balance our daily challenges most often through the quiet repose of his spirit, but like the stories mentioned, he can also do it through the ministering of angels, through our relationships with others, or through the healing balm of the Savior, himself.

Why Bad Things Happen

Earth life is filled with suffering and tragedy for everyone and not all of it is a blue printed plan of the devil. Some we bring on ourselves through the choices we make, but others come through happenstance and no fault of our own. Sometimes we're simply in the wrong place at the wrong time. No one who ever lived has escaped it, prompting the age old question "if there is a God, why does he let bad things happen to good people?" Some have turned their backs on God after being unable to reconcile the devastating events in their lives with the idea of a loving Heavenly Father.

Some perspective can be found in the words of Spencer W. Kimball to BYU students many years ago. He asked,

> "Was it the Lord who directed the plane into the mountain to snuff out the lives of its occupants, or were there mechanical faults or human errors?
>
> "Did our Father in Heaven cause the collision of the cars that took six people into eternity, or was it the error of the driver who ignored safety rules?
>
> "Did God take the life of the young mother or prompt the child to toddle into the canal or guide the other child into the path of the oncoming car?
>
> "Did the Lord cause the man to suffer a heart attack? Was the death of the missionary untimely? Answer, if you can. I cannot, for though I know God has a major role in our lives, I do not know how much He causes to happen and how much He merely permits ....
>
> "Could the Lord have prevented these tragedies? The answer is, 'yes.' The Lord is omnipotent, with all power to control our lives, save us pain, prevent all accidents, drive all planes and cars, feed us, protect us, save us from labor, effort, sickness, even from death, if He will. But He will not ....

> "The basic gospel law is free agency and eternal development. To force us to be careful or righteous would be to nullify that fundamental law and make growth impossible."[38]

Where so many people are told over and over that "God is Love," it truly is difficult for them to understand why, if he loves us so much, he doesn't stop tragedy and evil. The great apologist writer C.S. Lewis, once observed, "God has paid us the intolerable compliment of loving us, in the deepest, most tragic, most inexorable sense.... We are not metaphorically but in very truth, a Divine work of art, something that God is making, and therefore something with which He will not be satisfied until it has a certain character." Thus it is perfectly "natural for us to wish that God had designed for us a less glorious and less arduous destiny; but then we are wishing not for more love but for less."[39]

If you've ever shaken your fist at God for some trial you were experiencing, you're not alone. Everyone handles trials differently, but it's amazing how some people can come through a physical or spiritual ordeal of gigantic proportions, positive and grateful not only that it wasn't worse, but also that they learned something. Others feel the need to rant and rave a little and curse God before slowly working their way to a place of peace, that is, unless they decide to withdraw from God altogether.

Lewis, who wrote *Mere Christianity, The Screwtape Letters,* and *Chronicles of Narnia,* was an Oxford professor who became famous for helping a whole generation find God through his writing. But even he went through a dark period in his faith when his wife, Joy, whom, he married late in life at age 57, died of bone cancer after only three years of marriage. Before she died in 1960, they lived happily together, traveling and enjoying each other fully. Along the way, they went through the ups and downs of false hopes, remissions, temporary recoveries, all the while praying and trusting in God to make things right. But in just a few short years together, she died leaving him alone and embittered. He lashed out at God and questioned the rationality of believing in whom he called, "the cosmic sadist, the spiteful imbecile."[40]

He said after Joy died, "If God's goodness is inconsistent with hurting us, then either God is not good or there is no God: for in the only life we know He hurts us beyond our worst fears and beyond all we can imagine." In his pain and loss he wondered if the whole Jesus story as Savior of mankind was just a "trap" or a "vile practical joke."[41] Eventually, Lewis regretted his words and was able to renew his faith and continue connecting people with Christianity through his writing. But what we learn from this is how shakable the seemingly unshakable can be during times of real trial. We're told in the scriptures that Satan shall deceive "even the very elect" (Matthew 1:22).

Why do some people just fold and crumble in their faith during trials while others come out stronger? I think the answer is found in the degree to which we have internalized and applied the transformative power of conversion to the gospel of Jesus Christ.

Through living prophets we are blessed with a deeper understanding of God's true nature and his plan of happiness for his children. We learn that the true evidence of his love is found in two of his most exquisite and supernal gifts to mankind: Moral agency and the atonement of Jesus Christ. Until people fully understand the ramifications of these gifts, they will continue to blame God for their suffering and turn their backs on him.

When faced with evil deeds among men, the injustice of traumatic events in our lives, and the uncertainty of unanswered questions, we need only ask ourselves "is what I'm going through in this life worth it?" Apostle Richard L. Evans observed that some of the problems we face and have difficulty reconciling, will all work out in the end if we are patient. Such is the price we pay for the gift of agency. He said, "One of the cherished sentences I recall from the utterances of the prophet Joseph Smith is the one which says that 'an hour of virtuous liberty on Earth is worth a whole eternity of bondage.' So long as men have their free agency, there will be temporary injustices and discrepancies and some seemingly inexplicable things, which ultimately in our Father's own time and purpose, will be reconciled and made right."[42]

With the right attitude born from true understanding of God's plan, many have found peace and even triumph in their trials. One such person was Patricia P. Pinegar, former Primary General President, whose 17-year-old son, Cory, was killed in a car accident while she and her husband were serving a mission in England. They went home to Utah for his funeral, and then immediately returned to England to finish their mission filled with peace over their son.

She said, back in England, "I was walking down the street and an acquaintance who had heard of the death of our son said to me: 'Well, what do you think of your God now? You are serving a full-time mission for Him, and He has taken your son.' I was both shocked and hurt. I felt so sorry for this person who did not understand Heavenly Father's plan .... Trusting in His plan gave me peace during the time following our son's death. I knew where our son was, and I knew Heavenly Father loved him. I had a perfect hope that because of the Savior's atonement Cory lived, and we would be together again as an eternal family."[43]

In another example, gymnast Diane Ellingson worked hard and won U.S. championships while in high school and college. She was planning a gymnastics tour with several famous gymnasts when, during practice, she landed wrong off a vault and broke her neck. The injury paralyzed her for the rest of her life. Diane spent five months in the hospital filled with despair and frustration. But eventually she realized, "I can either give up or get on with my life." She learned to use a wheelchair and take care of herself. She even went back to college, graduated, and became an elementary school teacher. She also began speaking to groups of young people to help them overcome discouragement and adversity. Diane says, "People always think, 'You're so amazing, you're so incredible,' but I'm not .... You have to take whatever life gives you and deal with it, even if you might not want to .... You just learn and that's what's so great about time and the healing process ...."[44]

Other cases of tragedy involve abuse within families. Apostle Richard G. Scott shared one of many experiences he had with victims of abuse who found spiritual healing. He described how a young woman, who had been severely abused by her father, brought him with her to visit Elder Scott one day. She had already forgiven him and was moving on with her life, but her father was still wracked with pain and guilt. With love in her heart, she simply asked if Elder Scott could help him. She had come to understand the atonement and the Savior's ability to repair all damage and wanted the same healing influence for her father, whom she loved.[45]

These people, and many others like them, have found the key to unlocking life's ultimate treasure. In fact, Truman Madsen called this key the deepest secret of life. He said, "The awful tragedy of life, as of the next, is not suffering. It is suffering in vain. Or worse, it is suffering that could have been the elixir of nobility, transforming us into Godliness beyond description .... Think about it—pain becomes a laboratory of soul-nurture and we may count it all joy. The darkest abyss has its own revelations, its own chrysalis [metamorphosis in a cocoon] of higher promise. This is not myth! I testify it is the deepest secret of life."[46]

As we suffer through our trials, a nightmare voice whips us with "why," "if only," "how long." But in time, as the fever passes, we will be newly sensitive to flashes of revelation in the quiet surroundings of our souls. We simply can't avoid or escape the pain of trials because that is how we grow and learn and temper our souls to be more in line with Christ's. He suffered more than any of us can even imagine. If we are to be like him, we must suffer too. But more than that, we must be enlightened and transformed to elevated stations of Godliness that can come only through the lessons of tragedy.

Conclusion

Life is certainly not easy, and nobody ever finishes their sojourn on Earth without adversity. Many of these trials occur for no apparent reason, but many others come through the wickedness of others or when we let the influence of evil affect our choices.

Some would say the existence of evil is evidence that there is no God, when in fact, the opposite is actually true. When someone recognizes there is evil in the world, he is essentially making a moral judgment. Morality is a truth that is not material, in that it can't be tested in a laboratory but is nonetheless real. It belongs in with other non-material yet true realities in our existence such as logic, love, proposition, principles, and happiness. These are actual non-physical truths that populate our physical world.

Since evil falls under the category of morality and morality is not an illusion or an accident, then morals must be the result of divine design. Where else could moral judgment possibly have come from? It didn't just suddenly appear and become part of human existence. If God did not exist, then there would be no reason for man to have a conscience. Why would anyone behave morally if there was no God? Temptation to do evil at some level is a constant in this life, but so are all the other non-material truths to help us triumph over evil such as agency, motivation, and faith.

Historically, philosophers and theologians have puzzled over the existence of evil, some concluding that it is merely the absence of good. Scripture, however, depicts it as threateningly real, not just some relativistic notion. Isaiah warned, "Woe unto them that call evil good, and good evil; that put darkness for light, and light for darkness; that put bitter for sweet, and sweet for bitter" (Isaiah 5:20).

Through modern-day revelation, we know that God is not the source of any kind of evil, and we also know why he does not prevent it. The ancient philosopher Epicurus presented a famous dilemma: Either God is unwilling to prevent the evil that occurs or he is unable to prevent it. Mormons know both assumptions are false. In the first, we know that God allows opposition and temptation because they are essential to achieve the greatest good in our individual lives. We grow from the things that we suffer and from triumphing over difficult situations.[47]

BYU Professor David L. Paulsen explained why Epicurus' second assumption is also false. "God can't create out of nothing. Because of the coeternal entities in the universe [intelligences, chaotic matter, laws and principles, and evil], God's power must be used to bring about any state of affairs consistent with the natures of coeternal realities. An omnipotent God doesn't wield power to bring about any and everything including the eradication of evil because of its place as a coeternal reality."[48]

God did not create intelligences or control their development and sense of morality. He loves us for who we are and works within the framework of his creation to help us grow and advance, and that must include allowing evil and tragedies to happen. Things that occur in life do not always improve the world, like senseless massacres, rapes, or even natural disasters. However, if humans are to be genuinely free to choose, God cannot always intervene to stop bad things from happening because it would thwart his purposes. LDS writer Blake Ostler provided an appropriate example: "If steel-hard knives suddenly turned to rubber whenever a person wanted to use a knife to stab someone, the natural order necessary for God's plan to be accomplished would be frustrated. The possibility of morality through agency could not exist."[49]

Through prophets, God has given us the knowledge that one day soon, things will change. He is at the helm. Satan may have a colossal following and look like he's winning, but make no mistake about it—God will win the battle between good and evil. The apostle Paul declared, "Thanks be to God, [who] giveth us the victory through our Lord Jesus Christ" (1 Corinthians 15:57). Let us take comfort and hope in knowing the final outcome will be worth the challenges we face.

CHAPTER TEN

Inherited Attributes of Deity

When the Primary Children's Hospital was being built during the 1940s the "Buy-a-Brick" campaign was a very successful fundraising drive. Each Primary child was asked to contribute ten cents to buy a brick for the hospital. The drive raised more than $20,000, which was used to buy 203,303 bricks with mortar.[1] At one time, a Primary board member was leading a tour of children through the finished building when a little boy asked her, "Lady, can you tell me which is my brick?" This boy understood his individual worth.

In another story, the young daughter of William Howard Taft III was assigned to write a short autobiography, as was each child at the start of a new grade. Here's what she wrote: "My great-grandfather was president of the United States. My grandfather was senator from Ohio. My father is ambassador to Ireland. I am a Brownie."[2]

She too understood her individual worth. Both of these children knew intrinsically that who they were and what they contributed had value. They possessed a union with Heavenly Father that testified of this important fact, before the difficulties of life could erode away their confidence and self-esteem. We can hang onto that individual worth when we comprehend that we are the literal offspring of God endowed with his divine attributes. This endowment is also evidence of God.

Yes, we go through life conflicted because of Satan's influence, but our nature, the very core of what makes us children of God, is goodness. And just as there are abundant stories of human atrocities among us, there also are scores of stories rich in everyday courtesies, displays of compassion, and acts of heroism. These stories are all around us making societal coexistence possible, something that could not occur if people were intrinsically evil. The "charity" we so freely give to one another, individually and through organizations across the world, is more than just the act of giving. It is actually an inherited condition of the heart, as well as a gift of the Spirit, that leads us to love one another. "…because the love of God is shed abroad in our hearts by the Holy Ghost which is given unto us" (Romans 5:5).

Charity ranges anywhere from bringing a casserole to a sick neighbor to global relief efforts during natural disasters. For example, a 2004 tsunami in Indonesia killed about 275,000 people, injured tens of thousands more, and displaced another 10 million. The world responded with physical and monetary help. After the Gulf deluge from Hurricane Katrina in 2005, more than 70 countries provided monetary donations or other assistance, and individuals arrived in busloads from all over the country to lend a hand. Likewise, when a massive 2013 typhoon in the Philippines killed more than 6,000 and displaced another four million, U.S. marines responded immediately along with other governments and international aid groups. All participated in a multi-million dollar relief effort to help some 14 million people affected by the disaster.

We have all been recipients or providers of charitable service and have felt in either case, an intimacy with God that was unique and powerful. We learned that service to others is the same as service to God (see Mosiah 2:17), which can bring some of the greatest joy in mortality.

I'd like to share a story of my own that has had a lasting effect on my life. In 1999, when I lived in Las Vegas, a huge flash flood slammed into the city inundating whole sections of town. It caused two deaths, swamped and uprooted more than 350 homes and businesses, swept away cars, and shredded sections of roads. National disaster relief was received to help with the $26 million repair bill. The effects of the flood were particularly devastating to a trailer park nestled near one of the city's massive drainage ditches. As I watched news accounts of the utter ruination of these people, many of them elderly or disabled, something snapped in my head and I grabbed a shovel, got in my car, and headed to the scene.

When I arrived, the road into the trailer park was washed out. As I entered on foot, I was sickened by what I saw. Some two to three feet of mud and debris had filled the narrow trailer park streets and oozed from every trailer and driveway nearest the ditch. Two trailers had even washed into the ditch after torrential waters ate away the ground under their foundations. Many of these people, who had little to begin with, lost everything, while others lost more than they could ever afford to replace.

I saw a group of teenage girls shoveling out the mud on one driveway and went to join them. I was thrilled and impressed to learn they were all youth from a nearby LDS ward that had rallied some volunteers. As the day progressed we were joined by some 60 to 70 others, most of them Latter-day Saints, who spent the day shoveling, hauling out ruined furniture, and cleaning the muck from damaged rooms.

The public works department came by and supplied us with gloves and the Red Cross made sure we had plenty to drink. One grateful resident of the trailer park passed out sandwiches while another one, eyes filled with tears, passed out "God bless yous." But the singular moment for me during this incredible experience was when an old man, visibly moved with emotion, scurried up to me from his trailer as I worked on his driveway and asked, "Have you ever heard the sound of God?" I smiled and looked a little puzzled as to how to respond when he provided the answer himself. He said, "Just listen. It's in the clang of the shovels all around you."

That clang has echoed in the altruistic "shovels" of countless individuals across this country and the world, moved to save the lives or ease the suffering of people in need. Individual stories of heroism are everywhere reminding us with sobering intensity that the human race has an amazing capacity for love and selflessness. The following are a collection of moving true stories that are presented as examples of this innate human capacity.

In the Boston Marathon bombings in 2013, heroism took place everywhere. Runners kept on running after the blasts straight to nearby hospitals to give blood for the injured, and thousands of Bostonians posted on social media sites that their homes were open to stranded marathoners and their families. Hundreds nearby the two explosions jumped in to help, heroes, every one of them, like Carlos Arredondo. Despite the fact that he had lost two sons—one in the Iraq War, the other by suicide four years later—Arredondo came to the event to cheer on other veterans. Wearing a cowboy hat and handing out American flags when the bombs went off, Arrendondo flew into action. A photo of him rocketed around the world showing him running alongside a wheelchair holding on to a man whose legs had just been blown off in the explosion. "I kept talking to him," he told the *Portland Press Herald*. "I kept saying, 'Stay with me. Stay with me.'"[3]

Another tragedy in the news also produced heroes. When shots rang out at Sandy Hook Elementary in Newtown, Connecticut, Principal Dawn Hochsprung was in a meeting with school psychologist Mary Scherlach and others. Without hesitation, Hochsprung, 47, and Scherlach, 56, ran out into the hall to find the source. Hochsprung confronted the shooter and put herself between the shooter and her colleagues whom she cautioned to stay behind. She ran at the gunman in an attempt to subdue him, but was killed in the process. Scherlach, who followed Hochsprung into the hall, was also shot.[4]

In another incident, Officer Moira Smith, a 13-year veteran of the New York Police Department, helped rescue people when the planes hit the World Trade Center towers on 9/11. Witnesses say she went in and out of one of the buildings several times carrying people to safety. She had the opportunity to leave and she chose not to, ultimately dying when the building collapsed. She was posthumously awarded the New York City Police Department's Medal of Honor for her heroism that day.[5]

On that same day a room full of people sat bloody and petrified in the South Tower as smoke engulfed the room and pain from the intense heat seared their bodies. To them it appeared there was no way out. Then out of nowhere, a young man burst through the door and authoritatively directed them to the stairway. He showed them the way in the darkness and wreckage and told the healthy to help the injured to get down. The young man, Welles Crowther, saved at least 18 lives that day, if not more, by exiting and entering the building at least three times, helping evacuate trapped victims. Crowther was neither a policeman nor a firefighter—he was an investment banker who just wanted to help. He ultimately gave his life to rescue people he never even knew.[6]

And who can forget the incredible story of Arland Williams who, in 1982, was a passenger on a plane that plunged into the Potomac River in Washington D.C. The horrific accident killed 78 people. Arland was the one in the news who kept passing the lifelines sent out by rescuers on to others who were still alive in the freezing waters, rather than take one for himself. When he was the only one left and the line was extended, he was no longer there, becoming the only plane passenger to die from drowning. Another hero emerged that day also. Lenny Skutnik was standing on the bank at the scene when one of the survivors was struggling to hold on to the lifeline because of the cold that took away all feeling from her limbs. He jumped into the water and swam out to help her safely back to shore even at the peril of his own life.[7]

There are innumerable other less spectacular stories that are just as moving in their messages of compassion. They occur in every country, city, and neighborhood.

When Chy, a special needs student started high school in 2012, she was mistreated, shoved, and taunted as she walked to class, the victim of bullying. Some students even threw garbage at her. When school quarterback Carson Jones, an Aaronic Priesthood holder, became aware of the situation, he knew he had to help. He got some teammates to join him in sitting with Chy during lunch, walking her to class, and in general, becoming her friend. Needless to say, the bullying stopped.[8]

Amy and John Cervantes wanted to teach their three children about giving back and so they put together a birthday party for a homeless child in a shelter.[9]

Dr. Benjamin LaBrot started Floating Doctors, a nonprofit that travels by sea to provide free health care for people in remote coastal areas. In the last two years, LaBrot and his volunteer team have treated nearly 13,000 patients in Haiti, Honduras, and Panama.[10]

Sgt. Dennis Weichel, 29, died in Afghanistan as he lifted an Afghan girl who was in the path of a large military vehicle barreling down a road.

Stories of every day heroes are everywhere: A man saved a woman from being killed on the subway tracks; despite terrorist threats, a woman brought education to Afghan girls; an Ohio mom worked to save minority children from the tragic drowning fate that took her own son's life; a former heroin addict helped others struggling with drugs get clean.

The headlines are not just full of crimes and tragedy. They are overflowing with good news stories that are truly evidence of God through his children:

"Woman Soaks Self in Water, Enters Burning House to Save 3 Kids"

"Michigan Firefighter Loses Both Legs, Returns to Work"

"Vets Who Lost Their Lives in Tragic Texas Train Crash were Heroes Even in the Face of Death"

"'It Was Worth It': Good Samaritan Loses Leg Saving Man from Car Crash"

"Cop Who Bought Boots for Homeless Man: 'I Had to Help Him'"

"Homeless Veteran Saves Shooting Victim's Life"

"Humble Hero Rescues 6-year-old from Freezing Water."[11]

Movies have even gotten into the act such as the 2000 movie, *Pay it Forward*. This movie, and the book that inspired it, have captured the hearts and minds of people everywhere. The concept is that a recipient of a good deed should pay it forward instead of paying it back by doing a good deed for someone else. It's so simple and yet profound in its effects, and it speaks right to the heart of our eternal spirits. It's difficult to say how big the movement has become, but over the last five years, more than one million Pay it Forward bracelets have been distributed in some 100 countries sparking simple acts of kindness worldwide.

The Transforming Power of Forgiveness

People are following the Savior's counsel in droves to "love thy neighbor" (D&C 59:6), not only through their selfless acts of kindness but also in their amazing capacity to forgive. They are living examples of the transformative power that comes to both the forgiver and the forgiven when this tender admonition of the Savior is followed:

> "And behold it is written also, that thou shalt love thy neighbor and hate thine enemy;
>
> "But behold I say unto you, love your enemies, bless them that curse you, do good to them that hate you, and pray for them who despitefully use you and persecute you" (3 Nephi 12:43-44).
>
> "Wherefore, I say unto you, that ye ought to forgive one another; for he that forgiveth not his brother his trespasses standeth condemned before the Lord; for there remaineth in him the greater sin.
>
> "I, the Lord, will forgive whom I will forgive, but of you it is required to forgive all men" (D&C 64:9-10).

This is a formidable directive to those faced with the prospect of forgiving someone guilty of despicable crimes against them or a loved one. But Jesus led the way when he fully forgave those who brutally murdered him on the cross at Calvary. Where was the ram in the thicket that would spare him like there was for Isaac when he faced a sacrificial death? There wasn't one, for Jesus *was* the ram. At the very height of his suffering, he uttered words of forgiveness with such simple eloquence that their meaning would resonate throughout the centuries as the purest example of unconditional love. "Then said Jesus, Father, forgive them; for they know not what they do" (Luke 23:34).

The atonement of Christ made it possible for all of us to receive forgiveness through the process of repentance. Every time we choose not to forgive one of God's children, we make a mockery of the atonement. We, in effect, turn our backs on our Savior as if to say, "What you suffered in the Garden of Gethsemane was all in vain because I will not forgive." But such an attitude only hurts us the most, because it cuts us off from the greatest opportunity for growth available in this life.

The Savior knew that the harboring of grudges and the desire for revenge is like a cancer that can grow and spread to deaden the heart and destroy our spiritual growth. I've heard it said that when you are bitten by a snake, you have two choices: You can either chase the snake or get rid of the poison. All too often our first inclination is to chase the snake, or seek revenge. If we do that, however, the poison will then have a chance to work its way through our bodies and eventually kill us, just like the poison of revenge and animosity will eventually kill our spirits. It's difficult to just let the offender get off unpunished, but continued anger will ultimately cause us the greater harm.

This is a weighty topic for those looking for evidence of God because a person's ability to forgive is the purest reflection of the inherited traits of virtue we all receive as offspring of Deity. When we forgive, we take a giant leap toward the Godly potential that is our birthright and move ever closer to the celestial beings we were sent here to become.

One example of forgiveness is Gary Weinstein whose wife and two sons were killed by drunk driver Tom Wellinger in Farmington Hills, Michigan. During a jailhouse meeting between the two, Wellinger asked Weinstein if he could ever forgive him. Weinstein's unselfish and reassuring response: "Can you forgive yourself?" Weinstein offered to work with Wellinger's children to help them heal while Wellinger served his 19-30 year sentence for three counts of second-degree murder. He also formally agreed not to block attempts for an early release.[12]

In another story, Charles Carl Roberts IV, on October 2, 2006, shot 10 Amish schoolgirls before turning the gun on himself. Five girls died and five others were seriously wounded in addition to Roberts' suicide. The shooting shocked and horrified the rural community in Lancaster, Pennsylvania, as well as the rest of the country who heard about it through nonstop media coverage. For the shooter's parents, Terri and Chuck, the horror was unbearable. On the day of the shooting, Terri crawled into a fetal position, feeling as if her insides were being ripped apart. Chuck, a retired policeman, cried into a tea towel, unable to lift his head, and wore the skin off his face from wiping away the tears. Later, during the evening of the shootings, an Amish neighbor named Henry, whom Terri called her "angel in black," came over. Chuck, who had relationships with the Amish by driving them to places too far for their horses and buggies to go, feared he could never face them again. But Henry just looked at Chuck and said, "Roberts, we love you," then continued to comfort Chuck for nearly an hour.[13]

And what about those people who play the hand they're dealt in life by taking bad events and turning them into something good? These are those truly insightful people who managed to turn their trials upside down, and by so doing, discovered not only the secret to happiness, but also the key to the cosmos. They too, are exhibiting inherited Godly traits of resilience, perspective, and love. Their examples are priceless.

There's the story of Erin Merryn, whose sexual abuse at just six years old by a male neighbor and later a relative, was the inspiration for Erin's Law, which mandates schools teach sexual abuse awareness and prevention. Besides championing Erin's Law, Merryn travels around the country telling her story to law enforcement and social service workers and has written three books about her experiences.[14]

Cancer survivor Jonny Imerman wanted to ensure no young adult is ever alone in their battle against cancer, so in 2002, he started Imerman Angels, a nonprofit that pairs cancer patients with cancer survivors for one-on-one support. The group has made more than 8,000 matches worldwide.[15]

Anne Juhlmann's 7-year-old son and special needs child, Sam, died one day because paramedics didn't know what medical equipment he needed for his condition or that he should be immediately transported to a farther away children's hospital. Because they lacked understanding of these two needs, Sam died that day from mitochondrial disease. Instead of blaming and brooding, Anne became a champion for improving policies at the local fire department to avoid duplicating the incident for other families. She worked closely with the fire chief to change the policies and took it even further by sitting on a committee to establish a database identifying children with unique medical needs in the event of an emergency or disaster.[16]

What examples we find in all of these stories of the Savior's teaching: "Ye are the salt of the earth …. Ye are the light of the world …. Let your light so shine before men, that they may see your good works, and glorify your Father which is in heaven" (Matthew 5:13-14, 16).

All of these people and more have let their light shine in the world, and because of it others have looked to their example as evidence of God. To the Doubting Thomas who seeks to know God, can there be anything greater, more affirmative, or glorious in its confirming witness that God lives, than in the selfless acts of his children? We are endowed with the attributes of our Heavenly Father and therefore, have the innate capacity to be like him. And when those qualities emerge in our actions toward each other, they are living patterns after the greatest act of love and sacrifice ever recorded in history.

Jesus Christ suffered for our sins and died an unspeakable death so that we could all live again and have a chance at exaltation with our Father in Heaven. There was no other way that God could save his children, and so he directed the ultimate sacrifice—the life of his Only Begotten Son to save the rest of us. "For God so loved the world, that he gave his only begotten Son, that whosover believeth in him should not perish, but have everlasting life" (John 3:16).

The Reality and Mission of Jesus

It should behoove all doubters who really want to know God, to personally come to know the Savior. It is Jesus Christ, after all, who stands at the head of the Church and is our exemplar in righteous living. He is the hope of the world and leads the way to happiness in this life and eternal life in the world to come. To know him, is to know God, the Father.

But before we can build a relationship with him, it might help to begin with a foundation of fact that he actually lived. Some may question if Jesus ever really existed or if he was merely a fable handed down through the ages. It's difficult to have faith in a theology or religion based on a person that may be a myth. Despite evidence to the contrary, a "Christ myth theory" has been around for ages. It questions the authenticity of the existence of Jesus described in the four gospels. Frankly, those who cling to this theory are in a distinct minority because most scholars who study the historicity around Jesus, point to a mountain of evidence attesting to his existence.[17]

One argument in Christ myth theory is that there is a lack of first century, non-Christian sources about Jesus, but this is not true. Here are a few of many such sources:

- The writings of the 1st century Romano-Jewish historian Flavius Josephus include references to Jesus and the origins of Christianity. Josephus' *Antiquities of the Jews*, written around AD 93-94, includes references to Jesus in Books 18 and 20.[18]
- Roman historian and senator, Tacitus, referred to Christ, his execution by Pontius Pilate, and the existence of early Christians in Rome in his final work, *Annals,* [written AD 116], book 15, chapter 44.[19]
- *The Babylonian Talmud* [Sanhedrin 43a] confirms Jesus' crucifixion on the eve of Passover and the accusations against Christ of practicing sorcery and encouraging Jewish apostasy.[20]
- Mara, son of Sarapion, was a Stoic philosopher from the Roman province of Syria. Sometime between AD 73 and the 3rd century, Mara wrote a letter to his son, also called Sarapion, which contains an early non-Christian reference to the crucifixion of Jesus.[21]
- Julius Africanus quotes the historian Thallus in a discussion of the darkness which followed the crucifixion of Christ in *Extant Writings*, 18.[22]
- Pliny the Younger, in *Letters* 10:96, recorded early Christian worship practices that included the fact that Christians worshiped Jesus

as God. He also entered a reference to the "love feast and Lord's Supper."[23]
- Lucian of Samosata was a second-century Greek writer who admits that Jesus was worshiped by Christians, introduced them to new teachings, and was crucified for them.[24]
- The Gnostic writings [*The Gospel of Truth, The Apocryphon of John, The Gospel of Thomas, The Treatise on Resurrection,* etc.] all mention Jesus.[25]

Add to these the four gospels of the New Testament, written between AD 65 and 100, and the Epistles of Paul, written just 25 years after Christ's death, and you have some mighty convincing historical references to the existence of Jesus. Paul even records that the resurrected Lord appeared to more than five hundred men at once (1 Corinthians 15:6), most of whom were still alive at the time of Paul's writings. Afterward, he appeared to James, and then to all the apostles (see 1 Corinthians 15:6-7). As recorded in the Book of Mormon, he later appeared to about 2,500 people in the ancient Americas, who had gathered in the land Bountiful (3 Nephi 11:8-15; 17:25).

Paul devoted more than three decades to the spreading of the gospel of the resurrected Lord. He traveled far and wide, with little regard for his personal safety, until he was executed in Rome, and sealed with his death his conviction of the divinity of Jesus. Perhaps the greatest evidence of devotion and allegiance to the Savior is when literally thousands of Christians in the first century AD, including the twelve apostles, suffered imprisonment, torture, and death as martyrs for him. They gave up everything, rather than recant their stated beliefs in the life and resurrection of the Son of God.

And let's not forget the appearance of the resurrected Lord to the Prophet Joseph Smith (Joseph Smith-History 1:17), and again to both Joseph and Sidney Rigdon (D&C 76:22-24).

Building Testimonies

The historical record provides ample evidence that Jesus Christ lived, suffered for our sins, died, and was resurrected. We can be assured of that reality in order to take the next step toward building our testimonies of him and his sacred mission. Because modern day prophets and apostles are special witnesses of Christ, their words can serve as persuasive depositions in the trial of our faith to know our Savior.

The Prophet Joseph Smith clearly declared, "And now, after the many testimonies which have been given of him, this is the testimony, last of all, which we give of him: That he lives!

"For we saw him, even on the right hand of God; and we heard the voice bearing record that he is the Only Begotten of the Father—

"That by him, and through him, and of him, the worlds are and were created, and the inhabitants thereof are begotten sons and daughters unto God" (D&C 76:22-24).

More recently, the First Presidency and Quorum of the Twelve Apostles issued a moving affirmation on Christ. Titled "The Living Christ," this declaration bears witness of the Lord Jesus Christ and summarizes his identity and divine mission. It is a beautiful expression of who the Savior is, and what he means to the entire world. It reads in part:

> "As we commemorate the birth of Jesus Christ two millennia ago, we offer our testimony of the reality of His matchless life and the infinite virtue of His great atoning sacrifice. None other has had so profound an influence upon all who have lived and will yet live upon the Earth ....
>
> "We solemnly testify that His life, which is central to all human history, neither began in Bethlehem nor concluded on Calvary. He was the Firstborn of the Father, the Only Begotten Son in the flesh, the Redeemer of the world ....
>
> "We testify that He will someday return to Earth .... He will rule as King of Kings and reign as Lord of Lords, and every knee shall bend and every tongue shall speak in worship before Him. Each of us will stand to be judged of Him according to our works and the desires of our hearts.

> "We bear testimony, as His duly ordained Apostles—that Jesus is the Living Christ, the immortal Son of God. He is the great King Immanuel, who stands today on the right hand of His Father. He is the light, the life, and the hope of the world. His way is the path that leads to happiness in this life and eternal life in the world to come. God be thanked for the matchless gift of His divine Son."[26]

This is revealed knowledge from prophets and apostles who have been called and set apart to testify of Christ. When all is said and done in the world of theology, it is revelation that separates fact from fiction. It is revelation that teaches the true nature and mission of Jesus Christ. It is revelation that imparts the reality and persona of our Savior as a model to live by, and as an ensign of what we can become. We learn that Jesus was not, as many have suggested, merely a great man or a prophet; not a politician who stood up against the exploitations of Rome; not a revolutionary or social reformer; not a magician, charismatic teacher, foreteller of the world's end, or "marginal" Jew.[27]

He was much more than any of these. In his own inimitable way, C. S. Lewis summed it up well:

> "A man who was merely a man and said the sort of things Jesus said ... would not be a great moral teacher. He would either be a lunatic—on a level with the man who says he is a poached egg—or else he would be the devil of Hell. You must make your choice .... You can shut him up for a fool ... you can spit at him and kill him as a demon; or you can fall at his feet and call him Lord and God. But let us not come with any patronizing nonsense about his being a great human teacher. He has not left that open to us. He did not intend to."[28]

There are simply too many skewed interpretations in the Bible, historical records, and scholastic offerings to gain resolute knowledge as to the divinity of Jesus Christ. This is not to say there are no instances of truth within these sources, because there are. But they alone cannot be reliable conveyors of the true personality and Godhood of our Savior; revelation, both personal and from the Lord's anointed, can. People reject the true Messiah, replacing him with anti-Christs, false creeds, and permissive doctrines, because it is easier to swallow in a worldly setting to keep him vague, passive, and non-intervening. To accept Jesus as our Savior would require a rejection of worldly things too hard for many to give up.

But as we absorb these prophetic avowals of the True Shepherd from God's authorized servants, we begin to feel the whisperings of the Holy Ghost testifying that they are true. This is the final step in our quest to know Christ—developing a spiritual and intimate relationship with him. We do this by inviting his Spirit into our hearts through prayer, study, and obedience to the commandments. As we put our burgeoning faith to the test through actively living the gospel, we will feel his warm embrace and quiet assurance that he is there. We will come to know for ourselves that everything he lived and died for is true, and that we can all partake in the richest blessings of the Father through the sacrifice of our elder brother, even Jesus Christ.

During his ministry in the meridian of time, Jesus "went about doing good ... for God was with him" (Acts 10:38). He blessed those in need, brought sight to the blind, caused the maimed to walk, and made the deaf to hear. He exemplified forgiveness, compassion, devotion, and love of God in everything he did and then asked us all to follow his example. And we're doing that, as exemplified in the stories of service and heroism described above. It comes to us naturally, almost effortlessly, because he is our brother, and the attributes of Godliness in his nature are the same attributes in ours. We are all offspring of the same Heavenly Father who has endowed us with the same heavenly gifts and qualities. When we strive to emulate the Savior, we begin the process of perfecting ourselves—a process that seems far more achievable when we understand our divine heritage.

Sometimes, in our weaker moments, we put limitations on ourselves at the realization that Jesus Christ was a God and we're not. We may feel he set the bar too high. But that's when we should realize that in his perfection, he set a slow but steady pace to give us time to "experiment upon the word" (Alma 32) and even to stumble along the way. Elder Neal A. Maxwell once said, "I thank him for encapsulating his exquisite mind in both perfect love and perfect humility. His brilliance is not the 'catch-me-if-you-can' kind, but a pleading and patient 'Come, follow me.'"[29]

As we follow him and begin to exhibit his qualities we also begin to draw closer to God. Some have said they feel closer to the Savior than to God because Jesus actually lived on Earth and went through trials like we do. But we must remember that everything the Savior did or taught was so that we might come to know our Father in Heaven. "And this is life eternal, that they might know thee the only true God" (John 17:3).

Elder Jeffrey R. Holland explained that "to come to Earth with such a responsibility, to stand in place of Elohim—speaking as He would speak, judging and serving, loving and warning, forbearing, and forgiving as He would do—this is a duty of such staggering proportions that you and I cannot comprehend such a thing. But in the loyalty and determination that would be characteristic of a divine child, Jesus could comprehend it and he did it. Then, when the praise and honor began to come, he humbly directed all adulation to the Father."[30]

"The Father ... doeth the works," he said. "The Son can do nothing of himself, but what he seeth the Father do: for what things soever [the Father] doeth, these also doeth the Son likewise" (John 14:10; 5:19).

Attributes of God

Jesus then, through the examples of his life, gives us a perfect model of the Father and how he operates for the good of his children. Sometimes people have mistakenly viewed God as harsh and judgmental as it sometimes appears in the Old Testament, where faulty translations have led to such misconceptions. But through the example of the life of Jesus, who is in the express image of the Father, we learn how deeply interested God is in us and how ever ready he is to bless and comfort. The books of the restoration have helped to depict God in the correct light as in the Pearl of Great Price account of Enoch's vision. As Enoch is shown in vision the challenges of mortality, he turns to see the Father weeping and is stunned at the sight.

"How is it that thou canst weep[?] ... Thou art just [and] merciful and kind forever .... Peace ... is the habitation of thy throne; and mercy shall go before thy face and have no end; how is it though canst weep?"

God replies, "Behold these thy brethren; they are the workmanship of mine own hands .... I gave unto them ... [a] commandment, that they should love one another, and that they should choose me, their Father; but behold, they are without affection, and they hate their own blood .... Wherefore should not the heavens weep, seeing these shall suffer" (Moses 7:29-33, 37)?

Can anything illuminate the true nature of God and his abiding love for his children more than this singular and momentous passage of scripture? God's sorrowful grief over children unwilling to accept him or his gospel speaks volumes about how engaged he is in our lives. It wasn't until the Savior arrived, that mankind finally started to understand the depth of God's devotion to us all. It was then that we had a tangible example to follow. Again, Elder Holland said it well:

> "So feeding the hungry, healing the sick, rebuking hypocrisy, pleading for faith—this was Christ showing us the way of the Father, He who is 'merciful and gracious, slow to anger, long suffering and full of goodness.'[31] In his life and especially in his death, Christ was declaring, 'This is God's compassion I am showing you, as well as my own.' In the perfect Son's manifestation of the perfect Father's care in their mutual suffering and shared sorrow for the sins and heartaches of the rest of us, we see ultimate meaning in the declaration: 'For God so loved the world, that he gave his only begotten Son, that whosoever believeth in him should not perish, but have everlasting life. For God sent not his

Son into the world to condemn the world; but that the world through him might be saved' (John 3:16-17)."[32]

And the crowning witness to the truth and majesty of both these Deities was found in the Sacred Grove nearly 200 years ago. There, the boy prophet, Joseph Smith, actually saw them both and heard the voice of the Father introduce his Son: "This is my Beloved Son, in whom I am well pleased. Hear Him" (Joseph Smith 1:17). In that moment and all the revelation that followed, we have finally come to understand the true nature of God. Also in that moment, was the inception of endless controversy and even persecution toward the Saints who would dare to go against the widespread creeds about the Trinity.

Errors of Man-Made Creeds

These unfathomable man-made creeds proclaimed God to be unknown and unknowable, formless, passionless, elusive, ethereal, simultaneously everywhere and nowhere. The Athanasian Creed of the fourth and fifth centuries establishes the Trinity as one God. But this does not even remotely resemble passages in the very Bible Christians hold dear where the Father, Son, and Holy Ghost are plainly depicted as distinct and separate members of the Godhead. These passages include, "My Father is greater than I" (John 14:28); Stephen seeing Christ on the right hand of the Father (Acts 7:56); the three all in one place at Christ's baptism where the voice of the Father is heard introducing his Son, and the Holy Ghost is descending like a dove (Luke 3:22).

These creeds, which are accepted by most of mainstream Christianity, provide a view of God's nature that more closely resembles the teachings of ancient non-Christian philosophers and pagans than it does to teachings of the early Jews and Christians. Definitions that portray God as pure spirit, invisible, without body, parts, or passions, immutable, immense, eternally incomprehensible, coincide exactly with the Greeks.

Christians adopted these descriptions starting in the mid-second century. In so doing, they completely left behind their earlier Jewish and Christian views of God "as having a body and mind like our own, though transcending humanity in the splendor of his appearance, in his power, his wisdom, and the constancy of his care for his creatures."[33]

And as for the LDS tenet that "The Father has a body of flesh and bones as tangible as man's; the Son also" (D&C 130:22), people are offended and call us blasphemous that we would reduce God to the stature of man. But it's not God who was created to resemble man, but rather, man who was created to resemble God. His whole purpose is to redeem and elevate man to partake in his glory.

Scholars have determined that most Christians from the earliest periods believed in a God with a body. An article in the *Harvard Theological Review* suggested, "ordinary Christians for at least the first three centuries of the current era commonly believed God to be corporeal," or embodied. "The belief was abandoned as Neoplatonism [in the third century AD] became more and more entrenched as the dominant world view of Christian thinkers."[34]

In the third century, the Christian philosopher Origen wrote, "The Jews indeed, but also some of our people, supposed that God should be understood as a man that is, adorned with human members and human appearance. But the philosophers despise these stories as fabulous and formed in the likeness of poetic fictions."[35] From the writings of Origen we see that anthropomorphism [the ascribing of human characteristics] was standard Jewish thought in early Christianity.

This is backed up by what Christian philosopher Justin Martyr said in the mid-second century: "And again when he says 'I shall behold the heavens, the works of thy fingers,' unless I understand his method of using words, I shall not understand intelligently, but just as your teachers suppose, fancying that the father of all, the unbegotten God, has hands and feet, and fingers, and a soul, like a composite being; and they for this reason teach that it was the Father Himself who appeared to Abraham and to Jacob."[36]

Who is God?

Now that we've established the physical nature of God, the next thing to consider is who he is. One of the most transcendent teachings of the Church comes from the famous Lorenzo Snow couplet, "As man is God once was, as God is man may become."[37] This doctrine takes wings in Joseph Smith's King Follett Discourse: "God himself was once as we are now, and is an exalted man, and sits enthroned in yonder heavens. That is the great secret ... [Y]ou have got to learn how to be Gods yourselves, and to be kings and priests to God, the same as all Gods have done before you ...."

In a later sermon Joseph Smith boldly preached, "If Jesus Christ was the Son of God, and John discovered that God the Father of Jesus Christ had a Father, you may suppose that He had a Father also. Where was there ever a son without a father? And where was there ever a father without first being a son? Whenever did a tree or anything spring into existence without a progenitor? And everything comes in this way. Paul says that which is earthly is in the likeness of that which is heavenly, hence if Jesus had a Father, can we not believe that He had a Father also? I despise the idea of being scared to death at such a doctrine, for the Bible is full of it."[38]

Mormons have been greatly disparaged over this principle, but a deeper look into Christian history shows that this doctrine may not nearly be as "non-Christian" as our critics suggest. In fact, it makes us closer to original Christianity than any other religion. LDS commentator Jeff Lindsay's research on the topic has unfolded some telling material including two quotes from Saint Clement of Alexandria, one of the great early Christian fathers who wrote in the late second century and is recognized as an authentic early Christian leader and defender of the faith.

Quotation 1. "But if thou dost not believe the prophets ... the Lord Himself shall speak to thee, 'who, being in the form of God, thought it not robbery to be equal with God, but humbled Himself' ... yea, I say, *the Word of God became man, that thou mayest learn from man how man may become God.* Is it not then monstrous, my friends, that while God is ceaselessly exhorting us to virtue, we should spurn His kindness and reject salvation" (italics added)?[39]

Quotation 2. "It [the knowledge of the gospel] leads us to the endless and perfect end .... After which redemption the reward and the honors are assigned to those who have become perfect; when they have got done with perfection, and ceased from all service, though it be holy service, and among saints. They become pure in heart, and near to the Lord, there awaits their restoration to everlasting contemplation; *and they are called by the appellation of gods, being destined to sit on thrones with the other gods that have been first put in their places by the Savior*" (italics added).[40]

Another example of the Mormon doctrine of becoming Gods can again be found in the writings of Origen: "Men should escape from being men, and hasten to *become gods* ... [41] and "Thou shalt resemble Him ... having made thee even God to his glory."[42]

Even with real Christian history on our side, not man-made creeds, our critics still see this doctrine as taking away God's glory and giving it to ourselves. But they fail to understand the full teachings of the concept that keep us ever dependent on and subject to our Father in Heaven regardless of our own eternal progression. Elder Boyd K. Packer attempted to clear this up when he said, "The Father *is* the one true God. *This* thing is certain: No one will ever ascend above Him; no one will ever replace Him. Nor will anything ever change the relationship that we, His literal offspring, have with Him. He is Eloheim, the Father. He is God. Of Him there *is* only one. We revere our Father and our God; we *worship* Him. There is only one Christ, one Redeemer. We accept the divinity of the Only Begotten Son of God in the flesh. We accept the promise that we may become joint heirs with Him."[43]

It should be pointed out here that God is not progressing in knowledge, truth, virtue, wisdom, or any of the attributes of godliness because he already possesses them. But Joseph Fielding Smith said he is progressing in the sense that "His creations increase, His dominions expand, His spirit offspring multiply, and more kingdoms are added to His domains."[44]

For me, personally, the LDS view of God the Father not only makes sense, but also gives meaning and focus to why we're here. It provides an eternal goal with eternal outcomes equal to what one would naturally expect of the children of Deity. Just as earthly parents help, prod, and influence their children to excel in life and otherwise become like them as they mature, so also does a caring Heavenly Father seek for excellence for his children and the opportunity for them to become like him. No matter what we achieve in the eternities, we are still subject to him and will always be reliant upon him as our God and our Father. The doctrine is anything but blasphemous; it is a testament to a powerful yet loving God who wants his children to have all that he has.

We are not Alone

In the enormity of God and the cosmos, people sometimes feel lost. Maybe you have been there. Do you ever feel like you're a tiny speck in a "Where's Waldo World" such that God can't possibly think much about you, let alone find you? Do you view yourself as one among millions of shells on a seashore, each beautiful in its own way, but yours of less value because it is worn and chipped from the incessant erosions of life? Or maybe you just can't help but feel the universe is too vast for little ol' you to really matter. People often doubt the existence of God because they can't begin to fathom him and all his creations, or his ability to know and care about every individual soul who ever lived.

But God, who oversees the immensity of all things, has assured us that he is aware of the fall of one sparrow and even numbers the very hairs of our heads (see Matthew 10:29-30; D&C 84:80). He even told Moses that he knows each of us by name, (Exodus 33:12) a promise verified many times within the scriptures.

When Enos went into the woods to pray, he recorded, "There came a voice unto me, saying: Enos, thy sins are forgiven thee, and thou shalt be blessed" (Enos 1:5). God said to Moses, "I have a work for thee, Moses, my son" (Moses 1:6). In words of comfort to Emma Smith, God said, "Hearken unto the voice of the Lord your God, while I speak unto you, Emma Smith, my daughter" (D&C 25:1).

Elder Neal A. Maxwell said, "I testify to you that God has known you individually ... for a long, long time (see D&C 93:23). He has loved you for a long, long time. He not only knows the names of all the stars (see Psalms

147:4; Isaiah 40:26); He knows your names and all your heartaches and your joys!"[45]

Elder Jeffrey R. Holland added his testimony that, "No one of us is less treasured or cherished of God than another .... He loves each of us—insecurities, anxieties, self-image, and all .... He cheers on every runner, calling out that the race is against sin, not against each other."[46]

Individual stories also testify of how intimately God knows us, and that he will never leave us alone. One story is about Gayle Clegg, formerly of the Primary general presidency, and her husband, who lived for a number of years in Brazil. During a Primary assignment to speak in Japan, she worked her way through the chapel and noticed among the Japanese saints a Brazilian family. She knew the Brazilian people well, so could tell by the way they appeared that they were from that nation. She only had a minute to greet them and found the mother and children very enthusiastic but noticed that the father was rather quiet. "I'll have a chance to talk with them after the meeting," she thought as she was quickly ushered to the stand.

Her message in English was translated into Japanese, but she felt moved to bear her testimony in Portuguese as well. With concern that there were no translators for Portuguese into Japanese and that nearly 100 percent in the congregation who would not understand, she pressed forward. After the meeting, the Brazilian father came up to her and said, "Sister, the customs are so different here, and I have been lonely. It is difficult to come to Church and not understand anything. Sometimes I wonder if I would be better off just reading my scriptures at home. I told my wife, 'I'll give it one more chance,' and I came today for what I thought would be the last time. When you bore your testimony in Portuguese, the Spirit touched my heart, and I knew that this was where I belonged. God knows I am here, and He will help me."[47]

Some would say it was a coincidence that Sister Clegg was sent to Japan instead of to Portugal given her ability to speak Portuguese. But anyone who knows God and understands his love for "even the least of these," knows it was no coincidence. God brought her there and then relied upon her ability to follow a spiritual prompting that would bring comfort to someone feeling alone and forgotten.

Conclusion

We are all—mankind, Jesus, and Heavenly Father—a family. We share innate abilities and attributes through divine inheritance. And because we are a family, the head of that family, even God, will never cease to teach, protect, and engage with every single member. Like any mortal father, he cares about the details of our lives and will be there whenever we need him.

I'll never forget an incident in my childhood that captures God's love for each individual. Our family dog, a boxer named Penny, became lost after my older brother, Mike, peddled his bicycle across a country bridge in order to fish on the other side of the river. During the four-mile ride over, Penny had easily trailed behind him, but had to be coaxed when it came to crossing the bridge. After fishing for several hours, Mike realized how late it had become and took off on his bike without noticing if Penny was following. When he arrived home, the dog was nowhere in sight. A frantic search of the area in our family van after our dad got home turned up nothing. For three days we prayed together, drove up and down every street in the city, checked the animal shelter, and put signs up around town. Still, no Penny. My parents' six little children were deeply saddened and inconsolable.

The third day of our dog's disappearance was on Sunday. That afternoon between Church meetings, my mother awoke from a nap, gathered us all around, and said she'd dreamed that Penny was sitting under a street sign waiting for us to find her. She said she felt sure if we'd go look again that we'd locate her. We all knelt in prayer for guidance in finding our beloved pet, and then jumped in the van to hit the streets again. With a twinkle in his eye, my dad leaned over to my mom and asked, "You didn't happen to see the name of the street on that sign, did you?"

With high hopes, we cruised up street after street until the sun had nearly set and still no sign of our dog. When my dad was about to give up and head back across the bridge for home, we frantically reminded him that mom had had a vision. He wasn't going to deny that God had spoken to her in a dream, was he? But when all was nearly lost, we suddenly noticed a tiny little dirt road, nearly hidden by overgrown bushes, meandering near the bank of the river. We hollered at dad to follow it and he did. After just a few minutes we came upon a scene that will forever be etched in my heart. There was Penny sitting underneath a street sign at the end of this dusty little road, just as my mother had seen. We pulled up, jumped from the van in a solid bundle of sheer joy, and embraced our cherished dog. She leaped into the midst of us, tail wagging hard enough to churn butter, and shared in our elation and relief.

What a witness of the love of God. He even knows and cares about the tender feelings of children enough to help them find their family dog. Six little kids went away from that experience knowing that every single person, no matter how small or seemingly insignificant, is important to God.

Stories like this illustrate well the attributes of God, which are paramount for us to grasp so that we may better understand ourselves and our journey toward Godliness. Joseph Smith taught, "If a man learns nothing more than to eat, drink and sleep, and does not comprehend any of the designs of God, the beast comprehends the same things. It eats, drinks, sleeps, and knows nothing more about God; yet it knows as much as we, unless we are able to comprehend by the inspiration of Almighty God. If men do not comprehend the character of God, they do not comprehend themselves."[48]

We know the character of God because it is exemplified in the life and teachings of Jesus Christ. With perseverance and a desire born of inherited characteristics of love, we can serve each other by being aware of, figuratively, when a sparrow falls. We can be the first to smile, to bring a casserole, to fill a Church assignment, to care for the needy, or to give of our substance. We can let the "clang of our shovels" imbue the air in Godly service, even the pure love of Christ. By so doing, we fill the measure of our creation.

Our good deeds are the greatest evidence of God in mortality because we are his offspring. We are Gods in embryo. Let us declare to the world, by the light of our countenances, that God lives and that Jesus is the Christ!

Human beings are at the heart and center of an enormous plan that is simple in its design. All we have to do is align our hearts toward God's, and all that he has can be ours.

He knows and loves us all. Now let us know and love him too.

CHAPTER 11

Help for the Doubting Thomas

One can well imagine how some of Christ's apostles could be skeptical at the news that the crucified Jesus had come forth from the tomb alive and well with his resurrected body. Even though they had been taught this truth during the Savior's ministry, many thought him to be a spirit when they saw him.

He said, "Behold my hands and my feet, that it is I myself: handle me, and see; for a spirit hath not flesh and bones, as ye see me have" (Luke 24:39). When they were still doubtful, Jesus asked for and ate meat and honeycomb to help convince them.

Because Thomas was not present when Jesus first appeared to the apostles, he remained unconvinced. He told the others: "Except I shall see in his hands the print of the nails, and put my finger into the print of the nails, and thrust my hand into his side, I will not believe" (John 20:24-25).

This skeptical reaction saddled him for two millennia with the unflattering label, "Doubting Thomas." It's a characterization that unfairly implies that something was wrong with him or that he was somehow lesser than the other disciples. It branded him, and by extension, all others' whose faith may need a little help, as being deficient, lacking, or even rebellious.

But the Savior kindly acknowledged this disciple's doubt when he appeared to all of them, including Thomas, a week later. Jesus wasn't offended by the skepticism, nor did he ignore it, but instead, he lovingly offered Thomas what he needed in order to believe. After greeting them all, the risen Lord spoke to his doubting disciple: "Reach hither thy finger, and behold my hands; and reach hither thy hand, and thrust it into my side: and be not faithless, but believing" (John 20:27).

I love the artist Caravaggio's famous 1602 painting entitled "Doubting Thomas," which depicts Thomas using a single finger to feel the wound in the Savior's side, while at the same time, being touched by the Lord's full hand in return. In this tender moment, Jesus allayed Thomas' fears and answered his questions, as he will with all who doubt. Symbolically, we learn that faith comes when we can spiritually feel the wound of Christ through our own personal relationship with him.

Questioning is Not a Sign of Weakness

This account of Thomas teaches us that it is not a sin or a sign of weakness for Church members to question their beliefs. It can actually be the beginning of an exquisite expedition toward building faith. It was questioning and doubt, after all, that led Joseph Smith to answers that culminated in the restored gospel of Christ. Elder John A. Widstoe said, "Doubt of the right kind—that is, honest questioning—leads to faith" and "opens the door to truth."[1]

Dieter F. Uchtdorf, of the First Presidency, encouraged people to ask questions and seek answers to discover truth. "Inquiry is the birthplace of testimony. Some might feel embarrassed or unworthy because they have searching questions regarding the gospel. But they needn't feel that way. Asking questions isn't a sign of weakness. It's a precursor of growth."[2]

Many of us will have doubts about the gospel in varying degrees at some point in our lives, but the thing of greatest importance is how we deal with our misgivings. We can cave in to the sources of our doubt and turn our backs on the gospel, or we can dig into the literature provided by the scriptures, Church leaders, and LDS scholars, and learn and grow from them. Like everything else, it's all a matter of choice. Thomas could have continued to doubt, even after he saw the resurrected Jesus, if he chose to believe it was some kind of sorcery that produced the Lord that day. Instead, he chose to seek out the truth for himself, believe the evidence before him, and confirm and renew his faith.

Many Latter-day Saints are doing the same thing, according to research conducted by the Pew Research Center's Forum on Religion & Public Life. In its landmark "Mormons in America" study in 2012, center researchers found that among those identifying themselves as Mormons, 77 percent "believe wholeheartedly in all the teachings of the church." That number increases among those who attended college [81 percent], and goes even higher [85 percent] among those who are college graduates.

But 22 percent indicated that "some teachings of the LDS Church are hard for me to believe." That number goes down with increased education. Just 14 percent of LDS college graduates in the survey listed such doubts. But the survey also indicated that other Latter-day Saints feel frustration over items they find on the Internet that don't coincide with what they've been taught.[3]

Unfortunately, members get themselves into a quagmire of confusion when they listen to Church critics who may point out varying elements in our history that are made to sound incongruous with gospel teachings. They go on the Internet and lose faith after learning there are different accounts of the First Vision or that Joseph's translation of the Abraham manuscripts differ from those of Egyptologists. There are sound answers to these and other criticisms if Church members would but dig them out rather than give up altogether or let unanswered questions and unresolved issues haunt their lives.

One such person is Don Bradley, an editor and researcher specializing in Mormonism, and author of the *The Lost 116 Pages: Rediscovering the Book of Lehi.* He described his journey out of and back into the Church, because of a period in his life where he put more weight on intellectual processes than spiritual ones during his study of early Church history. "Spiritual inquiry wasn't an objective discipline," Bradley said. "There were too many unpredictable variables—like God—that couldn't be worked into a systematic methodology. But intellectual inquiry could always be worked into a systematic method. It was therefore easier to trust and rely upon the intellectual than the spiritual."[4]

Bradley left the Church, pursued other faiths, and eventually came back after re-examining the historical evidence that he had let damage his testimony. Only this time, he looked at it through the eye of faith. He said, "I came back focused on everything that is 'virtuous, lovely, or of good report or praiseworthy,' and determined to nourish the wheat until it choked the tares." With this new outlook, he found that "digging into Mormon history is ultimately favorable to faith. . . . The central claim of Mormonism is not that God spoke to a fallible human being in 1820. The central claim is that God can and will talk to fallible human beings today. When we reach out to Him, we will find His hand reaching out toward us, waiting."[5]

If we study the gospel and pursue answers to our questions with this kind of focus, we can alleviate doubt. A focus on the positive will most certainly reap positive results. Moreover, if we focus on what we already believe as opposed to what we don't believe or aren't sure we believe, we are, in effect, standing our ground against doubt.

Apostle Jeffrey R. Holland recalled the Bible story of the man who asked the Savior to heal his afflicted child. When Jesus asked the man if he could believe, the scriptures record, "And straightway the father of the child cried out, and said with tears, Lord, I believe; help thou mine unbelief" (Mark 9:24). Elder Holland observed,

> "when facing the challenge of faith, the father asserts his strength first and only then acknowledges his limitation. His initial declaration is affirmative and without hesitation: 'Lord, I believe.' I would say to all who wish for more faith, remember this man! In moments of fear or doubt or troubling times, hold the ground you have already won, even if that ground is limited. In the growth we all have to experience in mortality, the spiritual equivalent of this boy's

affliction or this parent's desperation is going to come to all of us. When those moments come and issues surface, the resolution of which is not immediately forthcoming, *hold fast to what you already know and stand strong until additional knowledge comes.* It was of this very incident, this specific miracle, that Jesus said, 'If ye have faith as a grain of mustard seed, ye shall say unto this mountain, Remove hence to yonder place; and it shall remove; and nothing shall be impossible unto you' (Matthew 17:20). The size of your faith or the degree of your knowledge is not the issue—it is the integrity you demonstrate toward the faith you do have and the truth you already know.[6]

There's an old idiom that's applicable here: "Don't throw the baby out with the bath water." In other words, don't throw out everything just because you don't know everything. Learning is a process. Spiritual growth is a process, so hold fast to that mustard seed of faith you do have. When you nourish it over time, through the fertilizer of prayer, Church attendance, service, prophetic counsel, and truths out of the best books, you can humbly experience it grow into an exquisite tree of life.

The Spiritual Value of Evidence

It appears to be human nature to need or seek out evidence of things that require belief. A broken window can be evidence of a burglary; a person's flushed look is evidence of a fever; a scientist weighs the evidence for and against a hypothesis. It is no less an important ingredient in testimony building.

"As all have not faith, seek ye diligently and teach one another words of wisdom; yea, seek ye out of the best books words of wisdom; seek learning, even by study and also by faith" (D&C 88:118). From this scripture we learn that scholarship plays a big role in the Church and that we should give proper weight to both intellectual and spiritual evidence to keep them in balance. Elder Boyd K. Packer said, "Each of us must accommodate the mixture of reason and revelation in our lives. The gospel not only permits but requires it."[7]

Reason and scholarship can help clear the air, fill the gaps, provide clarity, and illuminate truth. They are essential to true understanding. BYU Professor John W. Welsh, who is a law and religion scholar, explained how some things that might at first seem outrageous, resonate clearly on closer inspection.

> "The ancient Jaredite transoceanic migration that lasted 344 days (see Ether 6:11) ceases to seem so fantastic when that turns out to be exactly the length of time it takes the Pacific current to go from Asia to Mexico.[8] The oddity of Nephi's making new arrows when only his bow had broken suddenly becomes plausible when one realizes that arrows and bows must match each other in weight, length, and stiffness,[9] again making plain and plausible what the Book of Mormon has said all along.
>
> "In an important sense, evidence makes belief possible. I am very impressed by the words of Austin Farrar in speaking about C. S. Lewis and quoted by Elder Maxwell on several occasions: 'Though argument does not create conviction, lack of it destroys belief. What seems to be proved may not be embraced; but what no one shows, that ability to defend is quickly abandoned. Rational argument does not create belief, but it maintains a climate in which belief may flourish.'"[10]

The Lord told Joseph Smith, "let us reason together, that ye may understand" (D&C 50:10). He also said, "and I, the Lord, will reason with you as with men in days of old" (D&C 61:14). We each possess a mind capable of and expected to search out, assess, and reflect on the abundant avenues of knowledge all around us. Much of this book is based on that principle and has hopefully helped us achieve some realistic or, at least, plausible answers.

Science and Revelation Work Together

I have attempted to juxtapose science and theology in several areas to show the compatibility they share in sourcing God as a master chemist, physicist, astronomer, biologist, and artist. God reveals elements of science as much as he reveals elements of theology; all are eternal truths for the benefit of his children. But science alone should never be used as a replacement for things of the spirit. While there is a place for both, it's the spiritual eloquence of our experiences that provides true one-on-one connection with our Father.

Where science attempts to define reality through numbers, formulas, and facts, revelation looks at reality through elements of the spirit. Science strives to answer questions about the physical world, while revelation answers who we are, why we're here, and where we're going. The sheer vastness of it all, from the minute to the magnificent, makes us stand in awe at this intricately fine-tuned system that impels us to quest after all understanding. Because humans are so inclined to seek answers to their existence, they must be wary of getting on board any particular theory just because someone more learned than they, says it's so. Hugh Nibley once said,

> "The words of the prophets cannot be held to the tentative and defective tests that men have devised for them. Science, philosophy, and common sense all have a right to their day in court. But the last word does not lie with them. Every time men in their wisdom have come forth with the last word, other words have promptly followed. The last word is a testimony of the gospel that comes only by direct revelation. Our Father in Heaven speaks it, and if it were in perfect agreement with the science of today, it would surely be out of line with the science of tomorrow. Let us not, therefore, seek to hold God to the learned opinions of the moment when He speaks the language of eternity."[11]

For all the advancements of science, we still don't know how angels can defy gravity and go through walls (see Joseph Smith History 1:43); how heavenly beings can travel instantaneously (see D&C 130:6-7); how priesthood power can raise the dead (see 1 Kings 17:17-23); or how the atonement of Jesus Christ can possibly save us from our sins. We simply can't explain these events via the science of physics, but in due time all will be revealed.

The prophets tell us there will be a complete harmony between the gospel of Jesus Christ and science during the Millennium. Brigham Young said during that thousand year period, the political kingdom of God "grows out of The Church of Jesus Christ of Latter-day Saints, but it is not the Church." In much the same way, science will grow out of the Church, but will not be the Church.[12] Until then, we need to embrace the words of Alma: "These mysteries are not yet fully made known unto me; therefore I shall forbear" (Alma 37:11).

"This is a divine work in process," said Elder Holland, "with the manifestations and blessings of it abounding in every direction, so please don't hyperventilate if from time to time issues arise that need to be examined, understood, and resolved. They do and they will. In this Church, what we know will always trump what we do not know. And remember, in this world, everyone is to walk by faith."[13]

Avoiding Stumbling Blocks

As we turn to science and scholarship to add to our testimonies and growth, we must beware of false or misleading interpretations about the evidence. During my research for this book, I found seemingly reasonable arguments and, what appeared to be substantiated support, for nearly any point of view on any given topic. Library shelves, bookstores, and the Internet are filled with information that on the surface seem acceptable and verifiable. Scientists and scholars write volumes to support the slant they take on their findings and to some, they sound right. Various theologians, using scriptural backup, preach their interpretations of God and Christ and to some, they sound right. Historians and anthropologists provide physical evidence of the origins of life leaving no room for God in the process and to some, they sound right. Now, there is plenty out there that doesn't sound right, but you could basically throw a dart at a target filled with differing answers to a given question and any one of them could sound plausible to those lacking in spiritual certainty.

It's confusing to say the least. While truth can be found in a number of places, we must remain ever vigilant that Satan may be twisting things just enough to set us on the wrong path. He is just cunning enough to make something completely false sound as if it is basking in gospel light, and make something otherwise insignificant seem worth a lifetime of pursuit. He would have us chasing after vexing minutia to keep us from experiencing the uplifting totality of God's perfect plan. He basically keeps us from seeing the forest for the trees.

BYU Religion Professor Robert L. Millett said he was always amazed at how often students spent energy on unimportant questions. He said, "This one just has to know the exact location of Kolob. That one won't rest until he has calculated the precise dimensions of the celestial city seen by John the Revelator. Others wrestle with the present resting place of the Ark of the Covenant or Joseph Smith's seer stone .... There is such a thing as getting so tied up with little fly specks on the great canvas which depicts the whole plan of salvation that we lose sight of what the life and the light and the glory of eternal reward are all about."[14]

He also said he has "a conviction that some truths matter more than others. It is valuable to know of gravity or the laws of motion, but it is vital to know of the reality of a Redeemer. It is helpful to know the laws of thermodynamics, but it is essential to know how to repent and call upon God, in the name of his Son, for forgiveness."[15]

Even the words of modern-day apostles and prophets differ from one another on certain topics, which only serves to bewilder the Doubting Thomas all the more. After all, aren't we supposed to give heed to their words as prophets, seers, and revelators? The answer is, of course, yes, if they are speaking in that capacity. But they are human and fallible just like the rest of us and have proffered personal opinion from time to time that is not doctrine. Our critics pounce on this as evidence of a false church. But even

Joseph Smith was scolded by the Lord on several occasions in the Doctrine and Covenants and told to repent. Everyone is given the privilege of making mistakes and repenting, including prophets and apostles.

We are far from grasping the weight of responsibility shouldered by our Church leaders, but I love and admire them for their willingness to carry the load. I have confidence that any irregularities in their teachings or in the Church's historical record are from human foibles and not any impropriety. I also trust that someday the Lord will reconcile their words and actions to bring lasting harmony and understanding to us all.

In the meantime, there are guidelines we can follow to ensure the tenets we pursue are on the straight and narrow path of the gospel. In a talk during BYU Education Week, David B. Marsh, a curriculum manager in the Church's priesthood department, offered a "doctrinal safety test" to use as a guide while searching out information. The test consists of four questions:

1. Is it a pattern in the scriptures?
2. Do the living prophets and apostles teach it?
3. Is it in harmony with current practices and approved policies of the Church?
4. Does the spirit testify to me of its truthfulness?[16]

This is a great guide in our search for truth, but it must be pointed out again that the Church does not always have official doctrine for every question or topic. In that case, we would still benefit from Marsh's test questions, but would need to rely more heavily on question #4. Where doctrine does not exist we, must embrace answers that ring true for us personally and ultimately strengthen our faith. Marsh also provided ten tips for dealing with doubt:

1. It is okay to experience doubts, but don't let them linger.
2. Fortify your faith in Jesus Christ.
3. Seek to resolve doubts through sincere prayer.
4. Increase your knowledge of truth.

5. Remember that truth is learned a little at a time.
6. Doubt your doubts before you doubt your beliefs.
7. Consult reliable and authoritative sources.
8. Consider the motives of the source.
9. Detect half-truths and lack of context.
10. Neither science nor religion can answer all questions.[17]

This list can be a valuable reminder of how best to approach temporal evidences. While some of the answers and evidence brought forth in this book are derived from reason and scholarship, there is nothing offered that is contrary to revealed truths within the restored gospel. My goal was to use evidence as the groundwork for the personal spiritual journeys we all must take to be converted. I fully endorse the words of Bruce R. McConkie when he said a knowledge of truths discovered in a laboratory or looking through a telescope enable "man to learn truths which are faith promoting and which help him to understand more about Deity; but saving knowledge of God comes only by revelation from the Holy Ghost as a consequence of obedience to the laws and ordinances of the gospel."[18]

Elder Boyd K. Packer echoed this counsel when he said, "If you learn by reason only, you will never understand the Spirit and how it works—regardless of how much you learn about other things. The scriptures teach that 'great men are not always wise' (Job 32:9). Spiritually you may 'know not, and know not that you know not,' and be 'ever learning, and never able to come to the knowledge of the truth' (2 Timothy 3:7). Your spirit learns in a different way than does your intellect. For 'there is a spirit in man: and the inspiration of the Almighty giveth them understanding' (Job 32:8), and the Spirit of Christ 'giveth light to every man that cometh into the world'" (D&C 84:46).[19]

We are simply not going to find all the answers right now and a reasonable person will embrace that fact as a dynamic in the overall gospel plan. Scholarly evidence provides essential stepping stones to comprehension, draws attention to understated details, builds reverence for the truth, and nourishes and broadens faith. But it's our turning at last to God in the spiritual depths of our souls that ultimate answers will be found to our most perplexing questions.

Revelation through Pondering and Meditation

David O. McKay said, "Spirituality ... is the consciousness of victory over self, and of communion with the Infinite."[20] He also said, "In our worship there are two elements: One is the spiritual communion arising from our own meditation; the other, instruction from others .... Of the two, the more profitable ... is the meditation. Meditation is one of the most secret, most sacred doors through which we pass into the presence of the Lord."[21]

The Lord has told us to "ponder upon the things which you have received" (D&C 30:3), and that he leaves "these sayings with you to ponder in your hearts" (D&C 88:63). In fact, the scriptures are filled with similar passages that emphasize this principle as being a key to spiritual growth. If we approach greater spirituality through the typical Mormon avenues of goal-setting, scripture study, fasting, prayer, and priesthood blessings without sufficient pondering and meditation, our spiritual growth can, for some, come up short.

We have learned through the experiences of prophets that pondering has preceded any great revelation. Nephi pondered before his glorious revelation explaining the tree of life and other elements of Lehi's dream (1 Nephi 11:1). Joseph Smith was pondering about which church to join when he received his vision of the Father and the Son. He and Sidney Rigdon also meditated on the salvation of man when they received in vision the doctrine of the three degrees of glory (D&C 76). Joseph F. Smith was pondering before he received, what is now section 138 of the Doctrine and Covenants, a revelation of Christ's visit to the spirit world. Spencer W. Kimball said he went to the temple day after day to ponder and commune with God about making the priesthood available to all worthy male members. He received confirmation from on High to do so in 1978. President Thomas S. Monson announced in October 2012, that "through prayer and pondering," he was divinely directed to lower the age at which young men and woman can begin their missionary service.[22]

Our leaders have set the example about the power of pondering, and have counseled us over and over to immerse ourselves in quiet reflection on spiritual matters. Neal A. Maxwell taught, "Pondering, for most of us, is not something we do easily. It is much more than drifting or daydreaming, for it focuses and stirs us, not lulls us. We must set aside time, circumstances, and attitude in order to achieve it. In Alma's words, we must 'give place' (Alma 32:27). The length of time involved in pondering is not as important as the intensity given to it. Reflection cannot be achieved in the midst of distraction."[23]

Physical Benefits of Meditation

Church leaders are not alone in their wisdom on the topic because science has shown that meditation can benefit both the spirit and the body. Physically, it has proven to ease chronic pain, anxiety, stress, improve heart health, boost mood and immunity, and resolve pregnancy problems. Cardiologist Herbert Benson, well known for research into the health effects of meditation, said, "The relaxation response [from meditation] helps decrease metabolism, lowers blood pressure, and improves heart rate, breathing, and brain waves."[24]

Studies on Buddhist monks reveal that meditation produces long-lasting changes in brain activity in areas involved in attention, working memory, learning, and conscious perception.[25] Long-term meditators have shown increased volumes of gray matter in areas of the brain responsible for regulating emotion. Even non-meditators, who completed an eight-week course in meditation techniques, showed similar changes, demonstrating that even small amounts of meditation can produce significant results.[26]

Meditation even appears to slow the effects of aging. In another study, those who had meditated about an hour a day for six years displayed increased cortical thickness, which usually thins as we age and is associated with dementia. Older meditators also showed a decreased thinning in cortical thickness compared to those of the same age who did not meditate.[27]

If meditation can have such a profound effect on our physical bodies, imagine what it can do for our spirits. One study compared three groups that tested the benefits of spiritual versus secular forms of meditation. Participants were taught a meditation or relaxation technique to practice for 20 minutes a day for two weeks. After two weeks, participants returned to the lab, practiced their technique for 20 minutes, and placed their hand in a cold-water bath of 2°C for as long as they could endure it. The spiritual meditation group exhibited far less anxiety and a more positive mood, along with greater spiritual health and spiritual experiences than the other two groups. They also tolerated pain from the cold-water bath almost twice as long. Spiritual meditation appears to have a greater effect on spirituality because it shifts the mind away from physical and mundane concerns to focus on the larger universe and the individual's place in it.[28]

Within the Church, we don't always think of using a specific form of meditation to increase our spirituality, but rather pursue a course of daily scripture study, prayer, and personal worship. This is fine if we're truly finding spiritual transformation through these mediums. I suspect sometimes we do and sometimes we don't depending on the level of our effort. The reason why many of us probably don't practice real meditative techniques is because we tend to associate them with Eastern religions, which may somehow appear not in keeping with LDS practices. But anyone can meditate for 20 minutes a day, through quiet thought and pondering, and immediately afterward feel renewed, energized, and closer to God. It's a technique to help us clear the clutter from our minds so that our study and prayers are more focused and meaningful.

After struggling for 30 years to find true spiritual transformation as a practicing Mormon, Philip McLemore, former LDS Institute of Religion director and a retired Air Force chaplain, found it in meditation. He said his entire LDS belief structure became enhanced when he discovered "expanded states of bliss, peace, and spiritual connection.

"After seven months of devoted meditation practice, I began to have consciousness-expanding experiences that provided exhilarating moments in which I felt a deep sense of oneness with the universe and all of creation.

I also began to identify much more with my spirit instead of my body, thoughts, and emotions. These states of higher awareness are nicely captured in Pierre Teilhard de Chardin's phrase, 'You are not a human being in search of a spiritual experience. You are a spiritual being immersed in a human experience.'"[29]

McLemore went on to describe how, through meditation, his testimony grew and his relationship with the Father and the Son grew beyond measure. He achieved through this simple method of directed thought, the kind of spirituality that had often eluded him before, though he has always been a solid member of the Church.

If you are concerned about your personal level of doubt, daily prayer and scripture study may not be enough. You've probably already been doing that for years with varying degrees of success in your faith and spiritual growth. You may need to take a bigger leap into what Church leaders have been telling us to do for years: Take the time to ponder. The way we do that is through consistently spending time in Godly communion so the Holy Ghost can nourish and revitalize our inner selves. It is the spirit touching spirit phenomenon that has us soaring to the highest heights, while at the same time, keeping us grounded in the gospel. Symbolically, it's like the exhilaration of riding atop an ocean crest with balance and precision all the way to the calm and safety of the waiting shore.

Stories of Inspiration

Another way to help faith grow is through stories of inspiration from those around us. Because the Holy Ghost reveals and confirms all truth, individual stories of prayers answered, spiritual connections made, and lives transformed, can provide an opportunity for the Spirit to bear witness of truth. "For where two or three are gathered together in my name, there am I in the midst of them" (Matthew 18:20). We know that God often answers prayers and provides spiritual experiences through our relationships with other people. Imagine a fire pit of burning coals. Together, each ignited individual coal helps to fuel the intensity of the collective heat. Acting together, they become a roaring, powerful resource for providing warmth. But when you remove one coal and place it away from the others, its own individual heat diminishes and more quickly dies.

This is much like our own spirituality heat index. We often need each other to keep the fire of the gospel burning brightly within us. It is therefore, vital that those who doubt seek out opportunities to learn what others have experienced through the Spirit. Rub shoulders with them, get to know why they have testimonies, and be edified by their stories of personal growth. Such stories can ignite in us the tinder of testimony and elicit flashes of faith that touch our souls and draw us closer to God. I would like to share two stories of my own from experiences during my mission to Colorado. I hope by sharing them in this venue, the converting power of the Holy Ghost can enter your hearts and testify with fire.

John was a U. S. Army soldier who had already completed three tours in Vietnam when my companion and I began to teach him the missionary discussions. He loved our message and readily accepted every new concept we taught. But there was a prevailing problem at the end of every discussion that we tried to address and clear up without success. He couldn't and wouldn't pray. We couldn't finish the teaching process until he prayed and received a personal witness of the truth of our message, and so we continued to work with him. After weeks of meetings, lessons, filmstrips, and recordings of general authorities aimed at helping him pray, we finally learned one evening why it was such a problem for him.

With his head lowered in shame, John told us that during his time in Vietnam, he had killed dozens of the enemy, many of them point blank in the tumult of battle. He knew they too, were children of God and it was on his shoulders that their lives had been snuffed out, never to experience the full purpose of life. The memory of it all haunted him to such a degree that he felt tainted, dirty, and offensively unworthy to address his Heavenly Father.

The mere act of finally talking about it and hearing our responses of God's ability to forgive and wipe away the stains of our actions, seemed to break through to his soul. This time when we invited him to pray, he humbly nodded his head, addressed his Father in Heaven, and poured out his soul for the first time since his war experiences. My companion and I wept alongside this special young man as he begged for forgiveness and asked with an earnest heart if our message of the restored gospel was true. I have never heard a prayer more rich in vulnerable sincerity than this one, and because of it, John was rewarded with an unmistakable communion with God through his Spirit. At the end of his prayer, John, tears streaming down his face, told us he felt the presence of God in that room, knew that he was forgiven, and that our message was true. He was baptized the next week.

In another experience from my mission, Ann, a middle aged married woman and mother of four, was in the advanced stages of dying from a malignant brain tumor when we met her. A dear friend of hers who was a Church member asked us to visit with her and provide some comfort. Without really intending to do more than that, we soon learned that she had been exposed to the Church many years earlier and chose not to join because of her husband's opposition to it. But now she was dying, and had no reason to deny herself the blessings of our message. So we began to teach her the discussions in her friend's home, and as we watched her blossom in her love and acceptance of the gospel, we also watched her diseased body deteriorate rapidly.

When we first met Ann, she could still walk unsteadily with a cane, but within a few days she was using a walker, and in another week, was confined to a wheelchair. Time was running out in mortality for this wonderful lady, but it was only beginning for what was to come in the next life. She accepted the gospel with all her heart after receiving clear answers to her prayers and requested baptism. As her body grew more and more weak, we felt the urgency of ensuring her baptism before her death.

On the day of her baptism, the room was filled with her family, friends, and well-wishers from the ward who wanted to support this dying woman's last request. After talks of inspiration were given, two worthy priesthood holders lowered her into the baptismal font, wheelchair and all, and performed this most sacred ordinance that would culminate her life. Three weeks later, Ann succumbed to her disease and returned to her Heavenly

Father. How grateful I was that Ann would not have to wait for someone to perform a vicarious baptism after her death. Instead, she would be able to enjoy immediately the blessings of the gospel in the spirit world.

Suffice it to say, God is eager to help us find our way home and will provide the means for us to feel the spirit of conversion if we will but do our part and try. Let us seek out and embrace the stories of others and glean from their testimonies the fire of the gospel that will ignite within us a flame to our own conversion.

The Love of God is our Rudder

One of the greatest evidences of God is his love for us. The scriptures are full of assurances of that love: "We love him, because he first loved us" (1 John 4:19); "I am encircled about eternally in the arms of his love" (2 Nephi 1:15); "For God so loved the world, that he gave his only begotten Son …." (John 3:16).

We are creatures of love—both the giving and receiving of it. We need it as much as we need food and raiment to live a full and complete life. But the thing that matters most in our growth process is our ability to *feel* his love. We need to recognize and experience the kind of love that can only come from him, and when we do, our lives will be transformed. His love is the kind that envelopes us spiritually in our most salient moments of both hope and despair. His love is the infinite, limitless kind manifested in the blessings and miracles of our lives. We can feel this Godly love as we realize that the vastness of the universe was created solely for our use. We can feel this Godly love when we realize he has not left us alone but has provided prophets, a Church, and principles to live by so that we might return to his presence. All are evidence of his love.

I learned a valuable lesson about the love of God metaphorically, during an exciting but ill-timed vacation with friends many years ago, in the middle of Hurricane Floyd while at Cape May, New Jersey. The squall had lessened in intensity by the time it spiraled its way that far north, but it dumped enough rain on us the first day of our trip to make us start looking around for the ark. Despite our bad luck, we took pleasure in witnessing an interesting phenomenon as we watched the maelstrom from the sanctuary of our hotel.

After a full day of furious torrential wind and rain without a glimmer of respite in sight, suddenly to our amazement, everything stopped. The rain vanished, the wind subsided, and the sun emerged like a springtime flower, bringing with it blue skies and a surreal calm that was in stark contrast to the tumult just moments earlier. We stood in awe as we realized we were in the eye of the hurricane. It was amazing to comprehend that right in the middle of the same storm that had wreaked such havoc, could be found placid tranquility. We basked in it while it lasted. After only about 30 minutes, the serenity departed and the squall exploded upon us again making us victims to the furor of the raging tempest.

The love of God is much like the calm found in the eye of the hurricane in that it envelopes us like a safe harbor in the midst of the swirling and perilous destruction of our telestial world. We are never completely shielded from the world's storms because life demands that we brave the elements in our work, schools, and communities. But his love does provide an anchor and a foundation to hold us steady and save us from drowning in more treacherous waters.

Sometimes, in the storms of life, we deny God's love because we let adversity overshadow the comfort he's trying to send. Elder Andersen shared a story of such a circumstance when he visited a mission in southern Europe. He told of spending time with a missionary who, ticket in hand, insisted on returning home because of challenges in the mission he could not face. The elder added,

> "'Brother Andersen, I don't even know if God loves me.' As he said those words, I felt a sure and forceful feeling come into my spirit: "He does know I love him. He knows it.'
>
> "I let him continue for a few more minutes, and then I said, 'Elder, I'm sympathetic to much of what you've said, but I must correct you on one thing. You do know God loves you. You know He does.' As I said those words to him, the same

Spirit that had spoken to me spoke to him. He bowed his head and began to cry. He apologized. 'Brother Andersen,' he said, 'I do know God loves me; I do know it.' He didn't know everything, but he knew enough. He knew God loved him. That priceless piece of spiritual knowledge was sufficient for his doubt to be replaced with faith. He found the strength to stay on his mission."[30]

Remember that God and Christ are on our side. They want us to defeat the foes that would block the way of our triumphant return to their presence. They are providing every tool possible to help us make that journey home. To put it in sports terms, God is like a coach who gives us the training to succeed and make the score. We must listen to him and trust that he will see us safely around the bases in this baseball game of life. He will not lead us astray nor cause us to stumble if we will but follow his directions.

And at the top of his list of directions is "follow the prophet." After 50 years of service in the Church as a general authority, our prophet, Thomas S. Monson, is uniquely qualified to steer us in the right direction. He is the Lord's anointed, and we can be assured of his love. We can also trust that his counsel is the Lord's counsel. In words, imbued with melody and prose, President Monson described what we need to do to find our way back to our heavenly home: "Like the vital rudder of a ship, we have been provided a way to determine the direction we travel. The lighthouse of the Lord beckons to all as we sail the seas of life. Our home port is the celestial kingdom of God. Our purpose is to steer an undeviating course in that direction. A man without a purpose is like a ship without a rudder—never likely to reach home port. To us comes the signal: Chart your course, set your sail, position your rudder, and proceed."[31]

Conclusion

I hope every Doubting Thomas who reads these pages will find the strength to exercise what faith they already have and proceed to chart a course of true conversion. As we reexamine the biblical account of the Lord's doubting disciple, we learn another important lesson: Thomas stuck around. Despite his misgivings, he had faith sufficient to wait to see if Jesus would come back. Like so many who doubt, Thomas wanted to believe, and so he lingered in the shadows of his own unbelief for eight days, unwilling to give up until he knew for himself that Jesus had risen. His story is no different from other skeptics who find themselves alone in their doubts in a throng of believers. They too want to believe, and so they stick around hoping and looking for the spiritual experiences that will help them feel for themselves, the wound of Christ.

When Thomas received his witness, his questioning mind was instantly soothed and a glorious change took place. In penitent veneration, he bowed before his Lord and exclaimed "My Lord and my God" (John 20:28). Doubting Thomas doubted no more. Likewise, God is ever ready to strengthen us and dispel our unbelief. It is not a sin to question, and we are not deficient or rebellious if we do. We all come to the Savior's table with varying degrees of faith on our plates, but each of us brings something special that turns an otherwise ordinary dinner into a resplendent feast. There is a place for us all at the table, but we have to make the effort to pull up a chair and sit down before we can partake. Because none of us are the same, we are only expected to use the light we have to choose the better part, and if we stumble, to repent and try again.

If we truly want to know of celestial things, if we yearn to have an unshakable testimony, we have to open our hearts and do whatever it takes to receive that Spirit. Some of us need to literally stand at the crossroads of life hungering to know if this Church is true. Without that hunger we won't thrust in our sickle with our might, something doubters especially need to do to get a testimony. "Blessed are those who hunger and thirst after righteousness for they shall be filled with the Holy Ghost" (3 Nephi 12:6).

Until we truly hunger to have a resolute testimony of God and Christ, we'll always find ourselves standing on the sidelines, staying in the background, or being on the outside looking in. We'll never fully understand the joy that others speak of when the Spirit has touched them. We'll never feel the elation of watching others grow through the sharing of our own testimonies. We'll never feel the undeniable warmth of the Savior's arms encircled about us as we approach him in faith. We'll never feel the exhilaration of being at the forefront of building God's kingdom and preparing the way for the coming of his Son.

If we decide we want these things and are willing to go after them, will it be easy? No, because "unto whom much is given, much is required" (D&C 82:3), and "ye receive no witness until after the trial of your faith" (Ether 12:6). But we're also told to rely on the Lord for the help we need because his "yoke is easy and [his] burden is light" (Matthew 11:30). A testimony is a priceless gift, and I suspect God would prefer planting seeds of faith in fertile ground. That may mean some real sacrifice on our part, like a willingness to give up a few sins, a desire to serve others, a desire to feed our minds, and a commitment to righteous living. If we prepare ourselves to receive the Spirit by ostracizing the "gray areas" from our lives, spiritual experiences will come. And when they do, the sweet warmth of God's love will carry us through all the storms of life and into an eternal reward.

President Monson reminded us that "it is celestial glory which we seek. It is the presence of God in which we desire to dwell. It is a forever family in which we want membership .... He is concerned also for the lost child, the tardy teenager, the wayward youth, the delinquent parent. Tenderly the Master speaks to these and indeed to all: 'Come back. Come up. Come in. Come home. Come unto me.'"[32]

We don't have to know everything to come unto Christ; as Elder Andersen taught, we just have to know enough. If we can but marshal up faith no larger than a tiny mustard seed, we're told nothing shall be impossible unto us (see Matthew 17:20). Like Doubting Thomas, we need to stick around. We need to stay in close proximity to the Church and Kingdom of God, with our desire for knowledge intact, so that we're ready and waiting for the witness we seek.

If you have not received a spiritual witness that God lives and Jesus is the Christ, your time has come. Reach deep within your soul and do all you can to nourish that desire, that seed of faith budding within. When that personal revelation comes—and it will—you too will know what others in the Church are so excited about because you will have spiritual knowledge. You too will feel the power of testimony illuminate your soul when you stand in God's holy house. You too will be stirred from deep within at the blessing of a baby, the baptism of a new convert, or a boy's first sacramental prayer.

And when your natural inclination to doubt starts to push to the surface from time to time, you can find strength in the roots of your testimony to keep your inner gospel garden flourishing. Move forward, my friend, tethered to the iron rod and with faith to overcome doubt. Hold fast to the words of the Savior: "Look unto me in every thought; doubt not, fear not" (D&C 6:36).

Notes

Introduction

¹ Brigham Young, *Discourses of Brigham Young*, John A. Widtsoe (Salt Lake City: Deseret Book, 1966), 247.

² Brigham Young, *Teachings of Presidents of the Church: Brigham Young* (Salt Lake City: The Church of Jesus Christ of Latter-day Saints, 1997), 17.

³ Harold B. Lee, *Life under Control*, Brigham Young University commencement speech, June 4, 1951, L. Tom Perry Special Collections, Harold B. Lee Library, Brigham Young University, Provo, Utah, 19.

⁴ Spencer W. Kimball, *Modern Scientific Findings Harmonize with Revelation through the Ages* (Salt Lake City: Deseret Book, 1962).

⁵ Edward L. Kimball, ed., *The Teachings of Spencer W. Kimball* (Salt Lake City: Bookcraft, 1982), 391.

⁶ Ezra Taft Benson, *Conference Report*, April 1958, 60.

⁷ Walter Isaacson, *Einstein: His Life and Universe.* (New York: Simon and Schuster, 2008), 388-389.

⁸ Gerald Lund, "Countering Korihor's Philosophies," *Ensign*, July 1992.

Chapter One

¹ Neal A. Maxwell, *Deposition of a Disciple* (Salt Lake City: Deseret Book, 1976), 16.

² Gordon B. Hinckley, *Faith: The Essence of True Religion* (Salt Lake City: Deseret Book, 1989), 10.

³ "Big Bang Theory – An Overview." http://allaboutscience.org, www.big-bang-theory.com.

⁴ Hollis R. Johnson, "The Big Bang: What Does It Mean for Us?" *FARMS Review*: vol. 16, issue 2, 277-312; A review of *"Craftsman or Creator? An Examination of the Mormon Doctrine of Creation and a Defense of Creatio ex nihilo* by Paul Copan and William Lane Craig, (Provo, UT: Maxwell Institute, 2004).

⁵ John D. Barrow, *The Book of Nothing* (Cape, London, 2000), 216.

⁶ William Lee Stokes, *Joseph Smith and the Creation*, (Salt Lake City: Starstone Publishers, 1991), 59-60.

[7] *Times and Seasons,* (1844) vol. 5, 615.

[8] Daniel C. Peterson, "News from Antiquity," *Ensign,* January 1994, 16.

[9] Victor J. Stenger, *Has Science Found God? The Latest Results in the Search for Purpose in the Universe,* (Amherst, NY: Prometheus Books, 2003), 38.

[10] R.E.D. Clark, *Creation (London:* Tyndale Press, 1946), 20.

[11] Cornelius Hunter, "Darwin's God, How Religion Drives Science and Why it Matters," July 7, 2012, http://www.darwins-god.com.

[12] W. Knight, "Spinach Could Power Better Solar Cells," September 21, 2004, http://www.NewScientist.com news service.

[13] Richard Feynman, *The Meaning of it All: Thoughts of a Citizen-Scientist* (New York: BasicBooks 1998), 43.

[14] Dan Vergano, "Physicists Break Down Concept of God Particle," *USA Today,* July 6, 2012.

[15] Neal A. Maxwell, "Start Making Chips," *New Era,* September 1998, 6.

[16] Joseph Fielding Smith, *Teachings of the Prophet Joseph Smith,* (Salt Lake City: Deseret Book, 1974) 352-54.

[17] Henry Eyring, *The Faith of a Scientist,* (Salt Lake City: Bookcraft, 1967), 77-78.

[18] Bruce R. McConkie, *Mormon Doctrine* (Salt Lake City: Bookcraft, reprinted 1979), 218.

[19] Smith, *Teachings of Joseph Smith,* 350-352.

[20] James E. Talmage, *The* Articles *of Faith,* 42nd ed. (Salt Lake City: Deseret News Press, 1968), 33-34.

[21] Hollis R. Johnson, "The Big Bang: What Does It Mean for Us?" *FARMS Review* 16, no. 2, 2004, 296.

[22] Michael Bronson, "7-Day Creation: Figurative or Literal?" http://www.biblehelp.org/7day.htm.

[23] F. Kent Nielsen and Stephen D. Ricks, "Creation, Creation Accounts," *Encyclopedia of Mormonism,* 342.

[24] *Ibid.*

[25] Robert J. Woodford, "In the Beginning: A Latter-day Perspective," *Ensign,* January 1998.

[26] Brigham Young, *Journal of Discourses,* vol. 14, 1856, 115-6.

[27] Ross Anderson, "ATLAST: The Gargantuan Telescope Designed to Find Life on Other Planets," *The Atlantic,* October 11, 2012.

[28] Young, *Journal of Discourses,* vol. 3, 276.

[29] Orson Pratt, *Great First Cause,* pamphlet, January 1, 1851, 5.

[30] Orson Pratt, *Journal of References,* vol. 1, (March 14, 1875).

[31] Rodney D. Griffin, *Scientific Support for Scriptural Stories,* (Bountiful: Horizon Publishers, 1992), 226.

[32] McConkie, *Mormon Doctrine,* 169.

[33] Kathleen Duffy, "Religious Response to an Evolutionary Universe," http://waccglobal.org.

[34] "The Great Plan of Happiness," *Book of Mormon Teacher Resource Manual,* (2004), 290-293; "The Plan of Salvation," video https://www.lds.org/pages/the-plan-of-salvation-d-and-c-video?lang=eng.

[35] NASA, "Universe 101," http://map.gsfc.nasa.gov/universe/bb_cosmo_infl.html.

[36] John D. Barrow, *Impossibility,* (Oxford, UK: Oxford University Press, 1999), 171-72.

[37] Blake T. Osler, "The Doctrine of *Creation Ex Nihilo* is a Big Fuss Over Nothing: Part II: The Inductive Argument," *FAIR,* 2013, http://www.fairlds.org/reviews_of_the_new-mormon-challenge/a-response-to-copan-and-craig-part-2-the-inductive-argument.

[38] Brigham Young, *Journal of Discourses,* 26 vols. (London and Liverpool: LDS Booksellers Depot, 1862), vol. 9; 168; Joseph Smith, *The King Follett Discourse* (Salt Lake City: Magazine Printing Co., 1963), 8; 10; John Taylor, *Journal of Discourses* (February 19, 1860) vol. 8; 3.

[39] *Gospel Principles*, (Salt Lake City: LDS Church, 2009), 227.

[40] "Multiverse," *Reference.com*. Lexico Publishing Group, LL., 2005, retrieved January 29, 2005, from http://www.reference.com/browse/wiki/multiverse.

[41] Martin Rees, *Before the Beginning: Our Universe and Others* (Reading, Mass.: Addison-Wesley, 1997), 3.

[42] Kirk D. Hagen, "Eternal Progression in a Multiverse: An Explorative Mormon Cosmology," *Dialogue: A Journal of Mormon Thought*, 29.

[43] Robert Jastrow, "The Religion of Science," in *God and the Astronomers*, (New York: Readers Library paperback, 2000) 105.

Chapter Two

[1] Frank Newport, "In U.S., 46% Hold Creationist View of Human Origins," *Gallup Politics*, June 2012.

[2] Clayton R. Brough and Rodney D. Griffin, *Scientific Support for Scriptural Stories*, (Bountiful, UT: Horizon Publishers, October 1992), 32.

[3] *Improvement Era*, September 1925, 1090-1091; also in *Deseret News*, July 18, 1925.

[4] Duane E. Jeffery, "Seers, Savants and Evolution: The Uncomfortable Interface," *Dialogue*, vol. 8, no. 3 & 4, 22-23.

[5] D. Todd Christofferson, General Conference, Sunday Morning Session, April 1, 2012.

[6] Neil L. Anderson, "Trial of Your Faith," *Ensign*, November 2012.

[7] Letter to Dr. LaRele J. Stephens from David O. McKay, March 11, 1955.

[8] Letter from David O. McKay, *LDS Church Archives*, February 3, 1959.

[9] Kenneth J. Brown, "Distinguishing the Doctrinal, Non-Doctrinal and False Doctrinal Concepts of the Creation," paper presented to the Natural Science Division and Religion Department Seminar at Ricks College, November 21, 1974.

[10] *Ibid.*

[11] *Improvement Era*, April 1910, 570. Although there was no author's name attached to this statement, a number of scholars think Joseph F. Smith was responsible since he and Edward H. Anderson were the editors (see Duane E. Jeffery, "Seers, Savants and Evolution: The Uncomfortable Interface," *Dialogue* 8, Autumn/Winter 1973).

[12] Brown, *Distinguishing the Doctrinal*.

[13] Terry Ball to Nancy Browne, email, June 11, 2013.

[14] *The American Heritage® Dictionary of the English Language*, 4th edition, (Boston: Houghton Mifflin Harcourt Publishing Company, 2010).

[15] "Randomness," http://en.wikipedia.org/wiki/Randomness.

[16] William S. Bradshaw, "Biological Evolution: Toward a Reconciliation of the Science and Our Faith," *Sunstone*, issue 158, March, 2010.

[17] *Ibid.*

[18] M. J. Russell, and N. T. Arndt, "Geodynamic and Metabolic Cycles in the Hadean," *Biogeosciences*, 2, 2005, 97-111.

[19] Russell M. Nelson, "Thanks Be To God," *Ensign*, April 2012.

[20] Gary A. Strobel, letter to Boyd K. Packer, Oct. 10, 1984).

[21] "What Is a Whale?" *Science* 263, January 14, 1994, 180-81.

Notes

²² Jeffery, *Seers, Savants*, vol. 8, no. 3 & 4, 41-69.

²³ *Ibid.*

²⁴ Emmett L. Williams, editor, *Thermodynamics and the Development of Order*, (Creation Research Society Books, 1981), 18.

²⁵ Brigham Young, *Journal of Discourses*, vol. 18, (London: Latter-day Saints' Book Depot, 1856), 231.

²⁶ Rich Deem, "The Human Difference: How Humans are Unique Compared to *All* Other Animals," http://www.godandscience.org.

²⁷ Boyd K. Packer, "The Law and the Light," in *The Book of Mormon: Jacob through Words of Mormon, To Learn with Joy*, eds. Monte S. Nyman and Charles D. Tate Jr., (Provo, UT: Religious Studies Center, Brigham Young University, 1990), 1-31.

²⁸ Barbara Mertz, *Black Folk Here and There*, (Univ. of California Center for Afro, February 1991), 187.

²⁹ Arthur Custance, *Noah's Three Sons*, (Grand Rapids, MI: Zondervan 1984), 63.

³⁰ Young, *Journal of Discourses*, vol. 2, 79.

³¹ James E. Talmage, *The Earth and Man*, talk delivered in Salt Lake Tabernacle, August. 9, 1931.

³² First Presidency Minutes, April 7, 1931, 54; quoted in Jeffery, "Seers, Savants and Evolution," 64.

³³ Joseph Fielding Smith, *Man: His Origin and Destiny*, (Salt Lake City: Deseret Book, 1954), 279.

³⁴ Russell M. Nelson, "Standards of the Lord's Standard-Bearers," *Ensign*, August 1991, 5.

³⁵ Hugh W. Nibley, "Before Adam," in Hugh W. Nibley, *Old Testament and Related Studies* vol. 1 of *Collected Works of Hugh Nibley*, ed. by John W. Welch, Gary P. Gillum, and Don E. Norton, (Salt Lake City: Deseret Book, Foundation for Ancient Research and Mormon Studies, 1986), 82–83.

³⁶ James Strong, *Strong's Exhaustive Concordance of the Bible*, (Peabody, MA: Hendrickson Publishing, January 2009), 120.

³⁷ *Ibid.*

³⁸ Alonzo Gaskill, *The Savior and the Serpent*, (Salt Lake City: Deseret Book, 2005), 26-27.

³⁹ Larry A. Witham, *Where Darwin Meets the Bible: Creationists and Evolutionists in America*, (New York: Oxford University Press, 2002).

⁴⁰ Bradshaw, "Biological Evolution."

⁴¹ *Ibid.*

⁴² Harold B. Lee, "The Iron Rod," *Ensign*, June, 1971, 6-8.

Chapter Three

¹ Henry Eyring, *The Faith of a Scientist*, (Salt Lake City: Bookcraft, 1967), 32.

² *Ibid*, 49.

³ George H. Gallup Jr., "Religious Awakenings Bolster Americans' Faith, http://www.gallup.com/poll/7582/religious-awakenings-bolster-americans-faith.aspx.

⁴ Jonathan Clatworthy, "Religious and Near Death Experiences," http://www.clatworthy.org.

⁵ *Ibid.*

⁶ *Ibid.*

⁷ *Report on the China Project*, Alister Hardy Religious Experience Research Centre, http://www.trinitysaintdavid.ac.uk/en/lrc/librariesandcentres/alisterhardyreligiousexperienceresearchcentre/research/reportonthechinaproject/.

[8] David Miller, PhD., "The Brain Proof of God," Apologetics Press Inc., 2012, http://www.apologeticspress.org/apPubPage.aspx?pub=2&issue=899.

[9] John N. Johnson, Ph.D., "The Computer and the Brain," http://s8int.com/article-six-brain-power.html.

[10] Alicia Puglionesi, "God on the Brain, Does neuroscience hold the answers to life's biggest questions?" Center for Programs in Contemporary Writing, 2007-2008, http://writing.upenn.edu/awards/eisenberg/puglionesi.php.

[11] Eyring, *Faith of a Scientist*.

[12] Kelly Bulkley, *Forthcoming. The Wilderness of Dreams: Exploring the Religious Meaning of Dreams in Modern Western Culture*, (Albany: SUNY Press, 1994).

[13] Patrick McNamara, "Dreams and Religion," *Institute for the Bio-cultural Study of Religion*, (April 20, 2011).

[14] P. McNamara, P. Johnson, D. McLaren, E. Harris, C. Beauharnais, & S. Auerbach, "REM and NREM sleep mentation." *International Review of Neurobiology*, 92, (2010). 69-86.

[15] *Dream Science,* http://www.dreamgate.com.

[16] Richard G. Scott, "How to Obtain Revelation and Inspiration for Your Personal Life," *Ensign*, (April, 2012).

[17] Enyiche Martins, "You Better Pray First," *Ensign*, (July 2012).

[18] Patrick McNamara, "Visitation Dreams, the Neuroscience of our Night Life," Dream Catcher, *Psychology Today*, October 8, 2011.

[19] Trudy Harris, "Dreams Bring Peace after a Loved One's Death," Guideposts.org, October 10, 2011.

[20] Dr. McArthur Hill, Pro-Life Action League, http://www.prolifeaction.org/providers/hill.php.

[21] Bruce R. McConkie, *Mormon Doctrine*, (Salt Lake City: Bookcraft, 1966), 208.

[22] *Ibid*, 823-24

[23] Sharon Begley, "Your Brain on Religion: Mystic visions or brain circuits at work," *Newsweek*, May 7, 2001.

[24] *Ibid*.

[25] "That Religious Studies Website," http://www.thatreligiousstudieswebsite.com/Religious_Studies/Phil_of_Rel/God/religious_experience_intro.php.

[27] Mary C. Neal, M.D., *To Heaven and Back*, (Colorado Springs: WaterBrook Press, 2012), 139-41.

[28] Alvin Gibson, *Echoes from Eternity*, (Bountiful, UT: Horizon Publishers, 1993), 26.

[29] Russell M. Nelson, *From Heart to Heart*, (Salt Lake City: Quality Press, 1979), 188.

[30] Dennis Gersten, M.D., *Are You Getting Enlightened or Losing Your Mind*, (Harmony of Crown Books, May, 1997).

[31] Bill Guggenheim & Judy Guggenheim, "After Death Communication," *The ADC Project*, http://www.after-death.com/Pages/About/ADC.aspx.

[32] *Ibid*.

[33] David Kessler, "Do the Dead Greet the Dying?" CNN.com, October 19, 2010.

[34] Joseph M. Higgins and Chuck Bergman, "Hospice Workers' Stories," http://www.netplaces.com/evidence-of-the-afterlife/medical-personnel-witnesses-to-the-crossing-over/hospice-workers-stories.htm.

[35] "Deathbed Visions Study," Horizon Research Foundation, http://www.horizonresearch.org.

[36] Bruce Greyson, *Anthropology and Humanism*, vol. 35, issue 2, The American Anthropological Association, (December, 2010).

[37] R. Craig Hogan, Ph.D., *Your Eternal Self*, (Normal, IL: Greater Reality Publications, 2009), 66-76.

[38] Richard Lloyd Anderson, *Book of Mormon Witnesses*, BYU Neal A. Maxwell Institute for Religious Scholarship, http://maxwellinstitute.byu.edu/publications/transcripts/?id=21.

[39] http://www.lds.org.

[40] Joseph Fielding Smith, *Teachings of the Prophet Joseph Smith*, (Salt Lake City: Deseret Book Co., 1968), 328.

[41] *Teachings of Spencer W. Kimball*, ed. Edward L. Kimball, (Salt Lake City: Bookcraft, 1982), 457.

[42] David A. Bednar, "The Spirit of Revelation," *Ensign*, April, 2011.

Chapter Four

[1] Heber C. Kimball, *Journal of Discourses* 4, (1956), 135-36.

[2] Carol Zaleski, *Otherworld Journeys: Accounts of Near-Death Experience in Medieval and Modern Times*, (New York: Oxford University Press, 1987), 116-117.

[3] Plato, *The Republic*. (New York: C. Scribner's Sons, 1928).

[4] Dr. Jeffery Mishlove, transcript from the series Thinking Allowed, "Conversations On the Leading Edge of Knowledge and Discovery," http://www.intuition.org/txt/moody.htm.

[5] "Scientific Theories of the Near-death Experience," http://www.near-death.com/experiences/experts01.html.

[6] Raymond A. Moody, Jr., M.D., *Life After Life*, (New York: Bantam Books, 1975), 101-07.

[7] Arvin S. Gibson, *Fingerprints of God*, (Horizon Publication & Distribution Co., 1999); "Near-death Experiences of Groups of People at the Same Time," http://www.near-death.com/group.html.

[8] Jonathan Clatworthy, "Religious and Near Death Experiences," http://www.clatworthy.org/religiousexperience.html.

[9] *Ibid*.

[10] Bruce Greyson, "Anthropology and Humanis," *Journal of the American Anthropological Association*, vol. 35, issue 2, December 2010.

[11] P.M.H. Atwater, Ph.D., taken from her book, *Children of the New Millennium*, http://www.near-death.com/children.html.

[12] Dr. Melvin Morse, *Parting Visions*, (New York: HarperCollins, 1996).

[13] Diane Komp, *Images of Grace*, (Grand Rapids: Zondervan Publishing, Feb. 1, 1996).

[14] C. Hurovitz, S. Dunn, G. W. Domhoff, & H. Fiss, "The dreams of blind men and women: A replication and extension of previous findings," *Dreaming*, 9, (1999), 183-193.

[15] "Proof of Life After Death," http://near-deathexperiences.org/index.php?option=com_content&view=article&id=53&Itemid=43.

[16] Kenneth Ring, "People Born Blind Can See During Near-death Experience," http://www.netplaces.com/evidence-of-the-afterlife/science-seeks-an-explanation/near-death-experiences-of-the-blind-dr-kenneth-ring-and-sharon-cooper-phd.htm.

[17] Vickie Noratuk, "A Blind Woman's Near Death Experience," http://www.seattleiands.org/stories/blind.htm.

[18] Raymond Moody, *"The Light Beyond,"* (New York: Bantam Books, 1988), 135.

[19] Gerry Lougrhan, "Can there be life after life? Ask the atheist!" Letter from London, March 18, 2001.

[20] *Ibid*.

[21] *Ibid*.

[22] Kevin Christensen, "Nigh Unto Death: NDE Research and the Book of Mormon: in *The Journal of Book of Mormon Studies* 2/1, 1993.

[23] Craig Lundahl, Ph.D., Harold A. Widdison, Ph.D., "Social Positions in the City of Light," *Journal of Near Death Studies,* 11:4, Human Sciences Press, Inc., Summer 1993, 231-38.

[24] *Ibid.*

[25] John Pontius, *Visions of Glory*, (Springville: Cedar Fort, Inc., 2012), 3-23.

[26] George Ritchie, *My Life After Dying,* (Norfolk: Hampton Roads Publishing, 1991), 22-25.

[27] *Ibid.*

[28] Emanuel Swedenborg, *Heaven and Hell*, translated by George F. Dole, 58th printing, (New York: Swedenborg Foundation, 1990), 230, 241-42.

[29] Joseph F. Smith, *Gospel Doctrine*, 5th ed., (Salt Lake City: Deseret Book, 1939), 472-76.

[30] George Ritchie, *Return from Tomorrow,* (Old Tappan, NJ: Spire Books, Fleming H. Revell Co., 1978), 66.

[31] Lance Richardson, *The Message,* (Salt Lake City: American Family Publishing, 2000).

[32] *The Teachings of Ezra Taft Benson*, (Salt Lake City: Bookcraft, 1988), 35-36.

[33] *Journal of Near-Death Studies*, vol. 9, no. 2, Winter 1990, 94.

[34] Moody, *Light Beyond,* 58-59.

[35] Duane Crowther, *Life Everlasting,* (Salt Lake City: Bookcraft, 1965), 285.

[36] Smith, *Gospel Doctrine*, 455.

[37] Zaleski, *Otherworld Journeys.*

[38] Moody, *Life After Life*, 67.

[39] Gibson, *Fingerprints.*

[40] *Improvement Era*, November 1909, 77.

[41] Kimball, *Journal of Discourses* 15, 242-43.

[42] Bruce Greyson, "Vital Signs," *Encyclopedia Britannica, Part 1*, Jan-March, 1992), 2, 6.

[43] Pim van Lommel as quoted in *Brain Death and Disorders of Consciousness,* C. Machado and D. A. Shewmon, eds., (New York, Boston, Dordrecht, London, Moscow: Kluwer Academic/ Plenum Publishers); *Advances in Experimental Medicine and Biology* 550, 2004, 115-132.

[44] *Ibid.*

[45] http://www.near-death.com/experiences/experts01.html.

[46] Pim Van Lommel, M.D., *Continuity of Consciousness*, (Baltimore: The Johns Hopkins University Press, 1995), 69-79.

[47] *Ibid.*

[48] Rick Strassman, *DMT: The Spirit Molecule: A Doctor's Revolutionary Research into the Biology of Near-Death and Mystical Experiences*, (Park City, UT: Park City Press, 2000).

[49] Steven Kotler, "Extreme States," *Discover Magazine*, July 24, 2005.

[50] Susan Blackmore, "Near-death experiences: in or out of the body?" *Skeptical Inquirer* 16, 1991, 34-45.

[51] G. A.Woerlee, "Darkness, Tunnels, and Light, *The Center for Inquiry,* vol. 28.3, May, June, 2004.

[52] Question 28 about Near Death Experiences," http://www.aleroy.com/FAQz28.htm.

[53] http://www.horizonresearch.org/main_page.php?cat_id=164.

[54] *Ibid.*

[55] *Ibid.*

[56] Eben Alexander, M.D., *Proof of Heaven*, (New York: Simon and Schuster, 2012), 133, 147-48.

[57] J. Mauro, "Bright Lights, Big Mystery," *Psychology Today*, July/August 1992, 54-57, 80-82.

[58] Kenneth Ring, *Life at death: A scientific investigation of the near-death experience*. (New York: Coward, McCann, & Geoghegan, 1980).

[59] A. Foos-Graber, *Deathing: An intelligent alternative for the final moments of life*, (York Beach: Nicolas-Hays, 1989).

[60] Kevin Williams, *Nothing Better Than Death: Insights from Sixty-Two Near-Death Experiences*, (Bloomington: Xlibris Corp., Oct. 2002), http://www.near-death.com/differences.html.

[61] Osis, Karlis, and Erlunder Haraldsson, *At the Hour of Death*, (New York: Hastings House, 1977), 66.

[62] Zaleski, *Otherworld Journeys*, 198.

[63] Joseph Fielding Smith, ed., *Teachings of the Prophet Joseph Smith*, (Salt Lake City: Deseret Book, 1964), 162.

[64] Craig Lundahl, *A Collection of Near Death Research Readings*, (Chicago: Prentice Hall, 1982), 33.

[65] *Ibid.*; cf. Crowther, *Life Everlasting*, 81.

[66] Kevin Christensen, "Nigh unto Death," *NDE Research and the Book of Mormon, Journal of Book of Mormon Studies*: vol. 2, issue 1, (Provo, UT: Maxwell Institute, 1993), 1-20.

[67] *Ibid.*

[68] Arvin S. Gibson, *Echoes From Eternity*, (Bountiful, UT: Horizon Publishers, 1992), 67-71.

[69] http://blogs.standard.net/the-political-surf/2013/01/14/near-death-experiences-get-treatment-from-a-mormon-perspective/

[70] Brent L. and Wendy C. Top, *"Beyond Death's Door,"* (Salt Lake City: Bookcraft, Salt Lake City, 1993), 277-78.

[71] Smith, *Teachings*," 313.

[72] Mary C. Neal, *To Heaven and Back*, (Colorado Springs: WaterBrook Press, 2011), 219.

Chapter Five

[1] Robert McMinn, *Atoms and the existence of God*, LCG Commentary, LCG.org, July 28, 2011.

[2] Joseph Smith, *Lectures on Faith*, (Salt Lake City: Deseret Book, 1985), 1-8.

[3] *Ibid.*

[4] *Ibid.*, no. 7, par. 5.

[5] R. Schulz, J. Bookwala, J. Knapp, et al., "Pessimism and mortality in young and old recurrent cancer patients." Paper presented at the American Psychosomatic Society annual meetings, Boston, MA., April 15, 1994.

[6] "Positive thinking: Reduce stress by eliminating negative self-talk," 2011, http://www.mayoclinic.com/health/positive-thinking/SR00009.

[7] Harold B. Lee, *"Be Loyal to the Royal within You,"* in Speeches of the Year: BYU Devotional and Ten-Stake Fireside Addresses, 1973, (Provo, UT: Brigham Young University Press, 1974), 91.

[8] Richard G. Scott, "The Transforming Power of Faith and Character," *Ensign*, October 2010.

[9] Dave. S. Collingridge, *Truth and Science, an LDS Perspective*, (Springville, UT: Cedar Fort Inc., 2008), 116.

[10] *Ibid.*

[11] *Ibid*, 116-117.

[12] Carol Osman Brown, "Pathfinder: Prayer in Healing," *HealthLinks*, Fall, 1995.

[13] Cited in Jim Ritter, "Med Schools See the Spiritual Side," *Chicago Sun-Times*, September 28, 1997, 37.

[14] E. Bagiella, T. Powell, and R.P. Sloan, "Religion, Spirituality, and Medicine," *The Lancet* 353, no. 9153, February 20, 1999, 664.

[15] Randolph C. Byrd, "Positive Therapeutic Effects of Intercessory Prayer in a Coronary Care Unit Population," *Southern Medical Journal*, July, 1988, 826-29.

[16] H. G. Koenig, E. G. Hooten, E. Lindsay-Calkins, K. G. Meador, "Spirituality in Medical School Curricula: Findings from a National Survey," *Int. Journal Psychiatry Medicine* 40, 2010, 391-98.

[17] Reginald Cherry, M.D., *Healing Prayer*, (Nashville: Thomas Nelson, Inc., 1999), 132-133.

[18] *Ibid*, 137-138.

[19] David A. Bednar, "Ask in Faith," *Ensign*, April 2008. Adapted from H. Burke Peterson, "Adversity and Prayer," *Ensign*, January 1974.

[20] Thomas S. Monson, "Come Unto Him in Prayer and Faith," *Ensign*, March 2009.

[21] Marcos Walker, "The Restoring Power of Prayer," *Ensign*, January 2011.

[22] Julie C. Donaldson, "A Week to Go Until Payday," *Ensign*, June 2008.

[23] Gerald N. Lund, *Selected Writings of Gerald N. Lund*, (Salt Lake City: Deseret Book, 1999), 305-06.

[24] Joseph Fielding Smith, *Teachings of the Prophet Joseph Smith*, (Salt Lake City: Deseret Book),166-67.

[25] B.H. Roberts, *History of the Church*, 5, (Provo: Brigham Young University Press, 1965), 499.

[26] Brigham Young, *Journal of Discourses*, vol. 8, 1956, 162.

[27] Dallin H. Oaks, *The Lord's Way*, (Salt Lake City: Deseret Book, 1991), 16-17.

[28] Ursula Goodenough, "The Way of Science: Revelation with Errata Sheets," November 11, 2010, www.npr.org/blogs/13.7/20/10/11/11/131243975/the-way-of-science-revelation-with-errata-sheets.

[29] *Ibid*.

[30] David A. Bednar, "The Spirit of Revelation," *Ensign*, April 2011.

[31] Lund, *Selected Writings*, 275-79.

[32] Dallin H. Oaks, "Eight Ways God Can Speak to You," *Ensign*, September 2004.

[33] Thomas S. Monson, "Come Unto Him in Prayer and Faith," *Ensign*, March 2009.

[34] Op. cit., Roberts, 215.

[35] http://www.basicincome.com/bp/modernmiracles.htm.

[36] James E. Talmage, *Jesus the Christ*, (Salt Lake City: Deseret Book, 1982), 138-140.

[37] http://hangingout.hubpages.com/hub/natural-laws-and-miracles.

[38] David Durtschi to Nancy Phippen Browne, email, August 16, 2013.

[39] "Sometimes, 'Miracles' Are Just That," *Dallas Morning News*, (January 30, 2000), 31A.

[40] "13 *Miracles*," Brigham Young University Speeches of the Year (5 Apr. 1966, rebroadcast from a speech delivered Feb. 18, 1953), 9.

[41] http://mormonsoprano.com/2010/03/17/prepare-for-a-miracle/.

[42] James E. Talmage, *Articles of Faith*, (Salt Lake City: Deseret Book, 1984), 200-201.

[43] David A. Bednar, "Converted unto the Lord," *Ensign*, (October 2012).

Chapter Six

[1] *George Weigel, World Religions by the Numbers,* http://www.catholiceducation.org.

[2] "The Global Religious Landscape," Pew Research Religion and Public Life Project, http://www.pewforum.org/global-religious-landscape-exec.aspx.

Notes

³ Tom Henegham, "'No Religion' Is World's Third-Largest Religious Group After Christians, Muslims According To Pew Study," *Reuters,* December 18, 2012.

⁴ *Ibid.*

⁵ "Mormon Church Set to Become World's Largest," *Charisma News,* http://www.charismanews.com/us/34365-mormon-church-set-to-become-worlds-largest.

⁶ *Ibid.*

⁷ Statement of the First Presidency, February 15, 1978, from "Communion With the Holy Spirit," *Ensign,* March 2002, 4.

⁸ Stephen Prothero, *"God is not One, the Eight Rival Religions that Run the World and Why Their Differences Matter,"* (New York: HarperCollins, 2010), 333-335.

⁹ "Selected Death Tolls for Wars, Massacres and Atrocities Before the 20th Century," http://necrometrics.com/pre1700a.htm.

¹⁰ Prothero, *God is not One,* 337.

¹¹ Rabbi Marc Gellman & Monsignor Thomas Hartman, *"Religion for Dummies,"* (Hoboken, NJ: Wiley Publishing, 2002), 21.

¹² *Ibid.*

¹³ *Ibid.*

¹⁴ *Ibid.*

¹⁵ *Ibid.*

¹⁶ Sly Navreet, *"The Smiliarities in All Major World Religions, Closer Than You Think,"* August 31, 2006, http://voices.yahoo.com/the-similarities-all-major-world-religions-68721.html.

¹⁷ Neal A. Maxwell, "From the Beginning," *Ensign,* October 1993.

¹⁸ Will Durant, "Caesar and Christ," *The Story of Civilization,* part 3, (New York: Simon and Schuster, 1944), 595.

¹⁹ Joseph Fielding McConkie, *Watch and Be Ready, Preparing for the Second Coming of the Lord,* (Salt Lake City: Deseret Book, 1994), 41-42.

²⁰ James E. Talmage, *The Great Apostasy,* (Salt Lake City: Deseret Book, 1968), 97.

²¹ Brigham H. Roberts, *Defense of the Faith and the Saints,* (Salt Lake City: Deseret News Press, 1907), 1, 512–13.

²² Hugh Nibley, *Old Testament and related Studies,* (Salt Lake City: Deseret Book, 1986), 31, 34.

²³ *Ibid,*15.

²⁴ Brigham Young, *Journal of Discourses,* 15, 325; see also Alma 29:8.

²⁵ Nibley, *Old Testament,* 42.

²⁶ *Ibid,* 43-44.

²⁷ Charles F. Hockett and Robert Ascher, "The Human Revolution," *American Scientist 52,* 1964, 90.

²⁷⁸ Richard Vandagriff, "Noah versus Gilgamesh," *Christian Monthly Standard,* http://www.christianmonthlystandard.com/index.php/noah-versus-gilgamesh/.

²⁹ S. Michael Houdmann, http://www.gotquestions.org/Gilgamesh-flood.html#ixzz2QC4mGPL6.

³⁰ Shahul Hameed, "Between the Stories of Prophets & Mythology," http://www.onislam.net/english/ask-about-islam/faith-and-worship/quran-and-scriptures/167721-between-the-stories-of-prophets-aamp-mythology.html?Scriptures=.

³¹ "Alleged Similarities Between Jesus and Pagan Dieties," http://thedevineevidence.com/jesus_similarities.html.

³² *Ibid.*

³³ *Ibid.*

34 Joseph McConkie and Robert Millet, *Doctrinal Commentary on the Book of Mormon*, vol. 1, (Salt Lake City: Deseret Book, 1987), 168.

35 http://www.mormonnewsroom.org/ldsnewsroom/eng/commentary/reverence-for-the-bible.

36 M. Russell Ballard, "The Miracle of the Holly Bible," *Ensign*, April 2007.

37 Young, *Journal of Discourses*, 285.

38 Parley P. Pratt, *Key to the Science of Theology*, (Forgotten Books, August 21, 2012), 50.

39 Spencer W. Kimball, *Ensign*, March 1976, 70-73.

40 Boyd K. Packer, *The Law and the Light*, Book of Mormon Symposium, BYU, October 30, 1988.

41 "Eve and the Fall," in *Woman*, (Salt Lake City: Deseret Book, 1988), 60.

42 Bruce R. McConkie, "Christ and the Creation," *Ensign*, June 1982, 15.

43 John A. Widstoe, *A Rational Theology*, (Salt Lake City: Deseret Book, 2009), 50.

44 "What the Bible Says about Adam and Eve," http://whatthebiblesays.info/AdamandEve.html.

45 *Ibid.*

46 Darrick Evenson, *The Mormon Faith & Black Folks*, Ch. 24.

47 *Ibid.*

48 Frank B. Salisbury, *The Case for Divine Design*, (Springville, UT: Cedar Fort, Inc., Springville, 2006, 31.

49 Kathryn Wilkinson, project editor, *Signs and Symbols,* (New York: DK Publishing, 2008), 39.

50 Hugh Nibley, "Departure," *Neal A. Maxwell Institute for Religious Scholarship, BYU*, http://maxwellinstitute.byu.edu/publications/books/?bookid=59&chapid=561.

51 Michael R. Ash, "Challenging Issues, Keeping the Faith: Michael Ash: Is the Tower of Babel Historical or Mythological?" *Deseret News*, September 27, 2010.

52 *Ibid.*

53 Michael R. Ash, "Challenging Issues, Keeping the Faith: Michael Ash: Still Confounded at the Tower of Babel," *Deseret News*, Oct. 4, 2010.

54 *Ibid.*

55 James L. Krugel, *A Guide to Scripture, Then and Now*, (New York: Free Press, 2008), 136, 362.

56 Eric A. Eliason, https://byustudies.byu.edu/showtitle.aspx?title=7592.

57 Keith Basso, "Stalking with Stories: Names, Places, and Moral Narratives among the Western Apache," in *Western Apache Language and Culture: Essays in Linguistic Anthropology* (Tucson, AZ: University of Arizona Press, 1990).

58 *Ibid.*

59 Kevin Barney, "Poetic Diction and Parallel Word Pairs in the Book of Mormon," *Journal of Book of Mormon Studies*, vol. 4, issue 2, (Provo, UT: Maxwell Institute, 1995), 15-81.

60 Stephen D. Ricks, "The Book of Mormon and the Dead Sea Scrolls," (Provo, UT: Maxwell Institute).

61 Hugh Nibley, "Two Shots in the Dark," *Book of Mormon Authorship*, (Salt Lake City: Bookcraft, 1982), 103-04.

62 Jeff Lindsay, "Book of Mormon Evidences," http://www.jefflindsay.com/BMEvidences3.shtml#q5.

63 Cyrus H. Gordon, *Forgotten Scripts*, (New York: Basic Books, 1968), 102.

64 C. Wilfred Griggs, "The Book of Mormon as an Ancient Book," *Book of Mormon Authorship*, (Salt Lake City: Bookcraft, 1982), 79-81.

65 Jeff Lindsay, "Book of Mormon Evidences," http://www.jefflindsay.com/BMEvidences.shtml#geography.

66 D.W. Parry, D.C. Peterson, and J.W. Welch, eds., *Echoes and Evidences of the Book of Mormon* (Provo, UT: FARMS, 2002), 75.

[67] Noel B. Reynolds, ed. *Book of Mormon Authorship, New Light on Ancient Origins*, (Salt Lake City: Bookcraft, 1982), 3-4.

[68] G. Bruce Schaalje, Matthew Roper, and Paul J. Fields, "Stylometric Analyses of the Book of Mormon: A Short History," *Journal of the Book of Mormon and Other Restoration Scripture*, vol. 21, issue 1, (Provo, UT: Maxwell Institute, 2012), 28–45.

[69] B. H. Roberts, *Conference Report,* October 1923, 91.

[70] Hugh Nibley, *An Approach to the Book of Mormon,* (Salt Lake City: Deseret Book, 1964), 211.

[71] Catherine M. Thomas, "Types and Shadows of Deliverance in the Book of Mormon," *Doctrines of the Book of Mormon, 1991 Sperry Symposium,* (Salt Lake City: Deseret Book, 1992), 182-3.

[72] *Ibid.*

[73] John P. Livingstone, "Conflict in the Book of Mormon: Types and Shadows of Spiritual Battle Today," *The Book of Mormon: The Foundation of Our Faith, the 28th Annual Sidney B. Sperry Symposium,* (Salt Lake City: Deseret Book, 1999), 174-5.

[74] Title page of the *Book of Mormon.*

[75] Joseph Smith, *History of the Church,* 7 vols., ed. B. H. Roberts, 4 (Salt Lake City: The Church of Jesus Christ of Latter-day Saints, 1932-51), 461.

[76] *Ibid.* 4, 540.

[77] http://www.lds.org.

[78] Gordon B. Hinckley, in *Conference Report,* October 1999, 94.

Chapter Seven

[1] Alma P. Burton, http://eom.byu.edu/index.php/Salvation.

[2] Bruce R. McConkie, *Mormon Doctrine,* (Salt Lake City: Bookcraft, 1976), 669.

[3] Bruce R. McConkie, *The Promised Messiah,* (Salt Lake City: Deseret Book, 1978), 129.

[4] John Sanders, "Those Who Have Never Heard: A Survey of the Major Positions," in *Salvation in Christ: Comparative Christian Views,* ed. Roger R. Keller and Robert L. Millet (Provo, UT: Religious Studies Center, Brigham Young University, 2005), 299-325; http://rsc.byu.edu/pt-pt/node/2298.

[5] *Ibid.*

[6] *Ibid.*

[7] *Ibid.*

[8] George Q. Cannon, *Gospel Truth,* compiled by Jerreld L. Newquist, (Salt Lake City: Deseret Book, 1987), 60.

[9] George G. Ritchie, Jr., *My Life After Dying,* (Norfolk, VA: Hampton Roads Publishing Co., 1991), 22.

[10] Joseph Fielding McConkie, *Answers: Straightforward Answers to Tough Gospel Questions,* (Salt Lake City: Deseret Book, 1998), 98.

[11] Hugh Nibley, "Baptism for the Dead in Ancient Times," (Provo, UT: Maxwell Institute); Reprinted from "Mormonism and Early Christianity," vol. 4 of *The Collected Works of Hugh Nibley* (Salt Lake City: Deseret Book and F.A.R.M.S., 1987), 100-67.

[12] *Ibid.*

[13] Origen, *Against Celsus* II, 43, in *PG* 11,864-65.

[14] Joseph Fielding Smith, com., *Teachings of the Prophet Joseph Smith,* (Salt Lake City: Deseret Book, 1974), 366.

[15] Clement of Alexandria, *Stromata* 6:14, in ANF 2:506; http://en.fairmormon.org/Plan_of_salvation/Three_degrees_of_glory/Not_biblical#endnote_fn205.

[16] *Ibid.*

[17] Origen, *De Principiis* 2:10:2, in ANF 4, p. 294.

[18] John Chrysostom, *Homilies on 1 Corinthians 41*: 4, in NPNF Series 1, 12: 251.

[19] Brian E. Daley, "The Hope of the Early Church," *A Handbook of Patristic Eschatology* (Cambridge: Cambridge University Press, 1991).

[20] Eliezer Lorne Segal, http://www.ucalgary.ca/~elsegal/Shokel/891103_7th_Heaven.html.

[21] Clark, *The Origenist Controversy*, 131; http://en.fairmormon.org/Plan_of_salvation/Three_degrees_of_glory/Not_biblical#ref_fn217

[22] John Wesley as quoted in *A Life God Rewards: Why Everything You Do Today Matters Forever* by Bruce Wilkinson, (Multnomah; First Edition, August 29, 2002), 120-21.

[23] Boyd K. Packer, "The Mediator," *Ensign*, April 1977.

[24] Joseph Fielding McConkie, *Answers: Straightforward Answers to Tough Gospel Questions*, (Salt Lake City: Deseret Book, 1998), 98.

[25] Smith, *Teachings*, 218.

[26] M. Russell Ballard, "Suicide, Some Things We Know, and Some We Do Not," *Ensign*, October 1987.

[27] *Wilford Woodruff*, speech in General Conference, April 1894.

[28] Joseph Fielding Smith, *Doctrines of Salvation*, vol. 2, (Salt Lake City: Bookcraft, 1992), 133.

[29] *Lorenzo Snow, Millennial Star*, 56: 50.

[30] Melvin J. Ballard, "The Three Degrees of Glory," presented in the Ogden Tabernacle, September 22, 1922.

[31] Robert L. Millett, *Modern Mormonism, Myths and Realities*, (Salt Lake City: Greg Kofford Books, 2010), 79.

[32] Alonzo L. Gaskill, *Odds Are, You're Going to be Exalted*, (Salt Lake City: Deseret Book, 2008), 71.

[33] *Journal of Discourses*, vol. 9, (London: Latter-day Saints' Book Depot, 1854-56), 125.

[34] George Teasdale in *Collected Discourses Delivered by President Wilford Woodruff, His Two Counselors, the Twelve Apostles, and Others*, 5 vols., comp. by Brian H. Stuy, (Burbank, CA: B.H.S. Publishing, 1987) 4:40.

[35] Robert L. Millet and Joseph Fielding McConkie, *The Life Beyond*, (Salt Lake City: Bookcraft, 1986), 137.

[36] *Ibid.*

[37] Bruce R. McConkie, "Jesus Christ and Him Crucified," *Brigham Young University Devotional Speeches of the Year* (Provo, UT: Brigham Young University Press, 1977), 398-401.

[38] Boyd K. Packer, "The Great Plan of Happiness," address to CES Symposium, Brigham Young University, Provo, Utah, August 10, 1993.

[39] Gaskill, *Odds are You're Going to be Exalted*, 17-18.

[40] *Ibid*, 18.

[41] Dieter F. Uchtdorf, "A Matter of a Few Degrees," *Ensign*, May, 2008.

[42] Smith, *Doctrines of Salvation*, 2, 90.

[43] Smith, *Teachings*, 321.

[44] *Conference Report*, April 1929, 110.

[45] Ezra Taft Benson, "You Are a Marked Generation," *Ensign*, April 1987.

[46] H. Burke Peterson, "Your Special Purpose," *New Era*, October 2001.

[47] Larry Barkdull, *Rescuing Wayward Children*, (American Fork, UT: Covenant Communications, 2009), 40.

[48] John A. Widstoe, *Discourses of Brigham Young,* (Salt Lake City: Deseret Book, 1993), 208.
[49] *Journal of Discourses*, vol. 23, 186-87.
[50] Smith, *Teachings,* 356-57.
[51] Lorenzo Snow, *The Teachings of Lorenzo Snow,* (Salt Lake City: Bookcraft, 1984), 195.
[52] McConkie, *Mormon Doctrine,* 408.
[53] Colin B. Douglas, "Justification," in Ludlow et al., *Encyclopedia of Mormonism,* 2 (New York: Macmillan Publishing, 1992), 776.
[54] McConkie, *Mormon Doctrine,* 362.
[55] Orson F. Whitney, "The Three Great Teachers," in *Collected Discourses,* 5: 432. Compare D&C 76:71, 74.
[56] James E. Talmage, *Articles of Faith* (Salt Lake City: Deseret Book, 1984 ed.), 104.
[57] Dallin H. Oaks, "Love and Law," *Ensign,* October 2009.
[58] *Journal of Discourses* 1, 10-11.
[59] *Journal of Discourses,* 380–81.
[60] *Journal of Discourses,* 379.
[61] Widstoe, *Discourses of Brigham Young,* 132.
[62] Ezra Taft Benson, *Teachings of Ezra Taft Benson,* (Salt Lake City: Bookcraft, 1988), 35-36.
[63] Joseph F. Smith, *Gospel Doctrine, (Salt Lake City: Deseret Book, 1977),* 436.
[64] Smith, *Teachings,* 326.
[65] Smith, *Teachings,* 310-11.

Chapter Eight

[1] John Ayto, *Dictionary of Word Origins,* (New York: Arcade, 1990).
[2] John A. Widtsoe, "Temple Worship," *The Utah Geneaolgical and Historical Magazine* 12, April 1921.
[3] KathrynWilkinson, project editor, *"Signs and Symbols,"* (New York: DK Publishing, 2008), 8.
[4] Patrick Cramsie, *The Story of Graphic Design,* (British Library, 2010).
[5] Christian Bale and Michael Caine in *Batman Begins,* 2005.
[6] Clayton Moore and Ralph Littlefield in "The Lone Ranger Fights On," *The Lone Ranger,* (1949).
[7] Emile Durkheim, *The Elementary Forms of the Religious Life,* translated by J. W. Swain. (New York: The Free Press, 1965, 1915).
[8] *Ibid.*
[9] Randall Collins, University of Pennsylvania, http://www.thearda.com/rrh/papers/guidingpapers/Collins.pdf.
[10] Alonzo L. Gaskill, *The Lost Language of Symbolism,* (Salt Lake City: Deseret Book, 2003), 6-9.
[11] Joseph Fielding McConkie, *Gospel Symbolism,* (Salt Lake City: Bookcraft, 1985) ix.
[12] Joran Friberg, "Numbers and Counting," in *The Anchor Bible Dictionary,* 4, ed. by David Noel Freedman, 6 vols. (New York: Doubleday, 1952), 1139-46.
[13] J.C. Cooper, *An Illustrated Encyclopaedia of Traditional Symbols,* (London: Thames and Hudson, 1995), 59, 96, 190.
[14] *Ibid,* 112.
[15] McConkie, *Gospel Symbolism,* 146-60.
[16] Gaskill, *Lost Language of Symbolism,* 271.

[17] Parry, Donald W. and Jay A., *Symbols and Shadows*, (Salt Lake City: Deseret Book, 2009), 88-90.

[18] *Ibid*, 7-8.

[19] Gaskill, *Lost Language of Symbolism*, 293.

[20] *Bible Dictionary*, 740.

[21] *Bible Dictionary*.

[22] Hugh Nibley, *Temple and Cosmos*, (Salt Lake City: Deseret Book, May 1992, 15.

[23] Daniel H. Ludlow, ed., *The Encyclopedia on Mormonism*, (New York: Macmillan Publishing Company, 1992).

[24] Gaskill, *Lost Language of Symbolism*, 27.

[25] Michael E. Stone, "The Apocrypha and Pseudepigrapha," June 2001, http://www.jewishvirtuallibrary.org/jsource/Judaism/apocrypha.html.

[26] B. H. Roberts, *History of the Church*, 7, (Provo, UT: Brigham Young University Press, 1965), 240.

[27] Jeff Lindsay, http://www.jefflindsay.com/LDSFAQ/FQ_masons.shtml.

[28] "Martyrdom & Ascension of Isaiah," *Pseudepigrapha*, 10: 24-25, 27, 29, 31, as referenced at http://www.jefflindsay.com/LDSFAQ/FQ_masons.shtml.

[29] Todd Compton, "The Handclasp and Embrace as Tokens of Recognition," in *By Study and Also by Faith: Essays in Honor of Hugh W. Nibley on the Occasion of His Eightieth Birthday*, March 27 1990, John M. Lundquist and Stephen D. Ricks, eds., 2 vols. (Salt Lake City and Provo: Deseret Book Co., Foundation for Ancient Research and Mormon Studies, 1990), 1: 620-21.

[30] Bruce H. Porter and Stephen D. Ricks, "Names in Antiquity: Old, New, and Hidden," in *By Study and Also by Faith: Essays in Honor of Hugh W. Nibley on the Occasion of His Eightieth Birthday*, March 27, 1990. John M. Lundquist and Stephen D. Ricks, eds., 2 vols. (Provo: Foundation for Ancient Research and Mormon Studies, 1990), 1, 512.

[31] Erving Goffman, *Psychiatry: Journal for the Study of Interpersonal Processes*, vol. 18, 1955, 213-231.

[32] Durkheim, *Elementary Forms*.

[33] Nadine Sultana d'Osman Han, *Reflections of religious rituals and rites in theater. Impact of Religious & Theater Rituals on Humans*, prepared for the 2nd International Seminar of Religion and Theater, in Tehran, Iran, November 18-19, 2010.

[34] Ludlow, *Encyclopedia of Mormonism*.

[35] Webster's New World Dictionary of the American Language, 1962 ed.

[36] James Strong, *Strong's Exhaustive Concordance of the Bible*, (Iowa Falls: World Bible Publishers, 1989).

[37] Hugh W. Nibley, *Sacred Vestments*, (Provo, UT: Neal A. Maxwell Institute for Religious Scholarship) http://maxwellinstitute.byu.edu/publications/books/?bookid=103&chapid=1149.

[38] Moshe Levine, *The Tabernacle: Its Structure and Utensils*, tr. Esther J. Ehrmann (Tel Aviv: Melekhet ha-Mishkan, 1969), 124-31, from the 1968 Hebrew *Mele'khet ha-Mishkan: Tabnit ha-Mishkan ve-Kelav*.

[39] James H. Charlesworth, *Testaments of the Twelve Patriarchs, The Old Testament Pseudepigrapha* 1, (Garden City: Doubleday, 1983), 791, as cited by John A. Tvedtnes, "Olive Oil: Symbol of the Holy Ghost," *The Allegory of the Olive Tree*, ed. Stephen D. Ricks and John W. Welch, (Salt Lake City: FARMS and Deseret Book, 1994), 427-59.

[40] BYU Studies, 1996-7, 251-8.

[41] *Ibid*, 649, 663-64.

[42] Louis Ginzberg, *Legends of the Jews* vol. 5, (Philadelphia: Jewish Publication Society of America, 1967-69), 104.

⁴³ Douglas R. Edwards, "Dress and Ornamentation," in *The Anchor Bible Dictionary*, vol. 2, (New York: Doubleday, 1992), 232-38.

⁴⁴ Carol Meyers, "Apron," in *The Anchor Bible Dictionary*, 1, ed. David Noel Freedman, 6 vols. (New York: Doubleday, 1992), 219, 318-19.

⁴⁵ Donald W. Parry, "Garden of Eden: Prototype Sanctuary," in *Temples of the Ancient World*, (Provo: Foundation for Ancient Research and Mormon Studies, 1994), 145.

⁴⁶ John Tvedtnes, "Priestly Clothing in Bible Times," in *Temples of the Ancient World*, ed. Donald W. Parry, (Provo, UT: Foundation for Ancient Research and Mormon Studies, 1994), 665.

⁴⁷ J. C. Cooper, *An Illustrated Encyclopaedia of Traditional Symbols*, (London: Thames and Hudson, 1995), 29, 80.

⁴⁸ Nahum M. Sarna, *The JPS Torah Commentary: Exodus*, (Philadelphia: Fortress Press, 1991), 185.

⁴⁹ Hugh Nibley, Commencement Speech, 1, 2 in *Christian Envy of the Temple*, 391-434.

⁵⁰ Matthew Brown, *The Gate of Heaven*, (Covenant Communications, October 1999), 129.

⁵¹ *Ibid*, 151-52.

⁵² Donald W. Parry, "Garden of Eden: Prototype Sanctuary," *Temples of the Ancient World*, (Salt Lake City: Deseret Book, 1994), 126-51.

⁵³ Spencer W. Kimball, *Ensign,* March 1976, 72.

⁵⁴ Beverly Campbell, "Eve," *The Encyclopedia of Mormonism* vol. 2.

⁵⁵ Widstoe, *Temple Worship*, 62.

Chapter Nine

¹ Edward J. Larson and Larry Witham, "Scientists and Religion in America," *Scientific American* 281, September, 1999, 90-91, as cited by John Sutton Welch, "Why Bad Things Happen at All, A Search for Clarity Among the Problems of Evil," *BYU Studies*, byustudies.byu.edu.

² David B. Haight, *Ensign,* July 1973, 56.

³ Steven A. Cramer, *Putting on the Armor of God*, (Springville, UT: Cedar Fort, Inc., 1992), 45.

⁴ John Pontius, *Visions of Glory,* (Springville, UT: Cedar Fort, Inc., 2012), 104-5.

⁵ *Ibid*, 109-11.

⁶ Neal A. Maxwell, *Notwithstanding My Weaknesses*, (Salt Lake City: Deseret Book, 1981), 55.

⁷ Cramer, *Putting on the Armor of God*, 21-2.

⁸ McLeod, Saul, "Asch Experiment," *Simply Psychology,* 2008.

⁹ Kenneth Levin, "The Psychology of Populations under Chronic Siege," *Post-Holocaust and Anti-Semitism*, No. 46.

¹⁰ David Kupelian, How Evil Works, (New York City: Threshold Editions, 2010), 50, 62-64.

¹¹ Donald W. Parry and Jay A. Parry, *Symbols and Shadows,* (Salt Lake City: Deseret Book, 2009), 345-6.

¹² *Ibid*.

¹³ Dieter F. Uchtdorf , "You Matter to Him," *Ensign*, October 2011.

¹⁴ *Ibid*.

¹⁵ "Understanding Addiction: How Addiction Hijacks the Brain," *Harvard Health Publications*, http://www.helpguide.org/harvard/addiction_hijacks_brain.htm.

[16] "The Science of Addiction: Drugs, Brains and Behavior," *NIH Medline Plus*, Spring, 2007, 14-17.

[17] B. F. Grant, "Estimates of US children exposed to alcohol abuse and dependence in the family," http://www.ncbi.nlm.nih.gov/pmc/articles/PMC1446111/; *American Journal Public Health*, January, 2000, 90(1): 112-15.

[18] "Prescription and illicit drug abuse is timely new topic on NIHSeniorHealth.gov," National Institute on Aging, http://www.nih.gov/news/health/jun2012/nia-06.htm.

[19] Daniel Bortz, "Gambling addiction affects more men and women, seduced by growing casino accessibility," *U. S. News and World Report*, March 28, 2013, http://www.nydailynews.com/life-style/health/gambling-addicts-seduced-growing-casino-accessibility-article-1.1301339#ixzz2RFzbLd2H.

[20] Roxanne Dryden-Edwards, MD, "What are complications and negative effects of gambling addiction? "http://www.medicinenet.com/gambling_addiction/article.htm.

[21] "Pornography Statistics," http://www.familysafemedia.com/pornography_statistics.html.

[22] "Addiction to Internet Pornography a Growing National Problem; Wired.com States that 'Internet Porn is Worse Than Crack,'" http://www.prweb.com/releases/2012/1/prweb9085685.htm

[23] Jorge Moll, Ricardo De Oliveira-Souza, Griselda J Garrido, Ivanei E Bramati, Egas M.A. Caparelli-Daquer, Mirella L.M.F. Paiva, Roland Zahn, Jordan Grafman, "The Self as a Moral Agent: Linking the Neural Bases of Social Agency and Moral Sensitivity," *Social Neuroscience* 2(3, 4), 2007, 336–52.

[24] William P. Cheshire, "Does Alien Hand Syndrome Refute Free Will?" *Ethics in Medicine: An International Journal of Bioethics* 26(2), 2010, 71-76.

[25] "Milgrim Experiment," http://en.wikipedia.org/wiki/Milgrim_experiment.

[26] *Ibid.*

[27] Jeffry Ricker, PhD., *Comparing Milgram's Obedience and Zimbardo's Prison Studies*, November 25, 2011.

[28] P. G. Zimbardo, "On transforming experimental research into advocacy for social change," in M. Deutsch & H. Hornstein, eds., *Applying Social Psychology: Implications For Research, Practice, and Training*, (Hillsdale, NJ: Lawrence Erlbaum, 1975), 115.

[29] Agigail Tucker, "Are Babies Born Good?" *Smithsonian*, January 2013.

[30] Oliver Burkeman, "Meet 'Dr. Love,' the scientist exploring what makes people good or evil," *The Guardian*, July 15, 2012.

[31] *Ibid.*

[32] Harold B. Lee, *Stand Ye in Holy Places*, (Salt Lake City: Deseret Book, 1974), 138.

[33] *Latter-day Sentinel*, June 3, 1983, 16.

[34] Art E. Berg, *Some Miracles Take Time,* (American Fork, Utah: Covenant Communications, 1990), 22.

[35] *Ibid*, 22-3.

[36] *Ibid*, 28.

[37] Nancy Richardson to Nancy Browne, email, May 27, 2013.

[38] Spencer W. Kimball, *Faith Precedes a Miracle*, (Salt Lake City: Deseret Book, 1974), 96.

[39] C. S. Lewis, *The Problem of Pain*, (New York: Touchstone Books, 1996), 37-38.

[40] C.S. Lewis, *A Grief Observed,* (New York: HarperOne paperback, 2001), 30.

[41] *Ibid*, 29.

[42] *Conference Report,* April, 1952, 67-68.

[43] Patricia P. Pinegar, "Peace, Hope, and Direction," *Ensign*, January 2000.

[44] Kendra Kasl Phair, "A Champion Again," *New Era*, November 1988, 21–25; see also Renon Klossner Hulet, "Matters of Balance," *Ensign*, December 1992, 63.

[45] Richard G. Scott, "To Heal the Shattering Consequences of Abuse," *Ensign*, April 2008.

[46] Truman Madsen, *Eternal Man*, (Salt Lake City: Deseret Book, 1966), 60-61.

[47] David L. Paulsen, "Evil," http://eom.byu.edu/index.php/Evil.

[48] *Ibid.*

[49] Blake T. Ostler, "Evil: A Real Problem for Evangelicals," *FARMS Review* vol. 15, issue 1, (Provo, UT: Maxwell Institute, 2003), 201-13.

Chapter Ten

[1] *Utah Historical Quarterly*, vol. 76, no. 4, Fall 2008, 348, http://utah.ptfs.com/awweb/awarchive?type=file&item=13881.

[2] E. James Dickey, *The Amazing Power of the Holy Spirit*, (Bloomington, IN: WestBow Press, 2011), 79.

[3] Connie Schultz, 'One by One, Stories of Heroism Are Bubbling Up,' http://www.parade.com/5837/connieschultz/one-by-one-stories-of-heroism-are-bubbling-up/.

[4] Katie Kindelan, "Principal Dawn Hochsprung a '5-foot-2-inch Raging Bull' Lifesaver," http://abcnews.go.com/blogs/headlines/2012/12/principal-dawn-hochsprung-a-5-foot-2-inch-raging-bull-lifesaver/.

[5] Cassy Fiano, "5 Heroes To Remember This September 11," http://hotair.com/greenroom/archives/2010/09/11/5-heroes-to-remember-this-september-11/.

[6] *Ibid.*

[7] Christine Miller Ford, "Thirty Years Later, Recalling the Sacrifice of Arland Williams, Jr.," http://spiritofjefferson.com/blog/2012/09/thirty-years-later-recalling-the-sacrifice-of-arland-williams-jr/.

[8] David Beck, "Your Sacred Duty to Minister," *Ensign*, April, 2013.

[9] Michelle Lloyd, "Making Birthdays Special for Homeless Children," *The Charlotte Observer*, http://www.charlotteobserver.com/2013/02/25/3876824/making-birthdays-special-for-homeless.html.

[10] Allie Torgan, "Bringing health care to the world's most remote areas," *CNN*, http://www.cnn.com/2012/02/23/health/cnnheroes-labrot-floating-doctors.

[11] "American Heroes," http://www.huffingtonpost.com/news/american-hero/.

[12] Edward Lovett, "Three Stories of Extraordinary Forgiveness," *ABC News*, http://abcnews.go.com/US/cases-extraordinary-forgiveness/story?id=16065270#2.

[13] Daniel Burke, "Terri Roberts, Mother Of Amish Shooting Perpetrator Cares For Her Son's Victims," http://www.huffingtonpost.com/2011/09/29/terri-roberts-amish-shooting-victims_n_987525.

[14] Erin Merryn, http://www.erinmerryn.net/.

[15] Allie Torgan, "Pairing 'angels' with cancer patients," *CNN*, http://www.cnn.com/2012/08/23/health/cnnheroes-imerman-cancer.

[16] Jacqueline Seibel, "Family's tragedy spawns plan for action," http://www.jsonline.com/news/waukesha/29262764.html.

[17] Markus N. A. Bockmuehl, *The Cambridge companion to Jesus*, (Cambridge University Press, 2001) ISBN 978-0-521-79678-1, 123-124; Robert E. Van Voorst, *Jesus Outside the*

New Testament: An Introduction to the Ancient Evidence, (Eerdmans Publishing, 2000), ISBN 0-8028-4368-9, 16.

[18] "Historicity of Jesus," http://en.wikipedia.org/wiki/Historicity_of_Jesus.

[19] *Ibid.*

[20] "Did Jesus really exist? Is there any historical evidence of Jesus Christ?" http://www.gotquestions.org/did-Jesus-exist.html#ixzz2T8YGzw00.

[21] http://en.wikipedia.org/wiki/Historicity_of_Jesus.

[22] http://www.gotquestions.org/did-Jesus-exist.html#ixzz2T8YGzw00.

[23] *Ibid.*

[24] *Ibid.*

[25] *Ibid.*

[26] "The Living Christ," *Ensign*, April 2000, 2-3.

[27] Joseph Fielding McConkie, *Watch and Be Ready, Preparing for the Second Coming of the Lord*, (Salt Lake City: Deseret Book, 1994), 47.

[28] *Ibid*, 59.

[29] Neal A. Maxwell, *Even as I Am,* (Salt Lake City: Deseret Book, 1982), 114.

[30] Jeffrey R. Holland, *Broken Things to Mend,* (Salt Lake City: Deseret Book, 2008), 216-17.

[31] Joseph Smith, *Lectures on Faith*, lecture 3, (Covenant Communications, 2000), paragraph 20.

[32] Holland, *Broken Things to Mend*, 219-20.

[33] Christian Stead, *Philosophy in Christian Antiquity*, (Cambridge: Cambridge University Press, 1994), 120.

[34] David L. Paulsen, "Early Christian Belief in a Corporeal Deity: Origen and Augustine as Reluctant Witnesses," *Harvard theological Review* 83, 1990, 105.

[35] Origen, *Homilies of Genesis 3:1,* translated by Ronald E. Heine, The Catholic University of America Press, Washington, D.C., 1982, 89; http://www.mormonvoice.com/index.php/mormonism-vs-creedal-christianity/.

[36] Justin Martyr, "Dialogue with Trypho 114," *The Ante-Nicean Fathers 1,* Edited by Alexander Roberts and James Donaldson, 10 volumes, The Christian Literature Publishing Company, Buffalo, N.Y., 1885-1896, 256.

[37] Lorenzo Snow, *Teachings of Lorenzo Snow*, comp. by Clyde J. Williams, (Salt Lake City: Bookcraft, 1984), 1-2.; *Deseret News Weekly* x/y, November 3, 1894.

[38] *History of the Church*, vol. 6, 473-479.

[39] Jeff Lindsay, "The Divine Potential of Human Beings: The Latter-day Saint Perspective," http://www.jefflindsay.com/LDSFAQ/FQ_theosis.shtml.

[40] *Ibid.*

[41] Origen, *Commentary on John*, 29.27, 29, http://www.jefflindsay.com/LDSFAQ/FQ_theosis.shtml.

[42] Origen, *Refutations*, X.30, http://www.jefflindsay.com/LDSFAQ/FQ_theosis.shtml.

[43] Boyd K. Packer, "The Pattern of Our Parentage," *Ensign*, November 1984, 69.

[44] Joseph Fielding Smith, *Doctrines of Salvation*, vol. 1, (Salt Lake City: Bookcraft, 1976), 5-10.

[45] Neal A. Maxwell, "Remember How Merciful the Lord Hath Been," *Liahona* and *Ensign*, May 2004, 46.

[46] Jeffrey R. Holland, "The Other Prodigal," *Liahona,* July 2002, 72; *Ensign,* May 2002, 64.

[47] Sydney S. Reynolds, "He Knows Us; He Loves Us," *Ensign,* October 2003.

[48] *History of the Church of Jesus Christ of Latter-day Saints,* (Salt Lake City: Deseret Book, 1957), 6, 303-05.

Notes

Chapter Eleven

[1] John A. Widtsoe, *Evidences and Reconciliations*, 3rd ed. (Salt Lake City: Bookcraft, 1943), 29.

[2] Dieter F. Uchtdorf, "The Reflection in the Water," CES Fireside for Young Adults, BYU, November 1, 2009.

[3] Joseph Walker, "Mormons navigate faith and doubt in the digital age," *Deseret News*, July 26, 2013. http//www.deseretnews.com/article/865583665/Simple-faith-in-a-digital-age.html?pg+all.

[4] *Ibid.*

[5] *Ibid.*

[6] Jeffrey R. Holland, "Lord I Believe," *Ensign*, April 2013.

[7] Boyd K. Packer, "I Say unto You, Be One (D&C 38:27)," *Brigham Young University 1990-91 Devotionals and Fireside Speeches* (Provo, UT: Brigham Young University, 1991), 89.

[8] John L. Sorenson, *An Ancient American Setting for the Book of Mormon,* (Salt Lake City: Deseret Book and FARMS, 1985), 111, 368 n., 16.

[9] John W. Welch, ed., *Reexploring the Book of Mormon* (Salt Lake City: Deseret Book and FARMS, 1992), 41-43.

[10] John W. Welsh, "The Power of Evidence in the Nurturing of Faith," (Provo, UT: Maxwell Institute). See Austin Farrar, "Grete Clerk," in *Light on C. S. Lewis*, comp. Jocelyn Gibb (New York: Harcourt and Brace, 1965), 26; cited in Neal A. Maxwell, "Discipleship and Scholarship," *BYU Studies* 32/3, summer 1992, 5.

[11] Hugh Nibley, *The World and the Prophets,* (Salt Lake City: Deseret Book, 1987), 134.

[12] Dave S. Collingridge, *Truth and Science, an LDS Perspective*, (Springville, UT: Cedar Fort Inc., 2008), 114.

[13] Holland, *Lord I Believe.*

[14] Robert L. Millet, *I Will Fear No Evil,* (Salt Lake City: Deseret Book, 2002), 32.

[15] Susan Easton Black, ed., *Expressions of Faith – Testimonies of Latter-day Saint Scholars*, (Salt Lake City: Deseret Book, 1996), 94.

[16] David B. Marsh, "How LDS Church members can help themselves and loved ones deal with doubt," by Katie Harmer, *Deseret News,* August 27, 2013, http://www.deseret news.com/article/865585321/How-LDS-Church-members-can-help-themselves-and-loved-ones-deal-with-doubt.html?pg=1.

[17] *Ibid.*

[18] Bruce R. McConkie, *Mormon Doctrine*, (Salt Lake City: Bookcraft, 1966), 318.

[19] Boyd K. Packer, "Personal Revelation: The Gift, the Test, and the Promise," *Ensign*, November 1994.

[20] David O. McKay, "Gospel Ideals: Selections from the Discourses of David O. McKay," *Improvement Era,* 1953, 390.

[21] David O. McKay, *Conference Reports*, April 1967, 85.

[22] Thomas S. Monson, "Welcome to Conference," *Ensign,* October, 2012.

[23] Neal A. Maxwell, *That Ye May Believe,* (Salt Lake City: Bookcraft, 1992), 183.

[24] Jeanie Lerche Davis, "Meditation Balances the Body's Systems," *WebMD,* http://www.webmd.com/balance/features/transcendental-meditation?page=2.

[25] *Ibid.*

[26] Jonathan Krygier and Andrew Kemp, "Beyond spirituality: the role of meditation in mental health," January, 190, 2012, http://www.theconversation.com.

[27] *Ibid.*

[28] Amy B. Wachholtz and Kenneth I. Pargament, "Is Spirituality a Critical Ingredient of Meditation? Comparing the Effects of Spiritual Meditation, Secular Meditation, and Relaxation on Spiritual, Psychological, Cardiac, and Pain Outcomes," *Journal of Behavioral Medicine,* vol. 28, issue 4, August 2005, 369-384.

[29] Philip McLemore, "Mormon Mantras. A Journey of Spiritual Transformation," *Sunstone Magazine,* April, 2006.

[30] *Ibid.*

[31] Thomas S. Monson, "Sailing Safely the Seas of Life," *Ensign,* April 1982.

[32] Thomas S. Monson, *A Prophet's Voice: Messages from Thomas S. Monson,* (Salt Lake City: Deseret Book, 2012), 155.

About the Author

Nancy Phippen Browne is a retired journalist who has worked as an investigative reporter and editor for various newspapers and magazines across the country, including the *Church News*. Her writing background also took her into the field of public relations and marketing.

She earned a bachelor's degree in journalism in 1989 from the University of Wisconsin, River Falls, served a full-time mission to Colorado, and has actively served in ward and stake callings throughout her life. While this is her first book, she is also a freelance writer, with articles appearing in a variety of publications, including the *Ensign* and *This People* magazine.

Sister Browne and her husband, Raymond Browne, reside in St. George, Utah. Between them, they have seven children and 20 grandchildren.